Full Stack Recruiter

Diversity Sourcing Strategies

Jan Tegze

Edited by Sarah Lane.
Proofread by Katerina Nenkova.
Cover and book design by Euan Monaghan.

Published in 2023 by Net Image, s.r.o.,
Kumpoštova 7, Brno, 612 00, Czech Republic

ISBN (paperback): 978-80-908069-4-8
ISBN (hardcover): 978-80-908069-5-5

Contents

Disclaimer

Any opinions represented in this book[1] are personal and belong solely to the author and do not represent those of people, institutions, or organizations that the author may or may not be associated with in a professional or personal capacity unless explicitly stated. Any opinions are not intended to malign any religion, ethnic, group, organization, company, or individual.

This book is published for informational and educational purposes only. The publisher and/or the author make no representations or warranties with respect to the accuracy or completeness of the contents of this work and specifically disclaim all warranties, including, without limitation, warranties of fitness for a particular purpose. No warranty may be created or extended by sales or promotional materials. The advice and strategies contained herein may not be suitable for every situation. Publication of this book does not create a consultant-client relationship.

When you access this book, you agree that the author and/or publisher shall not be liable to you for any loss or injury caused by procuring, compiling, or delivering the information gained from the book. In no event will the author and/or publisher of the book be liable to anyone for any action taken on the basis of such information or for any incidental, consequential, special, or similar damages. The author and/or publisher expressly disclaim any and all liability for any direct, indirect, incidental, consequential, or special damages arising out of or in any way connected with the buying and reading of this book and/or any information contained in this book. The author and/or publisher disclaim all responsibility for any loss, injury, claim, liability, or damage of any kind resulting from, arising out of, or any way related to any information and content of this book. The information contained in this book is strictly for educational purposes. Therefore, if you wish to apply the ideas in this book, you are taking full responsibility for your actions.

Technology and services are constantly changing; therefore, this book might contain information that, although accurate when it was written, is no longer accurate by the time you read it. Your use of or reliance on the information in this book is at your own risk, and the author and/or publisher are not liable or responsible for any resulting damage or expense.

----

[1] In this disclaimer, the term *book* also includes the electronic version of this book.

Every possible effort has been made to ensure that the information contained in this book is accurate at the time of going to press, and the publisher and author cannot accept responsibility for any errors or omissions.

Acknowledgments

I want to thank everyone who contributed to this book, either by sharing their story or by reading and offering feedback. This book covers everything I learned about diversity and inclusion from people who are way smarter than me.

Writing this book would have been impossible without the help of all the amazing people who provided detailed and constructive comments on one or more chapters. These people include Maisha L. Cannon, Vanessa Raath, Reese Byrne, Mark Tortorici, Katerina Nenkova, and many other people from D&I and recruitment world. Thank you from the bottom of my heart!

There is one last person to whom I need to say thank you. And that person is YOU, the reader (whoever you are and wherever you are right now). Because of you, this book has a purpose and won't be left lying on a bookshelf. I hope that this book can help educate people about the importance of diversity and inclusion in the workplace.

I would greatly appreciate it if you could let me know what you think about the book, post a positive review on Amazon or LinkedIn, or share it with your friends and colleagues when you finish reading it.

I hope you enjoy this book.

Jan

About the Author

Jan Tegze[2] is an international recruiter and talent acquisition leader with more than eighteen years of experience in the recruitment industry.

He started his professional career in a recruitment agency and after that worked for several large corporations where he was responsible for global hiring initiatives. Over the years, he has interviewed more than 10,000 candidates, recruited hundreds of people, and trained and coached thousands of professionals from all walks of life and seniority levels in countries around the world.

He is a sourcing and recruitment trainer, blogger, keynote speaker, recruitment advisor, and author of several books including ***Job Search Guide***[3] and ***Full Stack Recruiter: The Ultimate Edition***,[4] which became an international bestseller in the recruitment industry.

To learn more about Jan Tegze, please visit jantegze.com[5].

---

[2] https://www.linkedin.com/in/jantegze/
[3] https://jobsearch.guide/
[4] https://fullstackrecruiter.net/
[5] https://jantegze.com/

Introduction

This book addresses the essential dilemma of diversity hiring. The dilemma is that, in the United States and other countries, it is illegal to hire people solely based on their membership in an underrepresented group, BUT diversity hiring is essential for your business's success and longevity— **studies have shown that diverse teams are more innovative and productive**[6].

If you hire a less qualified woman over a more qualified man, for example, the man could, technically, sue you. But the key point here is that you don't want to hire a *less qualified* woman, but you may want to hire a *differently qualified* woman. In other words, resolving the dilemma is all about expanding our notions of *qualification,* which is, in fact, the reason diversity hiring is so important.

For a long time, we have understood a person's qualification to mean that they went to one of the Ivy League schools, their experience is in line with what we have traditionally expected (with the right job titles and in the top companies), and they have references from what we have traditionally identified as other qualified people. But by clinging to traditional notions of the ideal qualifications, we are overlooking the power and resources that could be brought by people who are equally qualified but in a different way.

Maybe the ideal candidate for your job vacancy didn't go to an Ivy League school and didn't work for Google and didn't get a reference from the male CEO of another Fortune 500 company. Instead, maybe she went to a lesser-known school where she studied with excellent professors, she worked for a smaller company where she learned innovative strategies for solving complex problems, and she got references from brilliant CEOs of smaller, thriving companies. Those qualifications are not *less* valid. In fact, if your current employees are largely alike in terms of their experiences and skills, her qualifications may be *better*.

In this book we will examine the reasons diversity hiring is so important, what it really means, and, if done right, what it can do for you, your company, and your employees.

A diverse and inclusive environment is one where everyone feels like they belong and can be their authentic selves. This not only makes for a more fun and supportive workplace, but, as mentioned, also helps to boost

---

[6] https://www.forbes.com/sites/forbesinsights/2020/01/15/diversity-confirmed-to-boost-innovation-and-financial-results/

productivity and innovation. So next time you hear someone dismiss diversity and inclusion as "buzzwords," remind them of how important they truly are.

In recent years, employers have increased their focus on inclusion and diversity in the workplace. Although this is certainly a step in the right direction, there is still much work to be done.

In this book, I talk about the importance of inclusion and diversity and how recruiters can play a role in creating more inclusive environments in their companies. I also provide tips on how to find diverse candidates. By following these tips, recruiters can help create workplaces that are more inclusive and diverse. As a result, employees will feel more valued and respected, and companies will benefit from the wealth of talent and perspectives that diverse employees bring to the table, becoming better able to compete in the global marketplace.

What we're talking about is a win-win situation: When hiring managers build more diverse teams, companies succeed and the workplace becomes more equitable for everyone.

Ultimately, **diversity is good for business, employees, communities, and work teams**, so let's get started!

NOTE: *This book provides a number of examples of diversity and sourcing, many of which are based in the United States. However, the methods and strategies described in the book can easily be customized for any location. Whether you're searching for candidates in your own backyard or around the world, these techniques can help you build a more diverse and inclusive workforce.*

1. Uncovering Diversity

When we think about diversity, there are a few different factors that we should consider. Within the realm of HR and talent acquisition, we understand diversity as the variety of individuals within an organization representing different socioeconomic backgrounds, ages, ethnicities, races, religions, gender identities, physical abilities, and sexual orientations.

Throughout the past few years, more attention has been given to the way inequalities affect individuals' access to better-paying jobs, to certain forms of education, and to the same opportunities as others. More specifically, people have been focusing on privilege and ways to equalize the starting point so that everyone may have the same chance in the quest for employability. One of the strategies that has been used to address workplace inequalities is to introduce quotas, which are specific numbers or percentages of new hires who are in some way considered diverse.

However, opponents of quotas argue that, by actively changing hiring standards and requiring numbers of specific types of hires, employment practices are beginning to become disadvantageous to certain groups, specifically the ones who have until recently held an advantage. More precisely, people argue that in reserving positions for specific diverse members, people who are more qualified may be overlooked.

Although there is some merit to this perspective that more qualified people do sometimes get overlooked, the rationale behind diversity hiring is that a reset button needs to be hit: We need quotas to kickstart a "new normal" where a diverse workforce is simply the norm.

This reset also requires diverse individuals to be able to make hiring decisions. Although this process may temporarily disadvantage some who were previously not disadvantaged, it will ensure that all are given the same level of *opportunity*. Employment diversity practices lower the barriers that uneven privilege erects before certain candidates and introduce new talent acquisition models that incorporate a new hiring mindset.

Diversity Terms

Before beginning, it's important to work from a basic agreement on the definitions of *social justice, privilege, identity, quotaism, intersectionality, inclusion,* and *diversity.*

Social Justice

Social justice is a concept that emerged in the early 19th century. The term has been used in a variety of ways, but it generally refers to the idea that everyone deserves fair treatment, regardless of their social status or identity.

Social status and identity can include race, gender identification, sexual orientation, religion, and disability. In recent years, social justice has become a rallying cry for marginalized groups fighting for greater inclusion in society.

Although the term *social justice* is often used interchangeably with terms like *equity* and *fairness,* it is important to remember that it also includes the idea of taking proactive steps to eliminate inequality and injustice. This action component can involve everything from passing laws and policies to implementing educational initiatives and mentorship programs. Ultimately, social justice is about creating a society that is inclusive and accessible for everyone.

Privilege

In general, *privilege* refers to the advantages that one group of people has over another. The privilege can be conferred to higher economic classes, specific races, one gender, and heteronormative sexual orientations, for example.

Privilege[7] is another form of inequality. In the United States, many enjoy advantages that others don't have, such as access to better financial or social capital, which can influence one's access to certain social circles that open doors to employment in better jobs (i.e., nepotism[8]). Some forms of privilege are based on gender or group membership. For example, in certain industries or positions that require leadership, being a man often makes one more attractive to employers and more likely to be hired than a woman.[9]

According to the social psychology theory of privilege, individuals with more material advantages are more likely to become successful. Having opportunities begets more opportunities. If I go to a good high school, I'm more likely to get into a good college.

---

[7] https://www.merriam-webster.com/dictionary/privilege
[8] https://en.wikipedia.org/wiki/Nepotism
[9] https://www.bbc.com/worklife/article/20210108-why-do-we-still-distrust-women-leaders

Identity

Identity refers to the characteristics of an individual. They can include physical characteristics and cultural factors like religion or national origin. Identity is a personal concept and is established by each person—not imposed upon the person. For example, one person might identify as able-bodied, transmasculine, and neuroatypical. Another person might identify as queer, gender nonbinary, and Christian. Every single person possesses an individual identity and will define that identity in a unique way.

By understanding how privilege and identity interact, we can begin to create a more just and equitable society for all.

Quotaism

Quotaism is the concept of organizing society by a statistics-based system, whether in terms of race, gender, language, or some other demographic attribute. The basic premise is to represent specific demographics according to national statistics.[10]

In practice, quotaism involves setting hiring goals based on a protected characteristic. Although the practice may help meet a social objective, it is illegal under both state and federal law. In addition, quotaism can lead to a less diverse workforce, as qualified candidates are passed over to meet arbitrary numerical goals. Quotaism can even adversely affect morale by creating a feeling of resentment among employees.

Despite the potential negative outcomes, quotaism is official practice in some countries. For example, in South Africa the South African Police Service operates a quota system policy for hiring and promotion. Positions will be left unfilled if the appropriate demographic candidate cannot be recruited, even if a qualified person is available.[11]

Intersectionality

In 1989, Kimberlé Crenshaw,[12] an expert on critical race theory and co-founder of the African American Policy Forum, coined the term *intersectionality,*[13] a concept that has helped shape the approach to reducing inequalities within various societies, such as the United States.

Intersectionality is an analytical framework that examines how different social categories are connected through experience of systemic and overlapping discriminations and disadvantages. For example, a White

---

[10] https://en.wikipedia.org/wiki/Quotaism
[11] https://en.wikipedia.org/wiki/Quotaism
[12] https://www.law.columbia.edu/faculty/kimberle-w-crenshaw
[13] https://en.wikipedia.org/wiki/Intersectionality

woman experiences sexism; a Black woman experiences sexism and racism. A disabled Black woman experiences sexism, racism, and ableism. In other words, the disabled Black woman experiences more disadvantage than the White woman.

In human resources, it is crucial to understand the intersection of multiple challenges that might affect an individual. For example, in the United States, a single mother from a low socioeconomic background is much less likely to be eligible for a loan to access higher education than is a man or a higher economic class woman. Diversity hiring pinpoints how some people may be more disadvantaged than others and reduces as far as possible the effects that such inequalities have on their chances of succeeding.

Diversity

Most people think of *diversity* as simply the presence of people from a range of social groups, but it is so much more than that. Diversity is also a broad-based, goal-driven, strategic *plan* that focuses on discrimination prevention and workforce development.

The goal of diversity is to create an environment where everyone feels valued, respected, and able to contribute to their fullest potential. Diversity is focused on changing institutional policies and practices to make them more welcoming to all people.

By promoting diversity, organizations can create a more effective workforce. Studies have shown that companies with a diverse workforce are more successful and innovative.

Inclusion

Inclusion is about creating a welcoming culture that invites diversity. It is focused on changing the environment for the individual, taking social justice into consideration.

You can have diversity without inclusion. For example, you may make diverse hires but then not bother to help all the hires integrate as a team. You may hire a Black woman, but then, without a policy of inclusion, ignore her contributions and not look for ways to support her specific needs at work. Maybe she has to share a bathroom with all the other employees who are men. Maybe the company doesn't bother to take down the Confederate flag that's been on the plant walls for twenty years, and so every day the woman feels offended when she sees it.

Inclusion has been shown to increase employee satisfaction, and inclusive companies see higher revenue, lower turnover, and fewer complaints.

One study[14] found that happy workers are 20 percent more productive than unhappy workers.

Promoting diversity is important, but it is not enough on its own. Inclusion is crucial for positive workplace culture. An unhappy and unwelcoming workplace, even if it has a diverse workforce, will result in low morale, low productivity, and high turnover.

Diversity and *inclusion* are often used interchangeably, but they mean two different things. For example, diversity has traditionally been thought of as a right whereas inclusion isn't a right but a privilege. Diversity can be measured by the number of "diverse" persons in an organization or team, whereas inclusion has no quantifiable measure.

Whereas diversity means that many differences are represented in an organization, inclusion means all people are welcomed and recognized equally within an organization. A workplace focus on diversity will consist of recruiting from a broad range of groups and then supporting them with training and mentoring programs. But a focus on inclusion will ensure that there are no barriers to any employees being able to succeed and to apply their range of skills on the job.[15]

Diversity and Inclusion Language

Much of the language around diversity and inclusion has evolved over time, and there are some terms still in occasional use that can be viewed as outdated or offensive. For example, the term *minority* can be seen as a way of othering. Even the term *people of color,* which is often used to describe individuals who are not White, can be seen as divisive. After all, why should we group people based on the color of their skin? Wouldn't it make more sense to simply refer to people as individuals, without any labels? The term perpetuates the idea that skin color is the most important thing about a person. Besides, not everyone who is not White identifies as a person of color. In addition, many people feel that the term is simply too vague—there are many different shades of skin color, and it can be difficult to know who actually falls into a specific category.[16]

---

[14] http://www.smf.co.uk/wp-content/uploads/2015/10/Social-Market-Foundation-Publication-Briefing-CAGE-4-Are-happy-workers-more-productive-281015.pdf#page=9

[15] Roberson, Quinetta M. (2004). *"Disentangling the meanings of diversity and inclusion."*) Cornell Center for Advanced Human Resource Studies Working Paper Series. https://ecommons.cornell.edu/bitstream/handle/1813/76971/WP04_05.pdf?sequence=1

[16] https://www.npr.org/2020/09/29/918418825/is-it-time-to-say-r-i-p-to-p-o-c

A term currently being used is *underrepresented group.* This term acknowledges that, although certain groups may not be represented in equal numbers, they are still valuable members of the community. Another possibility is simply to use the name of the specific group you are referring to (e.g., "Black women"). This avoids any potential offense.

One way to show commitment to diversity and inclusion is to use language that is inclusive. For instance, rather than using the word *manpower* to refer to human resources, you could use the term *human capital, personnel, staff, or workers.* Similarly, using gender-neutral pronouns such as *they* and *them* can help to create a more inclusive environment.

By using language that is respectful and welcoming of all groups, organizations can signal their commitment to promoting diversity and inclusion in the workplace. Ultimately, the best way to choose inclusive language is to listen to members of underrepresented groups and use the terms they prefer.

Diversity and Inclusion in the Workplace

Diversity and inclusion go hand in hand, and one without the other simply does not work. Diversity without inclusion can give birth to a work environment that is toxic for an employee. On the other hand, inclusion without diversity is meaningless.

Categories of Diversity

We can talk about diversity in terms of four main categories:

- **External.** External diversity includes outside factors that affect an individual. This could be anything from work environment and education to religious beliefs and relationship status.
- **Internal.** These are factors that lie beyond the control of the individual such as race, age, ethnicity, gender identity, physical and mental ability, nationality, and sexual orientation.
- **Worldview.** This aspect of diversity is about an individual's perception of the world. It can change with time. It may include morals and political beliefs.
- **Organizational.** Organizational diversity is the kind of diversity that happens as a result of a person's workplace. This could include pay, management status, place of work, and job role.

Diversity Recruitment

Diversity recruitment is the practice of proactively seeking out and hiring a more diverse range of employees. This is important for all organizations in order to create a more inclusive workplace and to better reflect the diversity of their customer base.

Diversity encompasses the following (and more):

- Sexual orientation
- Race
- Religious beliefs
- Cultural background
- Political beliefs
- Gender identity
- Ethnicity
- Age
- Socioeconomic status
- Physical abilities or disabilities
- Neurodiversity

Diversity recruitment has gained special attention in the tech industry in recent years. This is because it has been common practice in the tech industry to choose and hire people from within one's own existing social and professional networks. People find it easier and more comfortable to hire people they know or who seem familiar; we humans like to surround ourselves with individuals who are most like us. As the *Harvard Business Review* explains, "It's important to accept that no one is pre-loaded with inclusive behavior; we are, in fact, biologically hardwired to align with people like us and reject those whom we consider different."[17]

This practice leads to a number of problems, including unchallenged and conventional decision- making as well as groupthink. And it means that many of the tech products that have been developed do not reflect the interests, needs, and wants of diverse customers—the result is that many potential customers are being overlooked.

Diversity recruitment is essential in order to create a more diverse and inclusive workforce. By proactively seeking out candidates from a wide range of backgrounds, organizations can ensure that they are attracting the best talent from across the sector. In addition, by promoting a more diverse and inclusive workplace, organizations can signal their commitment to equality and help to attract even more top talent.

Most people would agree that diversity is important, but it can be difficult to know where to start. That's where diversity recruitment marketing comes in. By specifically targeting underrepresented groups, organizations can not only increase the diversity of their workforce, but also send a

---

[17] https://hbr.org/2019/06/how-to-reduce-personal-bias-when-hiring

message that they are an inclusive and welcoming place to work. This, in turn, can help attract other diverse employees and create a more diverse and innovative workplace. So, if you're looking to prioritize diversity in your organization, start with your recruitment marketing strategy.

Diversity marketing is going to be covered in one of the chapters of this book.

The Rewards of Diversity

Inclusion of diverse backgrounds is key to the success of an organization, and there are many benefits of a diverse workforce. These can range from improved communication and innovation to improved productivity. In today's rapidly changing workplace, it is important to consider how to create a more inclusive environment for everyone. Workplace diversity is essential.

Although the differences among employees may not always be obvious, they can have a profound effect on work and may even spark conflict if some groups feel less represented than others or less valued than others. But these are hurdles that you have to try to overcome as there are compelling reasons to embrace diversity.

Better Decisions

A study[18] has shown that companies with diverse workforces make better business decisions 87 percent of the time. This leads to fewer meetings, as teams are able to come up with better solutions more quickly.

Better Performance

The Peterson Institute for International Economics conducted research[19] that shows that companies with more diverse leadership teams are also top financial performers. Another study found that businesses that are gender diverse are 15 percent more likely to perform financially above industry average.[20]

Better Employees

Diverse teams bring richness and energy to the workplace. A diverse workforce is also better able to recruit top talent, ensuring a positive brand

---

[18] https://www.cloverpop.com/hacking-diversity-with-inclusive-decision-making-white-paper

[19] https://www.piie.com/publications/working-papers/gender-diversity-profitable-evidence-global-survey

[20] https://www.stemwomen.com/blog/2017/12/Why%20Diversity%20Matters%20To%20Company%20Performance

reputation for the company. Companies that tend to have hierarchical structures that are overwhelmingly filled with White individuals, usually men, are often targeted by critics who point out their lack of diversity. Having a diverse team can also move the acquisition efforts of companies forward. According to data from Glassdoor,[21] 76 percent of people who are actively and passively seeking jobs, say that diversity is of great importance to them when evaluating job offers and the companies behind those offers. Conversely, a lack of diversity can drive talent away from a company.

A Variety of Skills and Ideas

A study[22] showed that people from diverse backgrounds tend to view information-gathering and knowledge-sharing differently, which helps bring a variety of resources, skill sets, and attitudes to a project. Ultimately, a diverse workforce is better able to solve problems. A diverse workforce is more innovative, and the quality of work is higher as more points of view and ideas are combined. Companies with more diversity in their teams often outperform others.

Appeal to Younger Employees

Another reason diversity and inclusion are key to any business, especially in recent years, is that many Millennials and Gen Z workers consider corporate social responsibility a must when they look at different employment options. A very significant factor involved in this is the diversity found within the company. According to a survey conducted by Glassdoor,[23] 67 percent of job seekers said a diverse workforce is important when considering job offers.

Greater Creativity

Having different cultures represented on staff means being more creative, having different perspectives around the table, and ensuring that these perspectives are represented in the products and/or services offered. Having a diverse workforce increases the chances of breakthroughs by enabling the sharing of widely different ideas.

Better Brand

Customers are starting to become more aware of where their money is going, choosing in increasing numbers to vote with their financial support

---

[21] https://www.glassdoor.com/employers/blog/diversity/
[22] https://www.researchgate.net/publication/256032015_Knowledge_Sharing_in_Diverse_Organisations
[23] https://www.glassdoor.com/employers/blog/diversity/

for companies that are more diverse. Boycotts are becoming more and more popular, and a small mistake can cost a company a lot. Here are some examples:

- **Abercrombie & Fitch:** A few years back, Abercrombie & Fitch's CEO made comments in an interview[24] that were repulsive to many customers. Explaining that the company was targeting only a certain demographic, he said, "That's why we hire good-looking people in our stores. Because good-looking people attract other good-looking people, and we want to market to cool, good-looking people." He added, "A lot of people don't belong [in our clothes], and they can't belong. . . Are we exclusionary? Absolutely. Those companies that are in trouble are trying to target everybody: young, old, fat, skinny. But then you become totally vanilla."[25] The CEO's comments were followed by a sharp decline in the company's stock. Sales fell dramatically in the following years.[26]

- **Victoria's Secret:** After enjoying an absolute blooming business throughout the early nineties to the early 2000s, the company started to decline in relevance as they neared the end of the 2010s. In 2018, as the CEO made remarks regarding including more transgender individuals in the runway show alongside more plus-size women as being "unnecessary" because the show was a "fantasy" and made for people to fantasize over a certain body type (i.e., the skinny, mostly White, and tall woman), the company went into a downfall. Shares fell and the CEO resigned. The new CEO pointed out the absolute lack of diversity in the board, which was made up of nine men and two women (remember that this company is a women's lingerie company). The company began hiring a more diverse team including a transgender model and a curvier model and paying attention to the feedback provided by its customers.

Although the company made solid progress and was able to increase sales slightly, they also received significant backlash, with critics noting that the company's behavior was not indicative of regret for their actions but instead of regret for being caught. The lesson here is that diversity and inclusion must come from an authentic desire to make things better and not simply to look as if things are better.

----

[24] https://www.latimes.com/business/la-xpm-2013-may-16-la-fi-mo-abercrombie-ceo-criticism-20130516-story.html
[25] https://www.chicagotribune.com/business/ct-xpm-2013-05-11-ct-biz-0511-abercrombie-ceo-20130511-story.html
[26] https://hbr.org/2019/06/how-to-reduce-personal-bias-when-hiring

Now Victoria's Secret is focusing on women leaders as its main representatives—again showing that the company is trying to keep up with the new world, which differs greatly from that of the early 2000s.

Diverse companies reap a greater share of the market as consumers are becoming increasingly aware of companies that take extra steps to make themselves more inclusive (such as by buying from Black-owned or female-led vendors and suppliers).

NOTE: *Workforce diversity has an impact on the acceptance rate of your offers. In a survey of 1,000 respondents, the job site Glassdoor[27] found that 67 percent of job seekers overall look at workforce diversity when evaluating an offer.*

Achieving Diversity and Inclusion

Throughout the next few sections, we will work on ensuring that your organization is openly pursuing workplace diversity. In general, as you embark on recruiting more diverse talent, keep the following principles in mind:

- Let your employees know that you value and are openly pursuing diversity and inclusion.
- Don't be afraid to ask employees about their experiences and suggestions. Your employees' concerns are important, and they need to be heard. You cannot achieve workplace equality if you don't allow people to voice their opinions. Create a feedback form or other mechanism to elicit input. Don't be afraid to invite participant in the discussion about workplace diversity.
- Break down geographic and cultural boundaries. With the growth of virtual collaboration and work-from-home practices, it is easier to gain perspectives from diverse locations and to hire an agile team without the limitations of physical location.
- Be open to and celebrate difference. If you give Christian employees time off to celebrate Christmas, why not give other employees time off to celebrate Eid al-Adha, Rosh Hashana, Yom Kippur, Navaratri, Ramadan, Chinese New Year, Passover, and/or Diwali? Instead of having an annual office Christmas party, why not celebrate the end of winter or the end of the year instead? For office parties, serve food from the different cultures of your employees.

---

[27] https://www.glassdoor.com/employers/blog/diversity/

2. Diversity Hiring

According to *The New York Times'* "Diversity and Inclusion Report,"[28] which was published in 2018, African-Americans, Hispanics, South Asians, and people with health conditions or impairments[29] were largely underrepresented in the company's workforce. However, the report also found that NYTs' employees spent a record amount of time on diversity and inclusion efforts, and the number of employees who felt they were treated fairly was also increasing.

In addition, the report found that more employees were being prepared for new management positions than ever before, and 6 of every 10 people who were promoted were women or minorities. Women made up 51 percent of the company's workforce, a 2 percent increase from the previous year. At the same time, White women also experienced a slight increase in representation. The number of Black females increased from 3 percent to 3.2 percent, Asian females increased from 6 percent to 7 percent, Latino males increased from 5 percent to 6 percent, and Latino females experienced a slight *decrease* by 0.1 percent in representation.

The report seemed to indicate that racial diversity was improving but had further to go. However, it also suggested that employees were not fully engaged because of fear of discrimination and the behaviors that may lead to discrimination as well as reluctance to let others know when they have been discriminated against. The recent report focused on the outlook for diversity in 2018 and what the NYTs could do to keep up with the evolving workforce.

Even though this report was solely about *The New York Times* staff, there are many other companies that publish similar data in their reports every year. A prime example is the company Deloitte, which views representation as a key indicator of the effectiveness of their equity efforts. In their 2022 report,[30] they' added new and expanded data elements to increase transparency. They reported increases in representation of Black, Hispanic/Latinx, and multiracial professionals as well as professionals

---

[28] https://www.nytco.com/company/diversity-and-inclusion/2018-diversity-inclusion-report/

[29] Don't automatically refer to 'disabled people' in all communications – many people who need disability benefits and services don't identify with this term. Consider using 'people with health conditions or impairments' if it seems more appropriate. https://www.gov.uk/government/publications/inclusive-communication/inclusive-language-words-to-use-and-avoid-when-writing-about-disability

[30] https://www2.deloitte.com/us/en/pages/about-deloitte/articles/dei/us-workforce-data.html

indigenous to the Americas. Deloitte's stated ambition is to set the standard for diversity, equity, and inclusion (DEI) by creating the culture and systems that empower everyone to thrive as their exceptional selves and reach their full potential. One of their goals is greater diversity hiring.

Diversity hiring is a set of practices implemented within organizations to increase the representation of underrepresented groups and women. Underrepresented groups can include ethnic minorities, people with disabilities, LGBTQ+[31] (lesbian, gay, bisexual, transgender, queer, and intersex) individuals, young people or older people, people of different religions, and people from lower socioeconomic backgrounds. Diversity hiring also recognizes the life experiences and cultural influences of employees. The aim is not to *tolerate* difference but to reflect within the workforce the makeup of society as a whole.

In the 1980s, corporations began to diversify their workforce by recruiting more women and minorities as well as by making concerted efforts to promote diversity. Today, 21 percent of corporations report having a formal diversity policy in place.

Diversity hiring assumes that employees who are diverse will bring a variety of experiences and viewpoints to the workplace, promoting innovation and more diversity.

Diversity in the Workplace

Karen Catlin in *Better Allies: Everyday Actions to Create Inclusive, Engaging Workplaces*[32] discusses the dynamics of a diverse workforce and the adjustments that need to be made for the diverse workplace to be accepted. She offers perspective on what the thought process is behind diversity hiring efforts and why diversity hiring is such a priority today. She discusses that many businesses are prioritizing a diverse workforce, even if they are not directly interested in increasing diversity.

The progression toward diversifying corporate environments has been slow, but progress is being made. Many organizations have implemented ways to recognize and address bias as well as to promote diversity in their workplaces. Unlike in the early '80s and '90s, when companies were afraid to try anything new, today's corporate environment is much more supportive of change.

---

[31] https://en.wikipedia.org/wiki/LGBT
[32] https://www.amazon.com/Better-Allies-Everyday-Inclusive-Workplaces/dp/1732723303

Catlin also notes that many workplaces require teamwork and collaboration in order to produce results and that these can be hindered by a lack of diversity. Catlin points out that having a diverse workforce can help companies improve performance as well as retain existing employees. She suggests that businesses must provide training for their employees that focuses on the formation of inclusive work environments, employee engagement, and diversity in general. Employers should be aware, she argues, of how to build an inclusive culture in their working environments.

Professionals from underrepresented groups may experience tension with their colleagues if they do not share their values and perspectives on work-related issues. Many employers have come to recognize this and have implemented programs to prioritize an inclusive workplace.

The ultimate decision by an employee to join or stay with a company is based on various factors such as the pay offered, the number of promotions and career growth opportunities, the company's culture, and whether or not there is a diverse team.

Diversity by itself cannot be the deciding factor because there are many companies that provide high-quality benefits to their employees and have an atmosphere that not only encourages teamwork but also encourages creativity and innovation. These factors are more important than diversity to determine whether someone will continue working for a company.

Arguments for Diversity Hiring

Diversity brings many benefits to companies, like higher revenue or cash flow.

- According to a survey conducted by Gartner,[33] highly inclusive organizations generate 2.3 times more cash flow per employee and 1.4 times more revenue and are 120 percent more capable of meeting financial targets. The companies in the survey that implemented diversity hiring also reported an increase in employee retention.
- Another reason for diversity hiring is that it is illegal in many countries to discriminate against certain protected classes. In the majority of countries, it is illegal to discriminate against people based on their religion or disability.
- Diversity hiring can help make employees feel more appreciated for their skills, talents, and abilities, which can have a positive effect on employee morale.
- Diversity policies can also encourage teamwork by ensuring that everyone is treated as an equal.

---

[33] https://www.gartner.com/en/human-resources/role/human-resources-leaders

- Barta, Kleiner, and Neumann (2012)[34] claim that there is a correlation between a diverse workforce and productivity. From a financial perspective, organizations are better off when there is diversity in their workforce because their teams are more productive, featuring different types of thinking and variation in the way work is done. Ilmakunnas and Ilmakunnas (2011) and Barta, Kleiner, and Neumann (2012) report a negative relationship between a lack of diversity and productivity.[35]
- Diversity can help employees improve their communication and collaboration abilities, which can lead to greater team productivity.
- Studies[36] have shown that diverse teams will usually be more effective than homogeneous ones in meeting work goals.
- A study from McKinsey & Company[37] found that the increase in women's overall share of labor in the United States—women went from holding 37 percent of all jobs to 47 percent over the past forty years—has accounted for about a quarter of current GDP.
- McKinsey's *Delivering Through Diversity* report[38] found corporations that embrace gender diversity on their executive teams were more competitive and 21 percent more likely to experience above-average profitability. They also had a 27 percent greater likelihood of outperforming their peers on longer-term value creation.
- Racially diverse executive teams provided an advantage of 35 percent higher earnings before interest and taxes and 33 percent more long-term value creation.
- Companies with a diverse staff are better positioned to meet the needs of diverse customer bases, and the cash flows of diverse companies are 2.3 times higher than those of companies with more monolithic staff. Diverse companies are 70 percent more likely to capture new markets than are organizations that do not actively recruit and support talent from underrepresented groups.[39]
- A diverse and inclusive workforce helps businesses avoid employee turnover costs. Businesses that fail to foster inclusive workplaces see higher turnover rates than businesses that value a diverse workforce

---

[34] http://jehdnet.com/journals/jehd/Vol_3_No_4_December_2014/7.pdf
[35] https://www.researchgate.net/publication/272364900_Diversity_in_the_Workforce
[36] https://hbr.org/2016/09/diverse-teams-feel-less-comfortable-and-thats-why-they-perform-better
[37] http://www.mckinsey.com/client_service/organization/latest_thinking/unlocking_the_full_potential.aspx
[38] https://www.mckinsey.com/business-functions/people-and-organizational-performance/our-insights/delivering-through-diversity
[39] https://www.marketwatch.com/story/the-numbers-dont-lie-diverse-workforces-make-companies-more-money-2020-07-30

because they foster a hostile work environment that pushes employees to leave.[40]

- Increasing a work team's racial, ethnic, gender, age, sexual orientation, and cultural diversity can help improve performance and create a more effective work environment for everyone. Research indicates that organizations that support diversity and inclusion are more likely to have employees who are productive, innovative, engaged, collaborative, and committed to their work.

- Studies also show that when organizations embrace diversity, they can improve their customer base. When businesses create a welcoming environment where everyone feels respected and valued, they are more likely to attract and retain customers from diverse backgrounds. Additionally, when businesses tap into the unique perspectives of their diverse employees, they can come up with new ideas that could be marketable to a wider audience.

- According to the World Economic Forum,[41] "the business case for diversity in the workplace is "now overwhelming." In an article in Forbes,[42] Vijay Eswaran says that the common assumption is that diversity is about tolerance and acceptance, but he explains that the business case for diversity is about "making the pie bigger."

- Employers gain a competitive advantage by tapping into the untapped talent pool that is often overlooked due to discrimination and bias toward race, gender, ethnicity, or sexual orientation. Deloitte Australia research[43] shows that inclusive teams outperform their peers by 80 percent in team-based assessments.

- In this day and age, considerable resources are spent on advertising and recruitment campaigns to find the best fit for any particular position. By advertising to a diverse audience of potential job seekers, companies open up their brand and make themselves recognizable to a wider audience.

- Employees who can relate to the employer and company values will be more motivated and loyal to the company, which will eventually lead to higher engagement and productivity. The overlap between diversity hiring and corporate social responsibility is also evident in diversity hiring practices.

---

[40] https://www.americanprogress.org/article/the-top-10-economic-facts-of-diversity-in-the-workplace/

[41] https://www.weforum.org/agenda/2019/04/business-case-for-diversity-in-the-workplace/

[42] https://www.forbes.com/sites/forbeshumanresourcescouncil/2019/08/21/the-business-case-for-a-diverse-workforce/?sh=64f2b4d34d4a

[43] http://www2.deloitte.com/content/dam/Deloitte/au/Documents/human-capital/deloitte-au-hc-diversity-inclusion-soup-0513.pdf

- Corporations committing to hiring and promoting diverse candidates show that they respect their employees and promote social justice.
- According to Josh Bersin's research,[44] inclusive companies are 1.7 times more likely to be innovation leaders in their market. McKinsey's research[45] shows that gender-diverse companies are 15 percent more likely to outperform their peers, and ethnically diverse companies are 35 percent more likely to do the same.

Arguments Against Diversity Hiring

- One of the most common arguments against diversity hiring is that it amounts to affirmative action. Critics claim that companies only care about meeting quotas for underrepresented groups, rather than actually finding qualified candidates. This means that White and Asian men are often passed over for jobs in favor of women and minorities, even if they're not as qualified.
- Another common argument is that diversity hiring is unfair to White men. This argument holds that White men are being systemically discriminated against in the job market, as companies give preference to women and minority candidates. While it's true that White men have historically been the dominant group in the workforce, this argument fails to take into account the fact that women and minorities have been systematically excluded from opportunities for many years. In other words, arguers against diversity hiring are essentially saying that it's unfair to level the playing field.
- Another common argument against diversity hiring is that diverse candidates aren't qualified for the jobs they're being hired into. This is based on the assumption that companies lower their standards when they're trying to meet diversity goals. Although it's possible that this happens in some cases, it's not necessarily indicative of the practice as a whole. In many cases, companies are simply expanding their recruiting efforts to include a wider range of candidates, which can only be a good thing.
- Some opponents of diversity hiring argue that a diverse workforce is harder to manage. However, this can be mitigated by hiring supervisors and managers who are diverse as well, are culturally aware, have the right communication skills, and are empathetic to all employees.
- Opponents argue that diversity can increase staff turnover rates because underrepresented people may feel that they do not function as well in a team as their colleagues in majority groups. This is why

---

[44] http://joshbersin.com/2015/12/why-diversity-and-inclusion-will-be-a-top-priority-for-2016/
[45] http://www.mckinsey.com/insights/organization/why_diversity_matters

it is important to hire managers who are highly educated in diversity training and who use inclusion strategies. In a diverse workforce, there is a higher likelihood that individuals from a majority group may identify with their colleagues from the same race or religion. Employers maybe left with the challenge of choosing between diversity and inclusion.

- Although diversity improves employee productivity, inclusion reduces staff fluency and productivity. This is because people from different cultures come with different communication styles, and it can be challenging to bridge the different styles.
- James Damore and David Gudeman filed a lawsuit[46] against Google for discrimination against conservative White men. According to the lawsuit, their viewpoints were suppressed because of their race, gender, and/or conservative political views.[47]

At the end of the day, **there are more pros than cons to diversity hiring**. The pros—including increased opportunity for underrepresented groups and a more representative workforce—outweigh any cons. Companies should continue to strive for a more diverse workforce, but they should also be aware of the potential pitfalls and make sure they're not discriminating against any group in the process.

Legality of Diversity Hiring

Diversity hiring is legal as long as it's done fairly and in a way that doesn't violate anti-discrimination laws. Let's take a closer look at what this means. First and foremost, when recruiting for diversity, companies need to make sure that they are not excluding qualified candidates based on protected characteristics like race, gender, or religion.

Second, they need to ensure that their diversity initiatives are truly designed to promote diversity and not simply perpetuate existing disparities. When done correctly, diversity hiring can be an immensely powerful tool for promoting equality and opportunity in the workplace.

Title VII of the Civil Rights Act of 1964, the Age Discrimination in Employment act of 1967, and the Americans with Disabilities Act are the leading laws safeguarding people of protected classes from discrimination in employment environments. Among other safeties, these laws prohibit discrimination in recruitment, hiring, firing, and retaliation involving

---

[46] https://techcrunch.com/2018/01/08/james-damore-just-filed-a-class-action-lawsuit-against-google-saying-it-discriminates-against-white-male-conservatives/
[47] Ex-Google engineer moves to end discrimination lawsuit against search giant. https://www.bizjournals.com/sanjose/news/2020/05/11/ex-google-engineer-moves-to-end-discrimination.html

persons in the protected classes, which include race, color, religion, sex, national origin, age, and disability.[48]

Affinity Groups

Any organization that is serious about diversity and inclusion needs to have affinity groups. What are affinity groups? Affinity groups are a way to unite people with similar backgrounds or life experiences to promote social justice and fight against prejudice and discrimination. They are voluntary groups of employees who share common life experiences or characteristics, such as race, gender, sexual orientation, religion, or ethnicity. Affinity groups have been around for centuries.

Affinity groups can provide support and a sense of community for members, while also serving as a valuable resource for the organization as a whole. For example, an affinity group can help to identify unconscious bias in hiring practices or work to create a more inclusive culture. In addition, affinity groups can be a powerful networking tool, providing members with the opportunity to connect with others who have similar backgrounds and experiences.

Many organizations and workplaces have affinity groups, which are similar to employee resource groups (ERGs). Affinity groups are an excellent way for employees to connect more deeply, form relationships, create networking opportunities, and boost morale. By forming affinity groups at the workplace, employers can create a more positive, productive, and welcoming work environment for employees of all backgrounds.

Affinity groups can be formed around an interest, such as a particular sport or hobby that employees share. Make sure that your company affinity groups are based on something that employees have in common and to which they can devote time outside of work.

To create an affinity group, follow these steps:

1. Set a goal.
2. Identify group members.
3. Describe your idea.
4. Set responsibilities of each member.

Once the affinity group is formed, find ways to work together and help each other succeed in the workplace.

Affinity groups yield many potential benefits:

---

[48] https://www.kcsourcelink.com/blog/post/blog/2018/05/01/how-to-recruit-and-hire-for-diversity-legally

- Increased collaboration
- Development of new ideas
- Increased understanding, bridged differences
- Increased confidence
- Inclusion and diversity
- Development of soft skills
- Employee empowerment
- Problem resolution
- Recognition of employee efforts
- Promotion of mutual support
- Development of leadership skills

When it comes to diversity and inclusion, affinity groups are an essential piece of the puzzle.

Diversity Training

Diversity training is a practice that tries to inform an organization about the value of cultural differences in teams as well as in business strategies. It is estimated that more than $8 billion dollars a year is spent on diversity trainings in the United States alone.[49]

Diversity training usually aims to make employees aware of the issues that underrepresented groups face. It also seeks to improve awareness of different cultures, increase cultural sensitivity, and limit the effects of unconscious bias. Through this type of training, employers hope that workplace discrimination will decrease in their organizations. In addition, diversity training provides an opportunity for companies to reduce staff turnover rates by improving employee morale.

Diversity training helps protect companies against discrimination lawsuits. Employees learn through the training that the business will not tolerate discrimination in any form.

A company can be more successful by helping employees gain more empathy toward different people and cultures. This development of empathy can be encouraged by the right kind of training.

---

[49] https://www.mckinsey.com/featured-insights/gender-equality/focusing-on-what-works-for-workplace-diversity

Diversity in Management

The most overlooked aspect of diversity hiring is management. According to Forbes,[50] 12.5 percent of the U.S. population is Black, yet only 3.2 percent of senior leadership positions are held by Black people.

Women leaders are more likely to be HR directors than they are to assume leadership in other roles. But their numbers have decreased from 2020 to 2021. In the same time frame, the proportion of women in other leadership roles like CEO, Chief Finance Officer, and Chief Information Officer has increased. In 2021, 26 percent of all CEOs and managing directors were women, compared to only 15 percent in 2019.[51] Fortune Global 500 reported an all-time high of twenty-three women CEOs in 2021, including six women of color.[52]

The Three Basic Types of Diversity Hiring

Numerous studies have been conducted to determine how best to embrace diversity in the workplace. Most of these studies suggest that companies should focus on three basic types of diversity. In incorporating these three into an inclusive work environment, employers can see substantial paybacks in terms of effective results as well as a more welcoming culture within their offices.

What are the basic types of diversity hiring?

1. **Minority Hiring:** focusing on racial and ethnic minorities in the workplace. Per the U.S. Bureau of Labor Statistics, Whites make up the majority of the labor force (77 percent). Black people and Asians constitute an additional 13 percent and 6 percent, respectively. American Indians and Alaska Natives make up 1 percent of the labor force, while Native Hawaiians and other Pacific Islanders account for less than 1 percent. People of two or more races make up 2 percent of the labor force.[53] People of color will be a majority of the American working class by 2032.[54] This is also one of the reasons many businesses are choosing to focus on hiring minority groups, especially Latinos and African Americans, as a way to promote diversity in their workplaces.

---

[50] https://www.forbes.com/sites/ashleystahl/2020/07/21/10-steps-businesses-can-take-to-improve-diversity-and-inclusion-in-the-workforce/?sh=148627d3343e
[51] https://www.grantthornton.global/en/insights/women-in-business-2021/
[52] https://fortune.com/2021/08/02/female-ceos-global-500-fortune-500-cvs-karen-lynch-ping-an-jessica-tan/
[53] https://www.bls.gov/opub/reports/race-and-ethnicity/2019/home.htm#table-1
[54] https://www.epi.org/publication/the-changing-demographics-of-americas-working-class/

2. **Women Hiring:** focusing on gender in the workplace. Women are an underutilized resource of talent, and companies must do what they can to include them in their diversity hiring practices. Many companies are currently focusing on getting more women in management roles as a way to improve diversity. One of the most successful gender diversity initiatives is Catalyst's Women's Executive Network (WXN[55]), which provides global executive business leadership. WXN offers a professional community to develop, engage, and advance successful women executives.

3. **LGBT+ Hiring:** focusing on sexual orientation in the workplace. Sexual orientation has been a controversial topic, but many companies are beginning to implement LGBT-inclusive strategies, mindful of the fact that diversity is crucial to the success of any organization. With this type of diversity hiring, organizations focus on welcoming people regardless of their sexual orientation or personal identity and give equal opportunity to all. According to the Human Rights Campaign Foundation,[56] LGBT-inclusive corporations are more likely to attract and retain top talent and see increased productivity, innovation, and financial performance.

---

[55] https://www.catalyst.org/
[56] https://www.thehrcfoundation.org/

3. How to Establish a Diverse Talent Pipeline

More and more companies are implementing programs and activities to promote diversity within their ranks. It is important for these initiatives to be driven by senior leaders within the company and essential that the CEO provides his or her full support. By doing so, the CEO sends a strong message that diversity is a priority for the company and that all employees are valued.

Building an inclusive work culture is not only an ethical move for companies, but it is also one that can have smart business implications. As we have seen, teams that are made up of individuals from diverse backgrounds and perspectives lead to better decision-making and greater innovation in the workplace.

Nevertheless, the majority of U.S. company boards of directors are still disproportionately White, despite greater overall diversity in the companies themselves. Just 2.7 percent of board directors at the start of the year 2022 were Hispanic, for example. That would need to soar to 18.5 percent to mirror the U.S. population.[57]

Executive data firm Equilar released its first racial breakdown of boards for companies in the Russell 3000 index, which covers about 97 percent of all investable U.S. stocks. The survey found that only 6.2 percent of directors are Black, even though Black people make up 13.4 percent of the population. And the 5 percent of directors who are of Asian or Pacific Islander descent also fell short of the Asian and Pacific Islander 6.1 percent makeup of the entire U.S. population.[58]

The lack of representation on boards has implications for diversity in hiring overall. According to the *Harvard Business Review,*[59] if there is only one woman or underrepresented candidate in a pool of four finalists, there is statistically zero chance that that person will be hired.

Although there is still a long way to go, more and more companies are now investing huge chunks of their revenue in diversity initiatives every year. According to data[60] by LinkedIn, the number of job listings that

---

[57] https://www.pbs.org/newshour/nation/boards-of-u-s-companies-are-still-disproportionately-white-despite-greater-overall-diversity
[58] https://www.pbs.org/newshour/nation/boards-of-u-s-companies-are-still-disproportionately-white-despite-greater-overall-diversity
[59] https://hbr.org/2016/04/if-theres-only-one-woman-in-your-candidate-pool-theres-statistically-no-chance-shell-be-hired
[60] https://www.linkedin.com/business/talent/blog/talent-acquisition/why-head-of-diversity-is-job-of-the-moment

showcase diversity and inclusion saw a 71 percent increase from 2015 to 2020. This is a good indicator that the corporate sector is headed in the right direction.

The biggest hurdle for companies seems to be in figuring out how to overcome their own unconscious biases that very often get in the way of hiring diverse talent. Change is uncomfortable. Because 95 percent[61] of CEOs are White men, they are naturally inclined to hire more White males for leadership roles and do so, whether intentionally or unintentionally.

For companies to bridge the gap in hiring, they need to start right from the beginning of their hiring cycle by building a diversity talent pipeline that attracts diverse candidates.

The Talent Pipeline

Talent pipeline refers to all of an organization's efforts to recruit, develop, and retain talent. The concept spans recruitment, hiring readiness, employee success, leadership development, and retention. A diversity talent pipeline initiative aims to identify talent pools with the tremendous potential to increase diversity in the workforce at large. A talent pool can include internal employees who show promise and have the potential to be promoted to better positions from within the organization.

By having a talent pipeline in place, organizations can be sure that they have a ready supply of qualified candidates to draw upon when vacancies arise. They can also reduce the high costs associated with recruitment and hiring. The pipeline helps to ensure that vacancies are filled quickly and efficiently, with minimal disruption to the business.

The pipeline can be made up of both active and passive candidates. Active candidates are those who are currently looking for a job, and passive candidates are those who are not actively looking for a job but would be open to the right opportunity.

Although the job market nowadays is largely led by candidates rather than employers, organizations often cannot wait for candidates to apply. They need to have prospective candidates ready to work before a need arises. Ultimately, a talent pipeline is an essential tool for any organization that wants to stay ahead of the curve in today's competitive marketplace.

In summary, a diversity talent pipeline offers key benefits:

- It saves the organization time, money, and resources by enabling a role to be filled as quickly as possible.

---

[61] https://www.catalyst.org/research/women-ceos-of-the-sp-500/

- It minimizes the disruption that is caused by the sudden leaving of an employee. Work on projects, especially critical ones, can continue smoothly.
- Managers can network with candidates in a way that nurtures positive professional relationships, even before they become employees at the company.
- It puts good communication at the forefront where both managers and candidates can work with each other collaboratively and comfortably.

How to Build a Talent Pipeline

In order to create a talent pipeline, you first need to build a strategy that supports your organization's business goals and company culture. This essentially allows you to build talent in the present while you keep an eye out for the future.

Talent pipelines should be as comprehensive as possible to cover a wide range of scenarios. Preparing for all potential outcomes that can impact your long-term planning is key. By being proactive and always looking for new ways to identify and attract top talent, you can ensure that your company has the resources it needs to be successful now and in the future.

Although a big part of creating a talent pipeline is attracting the right candidates, it's also important to look after those candidates once hired. You not only want to hire the best talent; you also want to retain them. Finding ways to tactfully engage these candidates helps them choose you over other companies.

It is also important to keep in mind that your talent pipeline should be flexible and adaptable. As your business goals change over time, so should your talent strategy.

Ensuring Your Talent Pipeline Is Diverse

The first step in having a diverse talent pipeline is to recognize and accept the vastness of the term *diversity* itself. This is because something as simple as the wording in your job description can create the wrong impression of your company for a candidate.

If you aim to create a diverse talent pipeline, understand that it takes time. Change does not happen overnight. Give yourself some time to modify things and cover all your bases.

It also helps to take a step back and reconsider previous recruitment techniques that you have used and how they can be improved upon to attract a more diverse applicant pool.

Remember that you are not hiring simply for the sake of diversity; instead, you are hiring to provide everyone with equal opportunities and reduce hiring bias.

With that said, let's have a look at how you can build your own diversity-oriented pipeline.

1. Begin with the Basics

It is important to start with the right mindset: Realize that building a diverse team is going to take time and hard work.

Once you are mentally committed to creating a more inclusive workplace, start by defining what *diversity, equity,* and *inclusion* (DEI) mean for you and your organization.

Craft a commitment to DEI as a business. Take stock of your staff and their backgrounds and demographics. Doing this will allow you to identify the gaps that exist within your system and give you direction on where to go next.

In addition to establishing a DEI mindset, make these additional changes:

- **Build a Diverse Search Committee.** We all have our inherent biases that close us out to certain people and make us feel drawn to others. To ensure that your biases are not interfering with the company's DEI efforts, create a diverse search committee that can provide insight and feedback during the recruitment process.
- **Commit to Create Transparency Around Pay.** Always pay your employees according to what the position entails and not relative to what they used to earn before. This is because women and people of color usually have lower salaries than White males and basing their current salary package based on their pay history can go against your diversity efforts.
- **Look at Transferable Skills.** Instead of focusing on the nitty-gritty of a candidate's technical skills, look at their transferable skills. This will allow you to build a robust diversity pipeline that will bring in talent from unexpected places.

2. Provide Recruiters with the Tools to Make Equitable Hiring Decisions

In order for recruiting to be equitable, companies need to broaden their range of platforms. By doing so, they will be able to tap into a larger pool of talent. Additionally, they will be able to identify qualified candidates who may have been overlooked in the past.

By using a variety of platforms, companies can send a strong message that they are committed to diversity and inclusion. As a result, they will be more likely to attract and retain the best employees.

If you utilize a selected few job portals and sites to post your job advertisements, the audience that ends up viewing your job posts will likely be from a specific class or group of people who use these platforms frequently. Today's job boards and websites allow businesses to help create a more inclusive work environment. Some of them also let you target a certain subsection of society that you want to hire from.

Automated screening software can help you narrow down the kind of applicant pool you are trying to target. These tools often help reduce bias at the screening stage of the hiring process.

3. Train Your Hiring Managers to Ensure That They Drive Your Diversity Efforts

If you want to increase diversity in your workplace, it's important to make sure that your recruitment managers are on board. All too often, unconscious bias can creep in and impact who gets hired, even if those making the decisions are not aware that they are being biased.

By providing training on how to identify and avoid bias, you can help ensure that your recruitment managers are driving your diversity initiatives instead of impeding them. In addition, regular check-ins and audits can help to ensure that progress is being made and that any setbacks are quickly addressed. With the right support, your recruitment managers can be an invaluable asset in increasing diversity in your workplace.

Diversity initiatives are sometimes difficult to manage. It's important to understand what your managers are looking for and then guide them along.

The best way to do this is to frame the conversation in a way that solves a shared objective: to find the best people possible with the best skills for a job role, regardless of their backgrounds. By focusing on this shared goal, you can help your managers see the value in diversity and how it can benefit everyone involved.

Since diversity and an individual's personal bias are delicate topics, it is imperative that you approach this conversation methodically and not in a way that feels accusatory or makes your hiring managers feel as if they are part of the problem.

This means having a conversation that is both open and honest.

This will help you to understand what biases your hiring managers have, and it will help you to address them and develop effective training.

4. Upskill Your Recruiters to Build Awareness Around Unconscious Biases

We all have unconscious biases, whether we like them or not. These are biases that we learn through patterns that occur around us throughout our lives. Essentially, they become automatic to us to the point that we don't recognize them as biases anymore.

We like to think of ourselves as rational beings, but the reality is that we are often driven by our unconscious biases. This is true for everyone, including recruitment managers. When recruitment managers are hiring staff, these biases can lead to an unfair job market that puts certain groups of people at a disadvantage. They lead to inaccurate decision-making and mismanagement.

For example, women and underrepresented groups have often been unfairly overlooked for senior positions because of inaccurate decision-making by those in charge who may assume that women are not strong enough to be leaders or that other underrepresented groups lack the necessary experience. This is not only bad for business, but it ultimately creates a workforce that does not reflect the diversity of society as a whole.

As anyone who's ever worked in an office knows, managers can sometimes be set in their ways. But when it comes to diversity and inclusion, it's important to encourage them to be open to new ideas. One of the more important steps in making your workplace more diverse and inclusive is to educate your managers on unconscious biases.

Help them recognize where they may be biased and how they can avoid making assumptions about people. Put them in touch with organizations that provide training in diversity recruitment. When team members are aware of their own personal preferences, they can make decisions that are more intentional and conscious. By being intentional about diversity in hiring, we can help build a workplace that is truly inclusive for everyone.

5. Go for Blind Hiring

In today's competitive job market, employers are increasingly looking for any edge they can get. As a result, many organizations have turned to blind recruiting, a process in which an applicant's identifying factors and nonessential information are removed from their resumés', information such as the following:

- Name
- Age
- Academic background
- Years of experience
- Location
- Address

The goal of blind hiring is to reduce unconscious bias and create a level playing field for all candidates. Although the practice is still relatively new, it is becoming increasingly common place in organizations globally.

Blind recruiting has been shown to increase diversity in the workplace and help identify individuals with the necessary skills and qualifications for the job. In a blind recruitment process, all resumés are anonymized, and candidates are evaluated based on their merits alone.

This ensures that factors such as gender, ethnicity, and education level do not influence the hiring decision. Although blind recruiting is not a perfect solution, it is a promising tool for creating a more diverse and equitable workforce.

6. Look Both Internally and Externally to Grow a Diverse Network

If you're looking to diversify your network and make your talent pipeline more inclusive, external organizations can be a great help. Reaching out to groups that focus on professional development, networking, and job placement can introduce you to individuals from a variety of backgrounds who can offer new perspectives. Reaching out to a management consultancy firm can help you get in touch with leaders from underrepresented groups.

In addition, these organizations can provide access to resources and opportunities that you may not have had before. By expanding your network, you can create a more diverse pool of potential candidates for your organization and help promote inclusion in the process.

In addition to acquiring external help, you can look within your organization. Reach out to your employee resource groups (ERGs) and get their advice on how you can make the workplace more inclusive. You should also ask your diverse employees for referrals and support.

7. Modify Your Job Descriptions to Make Way for Potential Over Credential

Job descriptions are often where organizations trip up when it comes to promoting diversity. If job descriptions are too specific, they can unintentionally exclude qualified candidates who might not have all the "right" credentials. On the other hand, if job descriptions are too general, it can be difficult for employers to identify the most qualified candidates. The key is to strike a balance between the two. Start by taking a close look at your current job descriptions.

Are there any areas where you could be more inclusive? For example, instead of listing "Bachelor's degree in XYZ" as a required qualification, you could simply say, "Bachelor's degree." This small change can make a big difference in attracting a more diverse pool of candidates.

Alternatively, you could list key qualifications rather than required qualifications. For example, instead of listing "3 years of experience" as a requirement, you could say "experience with XYZ software." By making these small changes to your job descriptions, you can help ensure that your organization is open to all qualified candidates, regardless of their background or credentials.

Many firms get tunnel vision and focus too much on the credentials the previous job holder had. They then compare those skills and traits with those of the new applicants.

This results in people getting weeded out of the hiring process only because they did not come from a similar background.

There is no need to try to duplicate the previous employee. Trying to find an employee who is just like the last one is a fruitless endeavor. Background, skills, and even personality can differ between two people with the same job title. Focusing too much on credentials can lead a company to overlook great candidates who would bring new and innovative ideas to the table.

Instead of trying to duplicate the previous employee, firms should focus on finding someone who is a good fit for the company culture and who has the skills necessary to do the job well. With the right mix of fresh perspectives and experience, any company can thrive. Look at what the potential new hire could bring to the organization. Figure out where that person is today and what they will need to be successful. This means looking at where your potential employee will be in two, three, four, five, or ten years.

8. Partner with Minority Institutions

A wide range of perspectives and experiences can help your company foster creativity, solve problems more effectively, and make better decisions. You also need to find the people who can bring those perspectives and experiences to your company. So if you're looking to increase diversity in your company, consider engaging with Minority Serving Institutions (MSIs).

MSIs are institutions that work to provide education solely to marginalized and underrepresented communities. Their support can help expand your network, fine-tune your diversity pipeline, and create a brand image that attracts diverse candidates. By investing in MSIs, you're also helping to ensure that everyone has an opportunity to succeed.

Many candidates nowadays choose whether to work with an organization based on the foundations and institutions that company follows and supports. Associating yourself with diversity institutions and choosing to partner with them will let people know that you are a business committed to providing a safe working environment for all your employees, regardless of their backgrounds.

9. Consider Relevant Data

When it comes to diversity, equity, and inclusion (DEI), looking at the right data is key to understanding the current status of your organization and where improvements need to be made. The data will also give you insights into any trends that are taking place. Without this information, it will be difficult to put together an effective diversity pipeline.

So what data should you be looking at? First, take a look at your employee demographic data. This will give you an overview of the makeup of your workforce in terms of gender, race, and ethnicity. Next, take a look at your retention rates. This will help you identify any patterns in terms of which groups are staying with the organization and which groups are leaving. Finally, look at your promotion and progression data. This will show you whether all employees are being given the same opportunities to progress within the organization.

By looking at all of this data, you will get a much clearer picture of your organization's DEI status and where improvements need to be made. You can collect data using questionnaires, surveys, and personality testing. When gathering data, always make sure to adhere to privacy laws and company policies surrounding the participants.

It is always good practice to go a step further and gain additional information using anonymous employee surveys. Doing this may uncover new concerns. Furthermore, you can consider conducting focus groups. They would encourage employees to open up and discuss whether their needs are being met within your company.

10. Diversify Your Interview Panel

It's important to have a diversity of perspectives on your interview panel when recruiting new employees. This way you can get a well-rounded view of each candidate and their fit for the role.

Having a diverse recruitment team also helps you avoid any potential unconscious bias in your hiring process. By taking steps to diversify your interview panel, you can ensure that you're getting the best talent for the job, regardless of background or identity.

This way, it will also be easier for diverse talent to envision themselves as a part of your organization because they will be more at ease and know that they wouldn't be the only diverse employees in the company.

If you cannot find a diverse employee to be a part of your interview panel, you should be honest with your candidates about why that is and what you are doing to overcome it. Most candidates are going to appreciate honesty and authenticity as it will represent your organization's ethics, who you are, and what you stand for.

11. Build a Strong Onboarding Process

A strong onboarding process is an important bridge between the candidate and the employees. As mentioned earlier, you don't just want to attract and hire diverse talent; you also want to keep talent from leaving. Creating an inclusive onboarding experience in which everyone feels like they can be themselves is a key part of this.

From the very first day, candidates should feel like they are a valuable part of the team. One way to do this is to make sure that their voices are heard and that their opinions are valued. It's also important to create an environment where people feel like they can be open about their backgrounds and experiences.

Onboarding is an important process for any new hire, but it's also an opportunity to get to know employees on a personal level and learn about their preferences. For example, you can ask employees about their preferred pronouns or whether they have any specific dietary needs or preferences.

By accommodating them, you'll make workplace integration much easier and more comfortable. Additionally, you'll get to know your employees, which can help to build a strong foundation for a productive and positive working relationship.

By making inclusion a priority from day one, you can help ensure that your diverse workforce feels engaged and respected.

12. Measure and Celebrate the Success of Your Diversity Hiring Programs

Fine-tune your diversity pipeline by measuring the success of your diversity hiring. Keep track of your progress and see how you are stacking up against the goals you set.

Share your results with the team and ask them for constructive feedback. If it is warranted, celebrate the success of your efforts. This lets your employees know that you truly care for inclusion and diversity in the company. It also creates a healthier and more positive environment for employees to work in. They will produce their best work because they feel appreciated, respected, and included.

13. Build a Company Culture That Is Inclusive

If you find yourself hiring many diverse candidates but they don't stay at your company for long, it might be time to take a look at your organization as a whole. It's possible that your workplace isn't conducive to a diverse workforce, and that needs to change.

There are a few things you can do to make your workplace more inclusive:

- Promote career development and growth opportunities for diverse employees.
- Publish diversity data.
- Offer awards and benefits that consider the needs of different groups.
- Support mentorship programs.
- Check-in on new employees.
- Encourage the formation of employee resource groups and their initiatives.

There are several other things you need to consider:

- Make an effort to connect with your employees to get to know them and their backgrounds and foster an environment where everyone feels comfortable being open about their cultures and experiences.
- Make sure that all employees feel like they have an equal opportunity to grow and advance in the company. That means creating pathways for promotions and offering training and development opportunities that are open to everyone.
- Be aware of unconscious bias in the workplace. We all have biases, but it's important to be aware of them so we can make an effort to overcome them. This includes things like not assuming that all new

hires are entry-level and not passing overqualified candidates because they don't fit the "corporate" mold.

14. Work with Colleges and Universities

One of the best ways to ensure a robust diversity pipeline is to partner with colleges and universities, especially when you are searching for university graduates. By collaborating with these institutions, companies can ensure that a steady stream of qualified candidates from diverse backgrounds is entering the job market.

In addition, colleges and universities can provide valuable resources and support to help employees thrive in their careers. As the workforce continues to become more diverse, companies that partner with colleges and universities will be well-positioned for success.

Final Thoughts

The candidate-employer relationship has transformed in the last few years. Applicants are now essentially consumers who are shopping for jobs. If organizations want to attract the best talent, they need to understand the expectations of every generation and know what speaks to them. There is no question that **diversity is important in the workplace**. It makes good business sense and helps foster a more creative and innovative environment. However, building a diverse workforce is not always easy.

One of the best ways to ensure success is to develop a robust diversity pipeline. This can be accomplished by partnering with community organizations, colleges and universities, and professional associations.

By building diversity pipeline, companies can position themselves as the employers of choice for diverse talent and build strong relationships with potential candidates. Additionally, diversity pipelines result in the professional and personal growth of the people involved. Finally, they enable companies to take an important step toward building a more diverse and inclusive workforce.

4. The D&I Strategy

In the wake of protests against racial injustice, many companies have made pledges to do better when it comes to diversity and inclusion (D&I). Although this is a step in the right direction, these sorts of pledges have been made before with little success.

In order to create lasting change, businesses need to take a hard look at their own hiring practices and make sure they're not inadvertently perpetuating bias and systemic racism. This means being intentional about seeking out qualified candidates from diverse backgrounds and making sure that everyone in the company feels like they belong. Only then will we start to see real progress when it comes to corporate diversity.

A diversity and inclusion strategy is important for any organization but can be especially beneficial for those that hire underrepresented groups. However, although diversity and inclusion strategies are fine to a point, they can also be problematic if they aren't developed properly. A diversity and inclusion strategy should be designed with input from the marginalized group and should reflect their needs. It should also be updated regularly to reflect changes in the community and the organization.

Developing an Effective D&I Strategy

According to a survey of Harvard Business School alumni,[62] 76 percent of those in senior executive positions believe that "a more diverse workforce improves the organization's financial performance." Other diversity surveys show that diversity hiring can be a good decision for businesses that are able to conduct market research and understand their needs.

When developing a strategy for diversity and Inclusion, it's essential that you develop an evaluation process that will help you get clear on the needs of your organization. The evaluation process should also take into consideration whether diversity hiring will be compatible with other existing business initiatives.

In addition, it's essential to incorporate your plan for diversity hiring into your overall business strategy. This is a particularly important aspect for companies that have multiple offices and locations across the world. Even though each office may have its own data set, there should still be

---

[62] https://hbr.org/2020/11/getting-serious-about-diversity-enough-already-with-the-business-case

some level of commonality among these data sets to ensure that you get an accurate representation.

There is no one-size-fits-all strategy for diversity hiring. However, there are some common best practices that can help organizations in their efforts. For instance, you could consider the diversity of your own workforce. This can be seen in a number of different ways. For instance, if your workplace is predominantly male, you may find it useful to consider hiring female staff members. This could also help reduce some of the gender-based wage gaps that exists between women and men.

However, simply hiring a few employees from underrepresented groups is not enough to create a truly diverse and inclusive workplace. To be truly effective, organizations need to consider their culture when developing a diversity hiring strategy. Otherwise, the new hires will quickly become disillusioned and leave. For example, if an organization has a history of sexual harassment, women will be reluctant to apply for jobs there, but even if they do accept a job offer, the sexual harassment will make them want to leave.

Similarly, if an organization is known for its discriminatory practices, people of color will be hesitant to join the team. If they do join the team, they won't stick around if they feel unwelcome. By taking the time to assess its culture and address any issues, an organization can create a more welcoming environment for everyone. Only then will it be able to attract and *retain* the best talent from all groups.

Any good D&I strategy starts with an understanding of the workforce. You need to know who your employees are, what they care about, and how they're different from one another. That way you can figure out what kind of D&I initiatives will resonate with them.

For example, if you have a lot of employees who are passionate about social justice issues, you might want to focus on initiatives that promote equity and inclusion. Alternatively, if you have a workforce that's highly engaged in their communities, you might want to focus on volunteering and community service opportunities.

Once you understand your workforce, you can start to develop targeted D&I initiatives that will make a real impact. And don't forget: The effort is not just about putting out the right messages; it's also about ensuring that your workplace is actually inclusive and welcoming to everyone.

That means making sure that your policies and practices are fair, that your environment is respectful and conducive to open dialogue, and that everyone has a chance to contribute their unique perspectives. It takes effort to create a truly inclusive workplace, but it's worth it. When everyone feels like they belong, they're more likely to be productive, engaged, and committed to your organization's success.

Building a strong diversity and inclusion strategy doesn't have to be complicated. In fact, there are really only a few key steps you need to take in order to set your company up for success. By following these simple steps, you can develop a strong diversity and inclusion strategy that will benefit both your employees and your business as a whole.

Step 1: Define What Diversity and Inclusion Mean to Your Organization

Diversity and inclusion are buzzwords that are often used in workplaces, but what do they actually mean? We know that, in general, *diversity* refers to the variety of people who make up the staff at your company. *Inclusion* refers to the effort of making sure that everyone can participate in and benefit from the workplace environment. But what do the terms mean specifically to *your* company? Start by understanding your own culture. What values do your employees hold dear? What does the company stand for? What does diversity look like in your workplace? What will make your employees feel valued and engaged?

Step 2: Identify the Stakeholders Involved

The stakeholders involved in developing a diversity and inclusion strategy are typically employees, customers, clients, suppliers, partners, and community members. It is important to identify these groups early in the process so that they can be included in the strategy development process. Also identify any potential barriers that may exist for these groups and create strategies to address them.

Step 3: Assess the Current Situation

Begin the strategy development process by assessing the current situation at your company. This means understanding your company's demographics, culture, and history. Once you have a good understanding of where you stand, you can develop a strategy for improvement.

Step 4: Develop a Strategy and Plan of Action

The best way to develop a diversity and inclusion strategy will vary depending on the organization's size, mission, and culture. However, there are some key steps that most organizations should take in order to create a comprehensive plan of action:

- Make sure that policies and procedures are in place to support diversity and inclusion. This includes things like anti-discrimination policies, equal opportunity/affirmative action programs, and training for employees on how to be respectful and inclusive of others.

- Understand the current climate and landscape of diversity and inclusion in the workplace. This can be done by conducting an assessment of the organization's demographics, including race, ethnicity, gender identity/expression, sexual orientation, physical challenges and differences, age group, and so on.
- Identify any gaps or disparities that exist within the organization based on these demographics.
- Develop a plan of action that addresses each gap or disparity identified.
- Define your goals. What are you hoping to achieve with your diversity and inclusion strategy? Do you want to increase representation of underrepresented groups? Create a more diverse leadership team? Improve employee satisfaction? It is important to be clear about your goals from the outset, as this will help you measure success.
- Consider your audience. Who do you want to reach with your diversity and inclusion efforts? Employees? Customers? Vendors? Make sure that your strategy is tailored to your target audience.
- Focus on recruiting a diverse pool of employees. This means not only looking for candidates who are from different backgrounds but also encouraging them to apply for open positions.
- Make sure you're marketing your products and services to a wider range of customers.
- Educate yourself and your team. Understand the key concepts surrounding diversity and inclusion and make sure that everyone on your team is on the same page. This will help create a common language.

Step 5: Implement the Strategy

Implementing a diversity and inclusion strategy can be a challenge. There are many factors to consider, such as creating an environment that is welcoming to all employees, creating training programs that are effective and accessible, and monitoring progress regularly.

There is no one-size-fits-all answer to how to implement a diversity and inclusion strategy, as the approach that is most effective for a given organization will depend on the size, culture, and mission. However, there are some general tips that can be useful in developing any such strategy:

- Many organizations believe that diversity and inclusion are critical to their overall success but do not have a clear understanding of what those goals actually are. It is important to articulate those goals clearly and unambiguously before beginning any implementation efforts.

- Develop an action plan for implementing the diversity and inclusion strategy. A D&I action plan should include specific goals and objectives as well as timelines for achieving them. Additionally, the plan should outline how employees will be evaluated based on their progress in implementing the strategy. The implementation should include milestones and measurements such as determining whether
  — the environment is inclusive for all employees,
  — effective training is provided, and
  — systems are in place to identify and address discrimination or bias. Encourage communication among all employees.

Elements of the D&I Strategy

Your D&I strategy should not be limited to one element of operations, like recruiting, for example. Instead, it should be comprehensive and touch upon *all* aspects of the workforce experience at your company. For example, you will want to consider at least some of the following elements:

1. **Diversity training.** This is crucial in maintaining a balanced team. It equips employees with the capability to understand, appreciate, and respect other cultures, religions, and ethnicities.
2. **Diversity management.** This is a proactive approach to achieving diversity at all levels within your company. It involves monitoring, encouraging, and supporting diversity all along the way. The result will be an inclusive team in a supportive environment where everyone can learn and be inspired.
3. **Mentoring.** Mentors help train and guide employees to keep them motivated and productive.
4. **Cultural integration.** This is necessary for fostering new ideas, perspectives, and opportunities that create a greater learning experience for your diverse team. It should be surrounded by policies, programs, or strategies that support active communication with employees.
5. **Culture change and development.** This is an effective way to ensure that your company's culture embraces the concepts of diversity and inclusion. Your company needs to change from one that is exclusive to one that is inclusive.
6. **Sensitivity training.** Such training helps your company avoid discrimination and hurtful behavior in the workplace.
7. **Fair employment practices.** This is an effective system that sets up equal opportunity for all employees regardless of their ethnic, racial, gender, and religious backgrounds.

8. **Improved recruitment process.** This is one way of ensuring that your company is making the best use of its diversity assets. It allows for greater representation and fairer promotion in the workplace.

Developing a D&I Policy

In the wake of increasing cultural, ethnic, and religious diversity in your company, you will find it difficult to run your business without a D&I policy that clearly spells out the expectations of your company for its diverse employees. This is about ensuring that everyone does their part to foster an environment where all employees are treated fairly and kindly.

Another benefit of such a policy is that it encourages open communication because everyone knows what's expected. The alignment of workplace policies with the culture of your business is key to a productive environment. This is best accomplished through clear communication, mutual understanding, and clear goals. Otherwise, the interpersonal differences and cultural gaps that exist in the workplace can be a fertile source for conflicts that disrupt both the atmosphere of work and the performance of employees.

According to the U.S. Bureau of Labor Statistics, cultural clashes in the workplace can be caused by language differences, different training and educational levels, different values and expectations, as well as different codes of ethics and business practices. If administrative routines are not followed properly, they can also lead to disharmony within your company's diverse team.

So how do you develop a diversity and inclusion policy?

Here are some guidelines:

1. Start by defining the values of your company to see how they align with the concept of diversity and inclusion.
2. Determine what office policies will promote diversity and how you will go about building a fair system for promoting policies that are unbiased or based on meritocracy rather than on race or gender quotas (which are illegal).
3. Create a culture of inclusion by advocating equal opportunities for the advancement of all employees.
4. Integrate employees from different cultures, age groups, genders, sexual identities, and languages by welcoming them as new additions to your company's workforce. Set up common channels that allow people from different cultural backgrounds to interact with one another—this will help create an open and honest environment where people can

engage in respectful dialogue about the issues that are common to their respective cultures or the differences in their needs and aspirations.

5. Work hard to ensure that everyone is treated equally and that your company's vision and mission are upheld by clear job descriptions.

6. Adopt a policy of inclusion; set up means for employees to share their contributions, work styles, talents, and aspirations within the company in order to help create a supportive environment for all workers.

The concept of diversity and inclusion at the workplace encompasses many different aspects and dimensions. In addition being about racial, gender, or sexual differences, it is also about how we define ourselves as individuals living in a culturally diverse society.

The globalization of markets has brought people of all races, ethnicities, and religions together to share the same working space. Workplace diversity is more than just a set of policies and practices; it is an ideal way to build an inclusive culture that allows everyone to be valued for who they are and their individual contributions.

A diverse and inclusive workforce can lead to innovation, creativity, and better decision-making. But without a diversity and inclusion (D&I) *strategy,* a company risks putting together a diverse workforce that cannot function at an optimal level.

The Four Types of Diversity in the Workplace

Workplace diversity can be classified into four major types: **internal**, **external**, **organizational**, and **world view**. Of these, *internal diversity* is the most important, as it sets the tone for the rest of the workplace.

Internal diversity is all about creating a workplace where everyone feels comfortable and respected. It includes efforts to insure gender equality, racial equality, and disability inclusion. Creating an inclusive environment starts with hiring a diverse workforce, but it doesn't stop there. You also need to ensure that your workplace policies are fair and inclusive, that your employees feel like they can openly discuss diversity issues, and that you're regularly assessing your progress on D&I.

External diversity is about engaging with people from different backgrounds and perspectives. This could mean anything from working with suppliers from diverse backgrounds to holding events that focus on topics like social justice or environmentalism to expanding the range of customers you serve. The goal is to broaden your company's horizons and get everyone thinking about D&I in new ways.

Organizational diversity is all about creating a company culture that values D&I. This could mean implementing D&I training for all employees, setting up Inclusion Councils or Employee Resource Groups, and actively monitoring your company's progress on D&I metrics. It also means being open to making changes to your organization if you find that you're not living up to your D&I values.

World view diversity is about taking a global perspective on D&I. For example, you might increase your awareness of international D&I trends and partner with organizations that focus on underrepresented groups. The goal is to build a workplace that truly reflects the world we live in today.

Final Thoughts

Diversity in the workplace is important for many reasons. It helps companies tap into a larger pool of talent, leads to increased creativity and innovative thinking, helps companies better understand their customer base, strengthens relationships with suppliers and contractors, and creates a more tolerant world.

No matter what type of workplace diversity you're looking to create, it's important to remember that the most important thing is to start with *internal* diversity. By hiring a diverse workforce and creating an inclusive environment, you'll set the tone for the rest of the workplace and lay the foundation for a successful D&I program.

From there, you can focus on external diversity initiatives, organizational changes, and global perspectives. By taking a comprehensive approach to workplace diversity, you'll ensure that your company is ready for anything.

Two Models for Workplace Diversity

There are a variety of ways to manage and measure diversity, but it can be difficult to know which approach is best.

One common model is the Diversity Management Model (DMaM), which focuses on increasing representation of underrepresented groups. The model is based on three functions of diversity management: recruiting and outreach, building cultural awareness, and promoting pragmatic management policy. These functions are linked to organizational performance through a series of intermediate steps. Quantitative analysis is then applied.[63] This model has been criticized for its lack of focus on inclusion as well as its potential to create a quota system.

Another approach is the Diversity Measurement Model (DMeM), which aims to track progress toward inclusion and identify areas that need improvement. This model has been praised for its ability to hold organizations accountable, but it can also be bogged down by data collection and analysis.

Both models have their strengths and weaknesses, and organizations must decide which approach is best for them.

There are a few key ways in which DMaM and DMeM differ. First, DMaM focuses on *creating* an inclusive environment within an organization, while DMeM collects data with the aim of *understanding* the current state of diversity within a company.

Second, DMaM is proactive, while DMeM is reactive; the former seeks to prevent discrimination and foster inclusion, while the latter simply gathers information about existing disparities.

Finally, DMaM is concerned with the long-term goals of an organization, while DMeM is more concerned with providing data that can be used to inform future decisions. While both approaches are important, it is clear that they serve different purposes.

Final Thoughts

The intricate relationship among diversity, inclusion, and the bottom line has been subject to debate by executives and scholars.

McKinsey's research[64] on diversity showed that companies with more diverse gender, culture, and ethnicity outperform employers that don't support diversity. The research found that companies in the top quartile for gender diversity experience outperform by 21%. For ethnic and cultural diversity, there was a 33% likelihood of outperformance.[65]

In order to promote inclusion in organizations, leaders must understand that creating diverse and inclusive workplaces calls for a broader understanding of diversity, one that sees the process

---

[63] https://journals.sagepub.com/doi/abs/10.1177/0734371X05278491
[64] https://www.mckinsey.com/business-functions/people-and-organizational-performance/our-insights/delivering-through-diversity
[65] https://haiilo.com/blog/diversity-and-inclusion-best-practices-focus-on-in-2020/

as ongoing and changing and one that takes into consideration successful integration of all employees in a company's processes and structure. Employers need to understand that diversity of staff is not the endpoint but merely a step along the way.

Creating a D&I strategy can be challenging, but it's worth it. To achieve such a strategy, you need to address a number of issues. One is that employees need to be aware of their own biases and the biases of others. Another is that organization needs to have D&I policies in place. These policies should address how employees can identify and address bias and how the company might promote diversity and inclusion.

By creating a D&I strategy, businesses can ensure that they are providing a welcoming environment for all employees. This can help to reduce discrimination and harassment as well as improve employee productivity.

5. SWOT Analysis in D&I

In order to create a successful diversity strategy, it is important to first understand your company's strengths and weaknesses. This can be done through a SWOT analysis. SWOT stands for **S**trengths, **W**eaknesses, **O**pportunities, and **T**hreats. By taking a close look at all four of these factors, companies can develop a more comprehensive and effective D&I strategy. A SWOT analysis divides the four categories into an organized list that is usually represented in a two-by-twrid pattern.

One of the advantages of using SWOT analysis is that it forces companies to take an honest look at their strengths and weaknesses. This can be difficult for some organizations, and a SWOT analysis is only as good as the information that goes into it.

A SWOT analysis is not useful only for understanding a company's internal workings. This analysis often proves to be extremely useful in recruitment too. Using the SWOT method, recruiters are essentially able to recognize what the candidates are looking for. They are able to analyze what their competitors are doing and how their own recruiting strategy stacks up against the industry standard, eventually leading them to enhance their sourcing efforts.

SWOT analysis can be used to study a number of varying situations in a business.

- Organizations can carry out a SWOT analysis for all of their products and services when deciding on the optimal way to achieve growth in the future.
- During the initial stages of a project, it is important to get a handle on the current situation. Using SWOT to appreciate your strengths, recognize weaknesses, study opportunities, and identify threats is a great way to kick off a project.
- A SWOT analysis can also be used to identify areas where the organization could improve its diversity.

To complete a SWOT analysis, collect the necessary information from interviews with key stakeholders, surveys, or focus groups. There are four steps you need to follow.

1. Build the Right Team of People

In order to create an effective SWOT analysis, it is important to have a team of people who are representative of the entire company. This team should ideally include someone from every department, as each person will bring a unique perspective to the table.

Having a variety of viewpoints is essential for productive and critical thinking, both of which are necessary for making the SWOT analysis a success. By bringing everyone together, you can create an environment where all voices are heard and considered, resulting in a more comprehensive and accurate assessment.

2. Conduct Brainstorming Sessions

Doing a SWOT analysis is quite similar to conducting brainstorming sessions and meetings. There is always a right and wrong way to run them in order to make them fruitful.

In order for your brainstorming meeting to be productive, it is good practice to provide everyone with a sticky note pad. To kick things off, have everyone jot their ideas down on the sticky notes.

This approach is better than allowing everyone to speak their ideas out loud first thing as it avoids groupthink. This method also makes sure that every department is heard.

After 10 to 15 minutes of brainstorming, put all the sticky notes on the wall, grouping similar ideas together. Allow for additional notes by employees at this stage.

When building your SWOT analysis, ask different types of questions to help guide the employees through the process.

Strength Questions

Strengths are things your organization is really good at; they are what sets your company apart from rivals and gives it an edge. Think about the benefits your organization provides over its competitors. They could be anything from a solid customer service base to a strong manufacturing process. Or, in terms of recruiting, they could include an attractive bonus package or a great work-life balance opportunity.

Your strengths are an integral part of your business. Along with asking yourself the questions mentioned below, analyze your company's Unique Selling Proposition (USP)[66] and add it to the *Strengths* section.

Remember at this stage to add only aspects of your organization that bring you a clear advantage over others.

Questions:

---

[66] https://www.entrepreneur.com/encyclopedia/unique-selling-proposition-usp

- What can you do well?
- What types of benefits are offered in your company?
- What are the qualities that separate you from your rivals?
- Is there an opportunity for work-life balance?
- What is the measure of growth per year in the industry?
- Is your brand image strong?
- How long has your organization been in business?
- Is there a unique focus?

Weakness Questions

Here, focus on your people, systems, resources, and procedures. Think about the things you can do to address the weaknesses. Also make a list of actions to avoid in the future that impact the organization negatively.

You want to find out how other people view you in the market. What is your brand image? Do they notice weaknesses that you are blind to? What is it that you are failing to see?

In your *Weakness* section, be honest. A SWOT analysis will only be as valuable as the information gathered.

Questions:

- **Company presence.** Where is your biggest presence? What part of the country is it concentrated in? Is that area one that candidates want to live and work in?
- **Company culture.** What is it like to work for you?
- **Attrition.** What is the rate of attrition per year? From which area do you tend to lose employees the most?
- **Credibility.** What is your company's standing in terms of credibility in the market?

Opportunities Questions

Opportunities are openings for something positive to take place, and you will need to seize them. You need to be able to spot and exploit opportunities that can make a difference in your organization and help you take the lead in your industry.

Questions:

- Could the benefits be made more competitive?
- What does your organization offer that your rival does not?
- How valuable is your rival's credibility?
- What type of developmental and career advancement opportunities are not available?

- How is modern technology affecting/changing your business?
- Are there new markets to apply your strengths in that you are currently neglecting?

Threat Questions

Threats consist of anything that can negatively impact your business. For your business to thrive, it is essential to take action against threats before they stall your growth.

When analyzing threats, always consider what your competitors are doing. Be willing to change your organization's focus to meet the challenge.

Questions:

- What is your competitor's growth forecast?
- Is your competitor expanding rapidly?
- What is their current industry ranking?
- What are your rivals developing?
- Is the introduction of new technology making your product or service obsolete?
- Is employee turnover high?
- Do you have a healthy cash flow?
- Are your employees satisfied?
- Are there any regulatory issues in locations where talent must be sourced?

3. Rank the Ideas

Once all the ideas are laid out on the wall, you should rank them. A great way to do that is through a vote. Based on the votes, you can then create a prioritized list of ideas. This list is then up for discussion, debate, and amendments.

Someone in the room should be appointed to make the final call. Usually, this person is the CEO. But the task can be delegated to a manager or someone else in the organization.

This process should be repeated for all four quadrants of your SWOT analysis: Strengths, Weaknesses, Opportunities, and Threats.

4. Create an Action Plan

Once you and your teams have analyzed the four aspects of SWOT, you will then want to do the following:

- Build on your strengths.
- Improve your areas of weakness.

- Exploit every opportunity.
- Get rid of any threats.

It is highly likely that after carrying out an analysis, you will have a long list of actions to undertake. But before you move ahead, make sure to develop your ideas further. Look for possible connections among the four different sections of your matrix. Might any opportunities open up because of your strengths? Are there any weaknesses that could lead to threats? Can you turn any weaknesses into opportunities?

Once that is done, it is then time to prioritize and fine-tune the list of ideas you have. You need to narrow your focus so that you can allocate the required time and money to the most impactful ideas.

It is important to note here that you need to apply the learnings you gain as a result of a SWOT analysis at the right level in your company, rather than simply companywide.

Example SWOT Analysis

Strengths	Weaknesses
• Low overhead from salary and benefits • Quick response to changes in the market • Lightweight and flat hierarchy resulting in faster decision-making	• Workload too high • Expertise missing from some key areas • No previous product planning experience
Opportunities	Threats
• Could convert existing products/services for new markets • Need to increase market share	• Loyalty issues with business partners • Cost of investing in new technology • Established competitors getting majority market share and brand-name recognition

Example D&I SWOT Analysis

Strengths	Weaknesses
• Employee diversity: 57% female in leadership roles, 38% minorities • Actively working with diverse groups and communities • Willing to accept, even if we do not agree (safe place) • Proactive responsiveness to change	• Not a clear commitment to diversity and inclusion across the organization. • Personal and institutional biases. • Lack of diversity among staff and in the community
Opportunities	**Threats**
• Expand the recruiting efforts to cover more diverse populations. • Tap into the energy, experience, and perspectives of our community. • Develop and communicate top-down support for diversity and inclusion across the whole company. • Develop diversity and inclusion performance aspects on performance reviews.	• Losing talented employees to other employers, based on the perception that our company does not embrace diversity and inclusion • Avoiding difficult discussions perpetuates bias, which makes us less effective • Lawsuits related to policy violations and unfair treatment of employees

In our example, the company needs to align positive elements of the organization to help take advantage of opportunities and identify gaps that occur due to the negative elements.

Final Thoughts

Organizational health and sustainability are why DEI topics are important. A SWOT analysis will provide a company with a comprehensive picture of their strengths, weaknesses, opportunities, and threats in relation to equity and inclusion. Once decision-makers have a better understanding of their knowledge base, limitations, and needs, they can analyze DEI in terms of organizational health and sustainability.

A healthy organization understands that its employee base is diverse and that taking steps to become more inclusive creates an environment where everyone can succeed. A sustainable organization knows that by being proactive on DEI issues they can avoid costly litigation and rebuild trust with employees, customers, vendors, and other stakeholders.

Organizations need to evolve their thinking on DEI from viewing it as something "nice to have" to something that is critical to organizational success. A SWOT evaluation can help get organizations started on that path by providing them with a snapshot of where they currently stand. From there, it will be up to leadership to give their employees the resources and support needed to create a more equitable workplace for all.

6. The Diversity Talent Mapping Plan

Diversity talent mapping is the practice of identifying and recruiting individuals from underrepresented groups. It is important to note that 'diversity' goes beyond race, ethnicity, and gender. Instead, diversity should be seen as a combination of experiences, perspectives, and thought processes. It includes people of color, women, LGBTQIA+ individuals, people with disabilities, and other groups that are traditionally underrepresented in the workforce. The mapping helps organizations build more diverse and inclusive workforces, which can lead to increased creativity and innovation, improved decision-making, and enhanced customer satisfaction.

In order to be effective, diversity talent mapping must be aligned with an organization's overall business goals and strategies. Additionally, it is important to have a dedicated team or individual responsible for implementing and overseeing the process. Finally, the involved staff need to learn how to prepare a diversity talent mapping plan.

Creating this plan will help develop strategies to attract, recruit, retain, and promote different talents. It will result in innovative ideas, collaborative problem solving, and increased innovation.

Creating a diverse talent mapping plan has many benefits for any organization. Let's examine a few:

- **Improved Workforce Quality.** Diverse groups produce more innovative ideas than do homogeneous groups. Having employees from various backgrounds improves the overall quality of the workgroup, and this, in turn, drives up company performance.
- **Enhanced Customer Satisfaction.** Including diverse employees in your organization's workforce can lead to increased product or services satisfaction among your customer base, helping to build strong relationships with them.
- **Excellent Problem Solving.** Diverse workgroups are better at solving problems together as they are more likely to consider multiple perspectives.
- **Increased Collaboration.** Diverse groups bring different ideas and experiences to the table.
- **Improved Retention Rates and Turnover.** Starting a diversity talent mapping plan can help drive internal retention rates and decrease turnover by removing diversity-related barriers to advancement.

- **Increased Hiring Potential.** By launching a diversity talent mapping plan, companies are more likely to increase their hiring potential by opening up communication channels.
- **Enhanced Organizational Success.** A diverse workforce leads to enhanced products or services offered by the company because diversity is associated with creativity, reduced biases, and greater engagement.
- **High-Quality Talent Pipeline.** Having a diversity talent mapping plan can help develop strategies that are targeted to attract, recruit, retain, and promote diverse talent, leading to an increased number of individuals who meet the company's requirements for jobs.
- **Reaping Rewards.** By developing your company's diversity strategy, you are investing in your employees and helping to build tomorrow. Why wait? If you have not already done it, take the first step towards a diverse culture in your organization today and open new doors to mutual success.

Starting a diversity talent mapping plan is crucial for future success in today's highly competitive job market. A talent mapping process can help organizations determine their existing pool of talent. Once organizations have an idea who they currently employ, they need to dig deeper and map out their demographics. These statistics will help determine if there is a problem. For example, if more than 20 percent of staff identifies as Chinese but there are no Chinese-identifying executives, there is a problem. Organizations can update their plans with new data as employees come and go each year.

Companies should do their best to create an atmosphere where people feel comfortable sharing information about themselves. This will allow companies to determine the root causes of gaps in demographics.

The Importance of Designated Leadership

Organizations must designate an authority to have the final say in hiring decisions. Depending on the company's size, this could include the CEO. It is also essential that hiring decisions are made not by an individual but rather by a group of people who represent the various levels of the organization.

Designated leadership can ensure that diverse hiring practices are implemented throughout an organization, updating their job descriptions, for example, to include words like *diversity* and *inclusion*. This will help them attract a vast pool of applicants.

Leaders must constantly keep an eye on demographics to see where improvements are needed. Organizations should continuously aim to increase the number of people from different backgrounds in their workforces. This diversity will help the organization grow and improve overall.

Diversity Hiring Practices Across the Board

Diversity hiring practices should not be limited exclusively to a specific hiring situation. It should be part of employee performance reviews too. This will help employees understand that diversification is vital for the organization's future success.

If diversity hiring is encouraged throughout an organization, it will become a natural part of the interviewing and selection processes. For example, interview panels should consist of people from varied backgrounds asking questions that explore diversity.

Managers should be trained on diversity hiring so they can lead by example. They should incorporate diversity hiring practices into their daily routine, such as by discussing diversification with colleagues outside of regular working hours, by encouraging diversity among work teams, and by planning events that celebrate diverse success stories.

How to Create a Diversity Talent Mapping Plan

A diversity talent mapping plan cannot happen overnight. It takes time and effort to identify the areas of need, develop a strategy, and implement changes. Organizations must have a clear vision of what they want to achieve and how they will achieve it before they can begin the process of mapping their diverse talent pool. The effort will require unified and coordinated participation of both HR professionals and leaders in the organization.

To create a diversity talent mapping plan, organizations should start by identifying the areas of improvement needed within their workforce. These areas could include

- types of candidates not currently targeted or attracted,
- geographic locations lacking diversity in the workplace, and
- groups underrepresented in the workforce.

Once these areas have been identified, organizations should create a plan to address them. Strategies include

- creating a diversity recruiting strategy that involves advertising employment opportunities across different media outlets and internally through employee networks and talent communities,
- developing plans for attracting diverse talent at job fairs or career expos,
- training supervisors to mentor and coach employees through promotion opportunities, and
- encouraging employees from diverse backgrounds to attend events or conferences that highlight their group's achievements in the workforce.

Final Thoughts

Talent mapping is a process that starts by identifying the underutilized and underrepresented groups within the organization, including different races and ethnicities, women, and veterans. Talent mapping helps companies understand the root causes of why employees from underrepresented groups leave, helping them improve retention. Talent mapping can also identify problems such as lack of training and mentorship or a hostile work environment.

For diversity talent mapping to work in your company, it's essential that company leaders value diversity in the workplace. They need to be on board with your strategy and committed to creating an inclusive environment where everyone can thrive. With the right leadership in place, diversity talent mapping can be an extremely powerful tool for success.

7. Common D&I Challenges

Diversity and inclusion bring a plethora of benefits to our workplaces, so much so that diverse companies are 1.7 times[67] more likely to be innovation leaders because they process data differently. Harvard Business Review[68] research found that more diverse companies are significantly better positioned—70 percent more likely—to capture new markets. And inclusive teams make better business decisions up to 87 percent of the time.[69]

With different perspectives and ideas comes more creative problem-solving. This helps companies better serve their customer base and gain a competitive advantage over their non-inclusive rivals. These are all good things. But D&I is not without its challenges. Let's explore what those are and how they might be overcome.

Communication Issues

Communication issues are common in diverse workplaces. Diversity can be accompanied by language barriers or differences in body language. It's important to address these communication challenges before they result in serious problems.

For example, if you have staff members in a primarily English-speaking environment who are nonnative speakers, you may see communication problems crop up in meetings, in written correspondence, or even in interface with customers. You will want to provide support to the nonnative speakers in the form of additional training and you will want to encourage the native speakers to monitor their own communication to make sure they are being understood. Staff can help identify particularly difficult types of interactions or easily misunderstood phrases and expressions.

Diversity Fatigue

Employees of a company who begin to experience diversity and inclusion efforts negatively could be biased and close-minded or they could just be experiencing what is known as *diversity fatigue*. This is a common

---

[67] https://joshbersin.com/2015/12/why-diversity-and-inclusion-will-be-a-top-priority-for-2016/
[68] https://hbr.org/2013/12/how-diversity-can-drive-innovation
[69] https://www.forbes.com/sites/eriklarson/2017/09/21/new-research-diversity-inclusion-better-decision-making-at-work/

development among employees who have been with a company for a long time and feel like they are suddenly not being heard or suddenly of less importance.

If unaddressed, diversity fatigue can lead to apathy and resentment, which can then lead to less productivity and more conflict.

Here are a few common indications of diversity fatigue:

- Employees say that diversity hiring "lowers the bar."
- Majority talent—such as White, cisgender men—may feel threatened because they view diversity initiatives as an effort against their own presence in the workplace.
- Employees overinvested in the cause of D&I can experience burnout from all the emotional energy required.

To confront diversity fatigue, you have to start with open communication and commitment to listening to *all* voices. When everyone feels like they are being heard, they are more likely to be engaged and invested in the company's success. It's also important to be careful not to frame D&I as a reaction against well-represented groups of people but instead as a positive, welcoming move toward underrepresented groups.

Remember that D&I is a long game. Setting unrealistic expectations early on in the process will only demoralize everyone in the long run.

Not Taking D&I Seriously

At some workplaces, employees perceive D&I initiatives as a joke. In these settings, the initiatives are often pushed aside and not taken seriously, which is a real shame. After all, these initiatives can have a real impact on an organization. They can help foster a more inclusive and more successful environment and promote understanding and respect for different cultures. Additionally, they can boost morale and help to attract and retain talent.

Diversity initiatives often get pushed aside for one or all of these reasons:

- The employees are prejudiced.
- The employees feel uncomfortable around the topic.
- The employees don't believe you're serious.

There are good strategies for addressing any of these problems:

- Remember not to rush things. Rushing will force people into situations before they're ready.
- Make sure the rationale for D&I is clear and that employees understand that statistics show D&I will benefit the bottom line.

- Make sure the D&I strategy doesn't sound too ambitious or inauthentic. Aim to start small, cut the unnecessary jargon, and get more concrete.
- Face opposition with direct communication, compassion, and a desire to understand what the underlying concerns are. Assume that the opposers are coming from a good place.
- Make sure to have the support of company leaders. Staff are more likely to sign on if they see upper management is behind the effort.

If your initiatives are not taken seriously, they're likely to have little effect. It's important for organizations to make sure that their diversity and inclusion initiatives are given the attention and resources they deserve. Otherwise, they'll just be another example of something that sounded good on paper but didn't amount to much in practice.

Ill-Defined Strategies

Often, diversity and inclusion strategies are enforced by a few teams in an organization but are continually undermined by other teams. This happens due to a lack of cohesive structure in D&I strategies. For example, your organization may be doing the diversity part of D&I right but failing to implement equity and inclusion in the workplace. If you overlook part of D&I, none of it will succeed.

Start your diversity initiatives by focusing on three primary areas more or less equally:

- Diversifying the talent pool pipeline.
- Ensuring each step in the hiring and interviewing process is free of bias.
- Improving inclusion (the sense of belonging).

Unconscious Biases

One of the hardest challenges to address in D&I efforts is that of unconscious biases. Because they're unconscious, it's very difficult for D&I leaders to get them out in the open where they can be dealt with.

Numerous studies back the presence of biases in even the most rational of thinkers. Everyone falls prey to the unconscious bias, and such beliefs are often deeply influential. For example, data[70] from 80,000 recruiters globally in 2017 revealed that when hiring managers source candidates on LinkedIn, they are more likely to click on male profiles. This statistic

---

[70] https://www.shrm.org/resourcesandtools/hr-topics/talent-acquisition/pages/five-steps-improve-diversity-recruiting.aspx

was confirmed by LinkedIn in its Gender Insights Report,[71] which showed that recruiters were 13 percent less likely to click on a woman's profile than a man's profile in a search result.

Even if you are the most well-intentioned recruiter, it's always worth double-checking your own biases. Take these extra precautions:

- Educate yourself on unconscious biases.
- Rather than using the term *cultural fit,* use *cultural add* to talk about future employees. This frees them from the expectation of needing to fit in with an existing culture and sets up the expectation among existing employees that they will be bringing something unique and fresh to the job.
- Challenge the recruiting team to provide a better reason to hire someone than a "gut feeling" or seeing a "cultural fit." Doing this will ensure that the key focus is on the employee's abilities, skills, and potentially unique contributions.
- Make sure every candidate is asked the same set of questions, providing an even playing field.
- Encourage everyone in the organization to address their unconscious biases through trainings.

Lack of Participation

One common response to D&I discussions and efforts is withdrawal. Although employees may appreciate that work is being done and see the benefits it will bring, they'd rather remain on the sidelines and not have to dive into any potentially uncomfortable or challenging situations.

For example, at a diversity seminar focused on women's issues, the fear among male employees of not knowing enough and consequently saying the wrong thing can kick in quite easily. So they sit through all the sessions quietly—not necessarily because they're interested and wanting to hear from their female colleagues but because they're afraid.

To tackle this issue, there needs to be a safe space in every organization for employees to voice their opinions without judgment. Managers should design and implement strategies that encourage discussion. You can start by clarifying the goal of your diversity program so that people have an understanding of what it's about. You can then set some ground rules and explain how issues can be addressed. For example, if someone uses the wrong language, they shouldn't be shamed but politely corrected.

---

[71] https://business.linkedin.com/talent-solutions/diversity-inclusion-belonging/gender-balance-report

Final Thoughts

Diversity and inclusion are deeply emotional topics and so they are accompanied by the potential for things to go wrong. Our workplaces are full of unconscious biases and misunderstandings, which makes the job even harder.

The effectiveness of your diversity programs is determined by how you address these D&I challenges. For your diversity and inclusion efforts to be fruitful, you should be ready to act promptly and with good intentions, taking into account everyone's feelings and opinions. Treat your diversity efforts with a business mindset and develop formal documentation, so that the rules and expectations of your initiatives are clear.

Don't be discouraged by mistakes or setbacks. With every setback comes a chance to look inward and figure out where things went wrong.

8. Hiring Strategies to Increase D&I

Rapid changes in the world of business have made it difficult for companies to recruit and retain local talent. With the help of cutting-edge technologies, companies can now target employees across countries and geographic regions, offsetting the problem of dwindling local talent pools and increased competition for foreign talent.

But the D&I hiring process is much more complicated than simply using technology to find and recruit talent. Your company needs a strategy for appealing to, targeting, recruiting, and then retaining a diverse workforce.

As the U.S. Bureau of Labor Statistics notes, diversity has been a challenge for many HR professionals because they lack the experience or training to manage it effectively. By offering talent recruiters inclusive, dynamic training and tools to assist them in their recruiting efforts, companies can continue to increase their workforce's diversity.

Sustainable development is a concept that was coined by the Brundtland Commission in 1987 as "development that meets the needs of the present without compromising the ability of future generations to meet their own needs." Sustainability plays a role in D&I too. In fact, many organizations like Samsung Electronics and the Toyota Motor Corporation recently embarked on a diversity hiring program to build an inclusive workforce that would serve as a sustaining resource for their business operations.

By understanding what constitutes sustainable development and its integral role in diversity and inclusion, companies can ensure that their diverse workforce will help them meet the needs of the present without compromising their ability to meet the needs of future generations.

As our society becomes increasingly globalized, the need for diversity in the workplace has never been more evident. Companies are starting to realize that in order to remain competitive, they need to reflect the diversity of their customer base. This means hiring a workforce that is representative of the many different cultures and backgrounds that make up our world.

Diversity hiring is not only the right thing to do from a social justice perspective, but it also makes good business sense. As mentioned, studies have shown that companies with diverse workforces are more innovative and successful than others. The future of work is diverse, and the sooner you start embracing it, the better off you'll be.

It's projected that over the next few decades, diversity within the workplace will change immensely. This presents tremendous opportunities for companies to tap into this potential if they can adjust their hiring strategies to accommodate these changes. Many Fortune 500 companies have already started efforts to cultivate a culturally competent workforce that can meet the needs of today and tomorrow.

Building Your Culture for Diversity Hiring and Inclusion

Establishing a culture that is favorable to the diversity hiring methodology requires a firm commitment from management and all employees. Management must understand that the success of the initiative rests primarily on the ability to foster an environment in which everyone has an opportunity to contribute and feel valued.

A company can develop tactics such as training employees in cultural competency, building collaboration among departments, coordinating efforts through training, creating mentoring programs, and sponsoring events that bring everyone together.

Diversity in the workforce can also be used to achieve better access to resources and career advancement.

A Comprehensive Plan for D&I in Hiring

Throughout the book so far, we have mainly focused on the *source* of the problem and how to spot when your organization is perhaps not as diverse as it should be or how to spot when you should be making more efforts to increase its diversity. Now it's time to think about concrete ways to increase your diversity through *hiring* that is diversity-minded.

This focus on hiring will be divided into four parts. First, we will be exploring how to map a candidate's journey in an inclusive manner to ensure that diverse candidates can apply and that you are not restricting the pool of applicants before the job is even posted. Second, we will be looking at *short-term* hiring strategies. Third, we will consider *long-term* hiring strategies. Fourth, we will be looking into how you can retain your diverse talent once you have hired new employees.

Mapping the Candidate's Journey

The traditional hiring process has been replaced with rapid technological advancements in the industry: Social media, mobile hiring, and cloud-based hiring platforms have revolutionized the industry. Each step of the process is now easier for candidates as well as employers.

With this new technology, the talent acquisition department can aim at simplifying the process of job hunters, including of candidates with different needs, requirements, and expectations. Creating an inclusive candidate journey could consist of building a holistic and participatory hiring process that is supportive of the diverse needs of talent acquisition professionals, candidates, and hiring managers.

From the HR perspective, the talent acquisition departments could be partners in the process of designing job postings as well as of creating advertising strategies including but not limited to social media and mobile applications. From the candidate's perspective, flexible working hours and remote work options are a few ways in which organizations can facilitate inclusive hiring practices. A truly inclusive practice acknowledges that people have diverse needs and expectations, different attitudes toward work, and a range of abilities (physical, intellectual, etc.).

As discussed earlier throughout the book, one of the key hurdles when it comes to hiring a diverse team is making sure that the people you are looking to employ can apply for your open position. More specifically, you need to think about the unique hurdles that some applicants may face. This may include having to find time to be interviewed when they are working a challenging schedule and maybe even balancing it with onerous family obligations or working in a precarious job setting that offers very little flexibility.

You will also want to think about diversity in terms of the tools needed to apply for your job. For example, is the software you are using very complex or expensive to acquire? Some applicants may not be applying from their own laptops but from an Internet café instead. As such, they may not be able to *access the application in the first place!*

Many applicants are likely to quit the application process midway through if it is too complex or too lengthy. In fact, interviewees at Forbes[72] outlined a few of the experiences that many candidates have struggled with:

> *"I spent three hours customizing my resume for the job opportunity and writing my cover letter. Then it took me over an hour to trudge through the online application process. I couldn't believe how difficult they made it."*

> *"The recruiter scheduled a telephone interview, then never called. After I emailed him, he rescheduled twice and blew me off two more times. You can be sure I'll never consider that company for employment again and I can't wait to share my thoughts in a Glassdoor review."*

---

[72] https://www.forbes.com/sites/lisaquast/2017/06/26/your-companys-candidate-journey-sucks-heres-why-and-what-you-can-do-to-improve-it/#4bb5c0d42a23

"Having gone through the lengthy interview process at many different companies and been treated so poorly, I now know where I don't want to work and the companies where I won't buy their products. It's truly shocking at the lack of respect for job candidates these days."

Improving Your Application Process

As you can see, there are more than a few issues at hand here. Not only is the candidate's journey through the application something that impacts their buying habits (which affects your bottom line), but it is also something that can affect your brand altogether. If the journey of applying to your company is frustrating, not optimized to save the applicant valuable time, and not organized in a way that makes them feel valued as an applicant (refer to the second testimonial), you are unlikely to attract high-quality applicants and, hence, you are less likely to hire a diverse team of individuals.

So what can you do?

Assess Your Own Application Process

First, take a look at your own application process and consider whether you are making it more difficult than necessary for your applicants. Data has shown that there can be real misunderstanding between the applicants and the company recruiting in terms of how the company expects the applicants to use their time. In many cases there is a large discrepancy between how long a company thinks their application takes and how long it actually takes the applicants to go through.

Some companies may feel that a challenging application experience is a good way to lower the number of applications and attract just the applicants with true dedication. This method of thinking is rarely accurate. The best applicants, in most cases, know that they are the best applicants. They are unlikely to want to jump through many hoops for a job because they have around a dozen open positions to consider. As such, they may go for the easiest option and/or the option that is being made more accessible to them (e.g., through recruitment).

Build Relationships with Applicants

Remember that each applicant is a person who is expecting a response. Rather than approaching hiring as a transactional process, such as filling a role, think of it as a relationship-building process in which you build value with the applicants, even if they are not hired. This ensures that you keep the customer behind the applicant as well, and it also ensures that you can go back to the applicant if a position opens that may be more appropriate for them.

Imagine the Application Journey

Think about the journey that you want your candidate to go through. Ask yourself the following questions:

- When you imagine the ideal candidate, what do they have in terms of skills? What does the candidate most optimized for your company look like? What is the best way to reach out to them and to communicate with them online?
- Think of the first time they come across your brand. What do you want them to feel like at that specific moment?
- Think about the logistics of hiring. How often can your team interact with the applicants? Can you use online tools such as automation and integrations to help you streamline the process and reduce the potential for mistakes?
- What steps can you take to make sure that the candidates feel valued when they are being considered for a position? How will you make them feel well-informed and welcome?
- Finally, to make sure you do not lose great potential candidates, how can you keep potential candidates interested in your company so they feel comfortable to apply again later, when they are more ready to apply and/or more qualified for the specific positions at hand?

Learn from Your Mistakes

Finally, you will want to learn from your mistakes! You can learn a lot by asking successful and unsuccessful candidates (or applicants who never finished their applications) about their experiences with the application process. Ask them what they feel needs work. They are the ones who will tell you exactly what has made them stop midway (if they did) or perhaps what made them hesitate throughout the process.

Creating an Inclusive Journey

Suppose you are a leader in an organization, and you have been tasked with increasing diversity in your workplace. How will you tackle the challenge? There are several ways that you can go about doing this.

Assess Your Employee Recognition Programs

To begin with, you can ensure that the employee recognition programs in your organization are inclusive. For instance, you can create a diversity award to recognize those employees who have done outstanding work in fostering and promoting diversity within your organization.

This will go far in increasing diversity at your workplace because it will show that management cares about the issue.

Develop a Culture of Inclusion

Strive to create an environment where all employees regardless of their gender identification or race or sexual orientation feel welcome and valued. The more inclusive your workplace is, the more inclusive it will become. That's because your company will attract greater diversity when it is showing that it is taking concrete steps to be more diverse.

Create programs at work that focus on empowering women and underrepresented groups so as to help them become more competitive in the job market.

Launch a mentorship program for women and minorities employed at your company. Such mentorships will help ensure these employees' success.

Dismantle the Concept of "Culture Fit"

To increase diversity, some companies have adopted a rather indirect approach known as "culture fit." This approach is based on the premise that people with similar belief systems, lifestyles, and educational qualifications are more likely to work well together. Culture fit is a logical application of the theory of homophily, or love for that which is the same, or familiar. The assumption behind culture fit is that companies that fill positions with employees who fit in with existing team members will be more successful. But research shows the opposite: that diverse teams are more creative, innovative, and stronger.

Short-Term Tips to Improve Your Diversity Hiring Efforts

Naturally, you will want to focus your efforts on creating an inclusive candidate journey throughout the process. This includes having a clear strategy and a solid vision for diversity and inclusion. You must make sure that your words are followed by actions.

Likewise, you will want to invest in diverse communities in a proactive manner. Don't wait for applicants to come to you, which can be problematic if your candidate journey is created in a way that only attracts a certain underrepresented group. Reach out to institutions that are historically diverse and focused on minorities (e.g., Black colleges and universities, organizations that help LGBTQIA+ individuals find employment).

When you are at the advertising stage and are looking for new employees, consider how your job ad may be targeting a specific demographic. Look at the ads you have used in the past and consider what you have learned throughout this book. Ask yourself whether these ads may have been less welcoming to diverse groups.

You may think that diversity hiring means that you should make job as non-targeted as possible. But this is not necessarily the case. You can write job ads that target a member of a specific group and you can explain that this is part of your diversity and inclusion strategy. Being explicit about your D&I efforts is a great way to show commitment. Similarly, by asking members of your team whether they have their own referrals or networks of people, you can increase diversity organically.

Try expanding the networks of underrepresented groups by bringing them into the company through a diverse candidate referral program, for example. Encourage your diverse team members to share your job ads with their networks to foster more diversity and inclusion.

Such short-term efforts will show that you are authentic and that your organization is serious about being more inclusive. Your company should also communicate the kind of culture that it has and what it is looking for in terms of candidates. It should also explain how it is trying to increase diversity. Finally, you will want to eliminate barriers that can be invisible in your hiring/application process (e.g., gendered language).

Your candidate journey should avoid bias right from the start (at the screening stage). First, select candidates who are not traditional, such as some that have the right skills, abilities, and knowledge even if their education is not necessarily what you would expect. Second, ask that personal information be removed from resumes before CVs are shared with the hiring team to reduce unconscious bias, or you can use software so resumes are screened with less bias. Be aware, however, that some such software has been shown to be biased![73]

Train your hiring managers to ensure that they know what to avoid in terms of interview bias and what to do to make hiring practices inclusive. This may also include establishing protocol with interviewers so that the hiring process is consistent and reduces interviewer bias. As mentioned, you will want a diverse interview panel—not only to have a different perspective in the room but also to make the candidate feel more comfortable.

Then, when you get to the offer point, make an equitable offer. This is where you can truly show your commitment to advancing diverse candidates within your organization.

Offer internships to targeted groups and reach out to diverse applicants in order to level the entry field. For example, your company can reach out

---

[73] https://www.reuters.com/article/us-amazon-com-jobs-automation-insight-idUSKCN1MK08G

to specific schools or diverse communities. Such communities usually have programs that try to push personal growth and development, so by teaming up with them you can boost your diversity in a way that is *sustainable* and authentic.

Long-Term Strategies for Diversity Hiring

There may be a bit more work to do when it comes to developing long-term strategies. To increase diversity and inclusion in your team and overall organization, you will want to develop a brand as an employer that showcases how dedicated you are to improving diversity in the long-term and not only on paper for the next few months.

You want to show that you value people and opinions from all sorts of backgrounds and that your actions follow your words. Valuing people and their uniqueness should be ingrained in your company culture, and it should be made clear and obvious with your employees. Talk openly about diversity and inclusion in the workplace and don't shy away from sharing the stories of your diverse employees if they agree to it. The key here is to be authentic.

Likewise, by developing company policies that are interesting and appealing to all kinds of candidates, you are creating a working environment in which all kinds of employees feel at home, welcome, and understood. For example, if you are truly interested in your employees' commitment to their communities, allow them to work flexibly so they do not have to give up this commitment.

Ask your employees how you could be more attentive to their needs. Parents may need to leave early to get their children out of school; individuals with disabilities may need to attend more doctor appointments than others do or may need to be able to work from home more often. Ultimately, it is up to you to make your company as approachable, enjoyable, diverse, and people-focused as possible.

The general assumption that companies are only interested in the bottom line (profits) is not entirely correct. The truth is that organizations need to focus on both increasing their profits *and* on engaging with their local communities. For example, there are many benefits to hiring women into leadership roles. These benefits include less workplace stress and more effective management styles.

These long-term strategies are mostly centered around creating a basis for company growth. Central to all long-term strategies is changing how companies recruit. Another facet of long-term diverse hiring is ensuring your company is represented well in the media and in the Internet. A positive and diverse presence in the media can be used by companies as a way to attract new employees.

Multinational companies are generally perceived as having more liberal values than are local businesses, which implies a tolerant workplace. This type of media exposure helps to attract more customers.

Retaining Diverse Talent

Why do we lose talented employees and what can we do about it?

A report from Deloitte—"Unleashing the Power of Inclusion: Attracting and Engaging the Evolving Workforce"—revealed the most important cultural aspects when choosing an organization to work for. The top three aspects cited were "An atmosphere where I feel comfortable being myself" (47 percent); "An environment that provides a sense of purpose, where I feel like I make an impact" (39 percent); and "A place where work flexibility (parental leave, ability to work remotely, flexible scheduling, etc.) is provided as a top priority" (36 percent).[74]

According to Bloomberg,[75] there are many ways to encourage the retention of diverse employees. This includes teaching executives diversity and inclusion strategies, focusing on conflict resolution programs, encouraging managers to be mindful of the words they use, providing employees with a support network, and providing training to managers and employees.

The things that attract people to a company are often the same things that make them stay. A positive company culture can lead to increased job satisfaction, higher productivity, and lower turnover rates. It can also help to attract top talent and create a more supportive environment.

If a company has a culture where employees feel like they can make decisions, then this will be a catalyst for their growth and development. The drive for growth and development also plays a significant role in the retention of diverse talent. In fact, many people will choose one job over another based on the company culture and whether it aligns with their own values.

An organization that is focused on growing and developing its workers is more likely to retain its employees. When an employee feels that they can develop within the company and that the company has an open plan

---

[74] https://www2.deloitte.com/content/dam/Deloitte/us/Documents/about-deloitte/us-about-deloitte-unleashing-power-of-inclusion.pdf
[75] https://sponsored.bloomberg.com/article/synchrony/how-to-retain-diverse-employees

for them to take on new challenges, they will be much more likely to stay put. The combination of management training, workplace culture, and incentives are key factors in boosting employee retention.

Management training should teach managers to be committed to diversity in the workplace. If a manager is not committed to the culture of their organization, then they will never be able to motivate the employees under their wing.

9. Diversity Metrics and Frameworks

The idea of measuring D&I has become increasingly important in recent years, with many firms and organizations developing special metrics. Some people believe that a certain level of diversity hiring is necessary in order to bolster the overall health of an organization. Others believe that this is just a way to make sure that firms look good on paper so that they can keep up with competitors in terms of their diversity credentials.

Whatever your personal opinion on the matter, it's important to understand how these metrics work, before you decide on whether to use them. Calls for diversity and inclusion have been increasing at a rapid rate. More than half of all millennials have stated that they'd be more likely to buy from a company if they supported diversity hiring. Social media has played a big role in raising awareness of how these hiring practices impact our world.

The metric most commonly used to measure organizational diversity is the Diversity and Inclusion Index (DII). The DII was created in order to standardize the way that organizations measure and report their progress on diversity initiatives. It is a holistic metric that takes into account a variety of factors, including gender, race, ethnicity, and sexual orientation.

The DII is meant to be used as a way to track an organization's progress over time, and a company's DII is often compared against that of other organizations in order to benchmark progress.

Although the DII is the most popular metric for measuring organizational diversity, there are other metrics that are used. These include the Cultural Diversity Index (CDI) and the Racial Equity Index (REI). The CDI was developed to measure the cultural diversity of leadership using a modified Herfindahl-Hirschman Index methodology. The CDI is applied by measuring the concentration mix of all the cultures in the employee population.[76] The REI[77] is a data tool designed to help communities identify priority areas for advancing racial equity, track progress over time, and set specific goals for closing racial gaps. It provides a snapshot of overall equity outcomes for cities, counties, regions, and states.

The DII is generally considered to be the most comprehensive and accurate metric.

---

[76] https://www.dca.org.au/sites/default/files/synopsis_-_cracking_the_glass-cultural_ceiling_available_to_public.pdf
[77] https://nationalequityatlas.org/research/racial_equity_index/index#/

Measuring D&I

The degree to which diversity exists in an organization's workforce is often measured by demographic variables such as gender, race, or ethnicity (or by other proxy variables); employment status; and in some cases even citizenship.

The most obvious measure of diversity involves the racial background of a firm's workforce. However, not all firms have a diverse workforce racially and there are many diverse populations in the workforce such as women, people with disabilities, and veterans. These populations often do not show up in racial or ethnic diversity statistics. Paid leave policy or maternity benefits can also be used as proxies for diversity.

As with all statistics, there are several factors that can affect the data collected and presented. For example, if a large manufacturer is located in New York City or Los Angeles, it may have more diverse workers than if it were in Kansas or Maine.

Consequently, the percentage of a workforce that identifies with a particular racial/ethnic group can be an unreliable indicator of the overall diversity of a company. The better way to measure diversity is the method that a company uses to select employees for hire. How well the company recruits, interviews, evaluates, and promotes employees is often used as a proxy measure for diversity. The next most common proxy is gender.

Diversity and inclusion have, in certain cases, become buzzwords— they are used by corporations to boost their status and to show to their customers and clients that they hold a certain sense of corporate responsibility. Having discussed what diversity and inclusion are and why they are crucially important to any organization that aims to lower its turnover rate and avoid being stuck in the "Great Resignation,"[78] it's time to get into the nitty-gritty details. The general public is becoming suspicious of diversity window dressing that is not backed up by real change. Aiming just to meet internal diversity quotas (which are illegal[79] in many countries) for show is not going to cut it anymore.

The Four Categories of Diversity

Categories of diversity refer to work diversity of a company and the employees who work there and have different traits, backgrounds, and abilities. Some of these categories are more visible than others, and some

---

[78] https://en.wikipedia.org/wiki/Great_Resignation
[79] https://www.lexology.com/library/detail.aspx?g=de679347-c94d-4676-a1ba-f5dd9e1755cf

are more salient in the United States than in other parts of the world, given the history of discrimination and exclusion.

When measuring diversity, there are four key categories to pay attention to:

- the basic characteristics of diversity, which include age (also known as generational diversity), racial background, gender identity (not the same as biological sex), and sexual orientation;
- the educational background, marital background, and/or parental status of the person as well as their religious beliefs;
- work experience, which includes the individual's level (i.e., their ranking), their shift, and the number of years that they have spent at the organization; and
- the style (mainly their work habits), such as how they lead and how they communicate.

Some categories are easier to measure than others; for example, you can easily measure the age ratios or the racial and ethnic background of your team. However, measuring diversity within the third and fourth categories can be trickier. Nevertheless, it is still important to do so.

Category One: Basic Characteristics

Generational Diversity

Generational diversity is one of the aspects of diversity that can be overlooked. Some organizations prefer young and fresh minds, which is understandable (especially in startup environments, for example), but there is also age bias surrounding newer employees who may be perceived as too inexperienced. On the other hand, older employees may be seen as inflexible and untrainable, as unskilled with technology, even as their years of experience may be considered a desirable quality.

A diverse workforce is more likely to come up with innovative solutions when it has a range of age groups as the varied experiences and lifestyles can promote a more open discussion.

For example, someone with decades of experience in change management may benefit greatly from speaking to a young employee aware of current trends and social media strategies. On the other hand, a newer employee may not have the experience to know how to implement workplace successfully.

Ageism can occur in the workplace and lead to discrimination against older or younger workers. This can be a costly mistake and can lead to expensive lawsuits as well. It's vital to be aware of the laws regarding age discrimination within your state. Even aside from protecting your company from a legal standpoint, age diversity holds a lot of value.

Communication is the most common barrier to intergenerational diversity. Different generations have different preferences for how they communicate. Some prefer face-to-face meetings and phone calls, while others use email or messaging apps. If you're not sure which method works best for your team, ask them about the different ways they prefer to communicate and make sure to compromise.

You can use various methods to keep the lines of communication open, and you can encourage both young and older employees to adapt to each other's style of communication. Although certain things may be nonnegotiable (e.g., learning to use Slack, if this is your company's preferred method of communication), other procedures can be set up to met your team's specific needs.

Generational diversity can help your business become more innovative and competitive. It can also help you attract talented individuals. When you establish generational diversity in your workforce, you become better able to find a diverse workforce faster and more efficiently.

Ultimately, a combination of skills and perspectives is likely to yield more creative solutions, and the opposite can cost your business its sustainability. The experience of older employees will keep a company on solid footing, and the fresh ideas and perspectives of younger employees can open the organization to new solutions.

When hiring a multigenerational workforce, employers should avoid language that limits the pool of candidates. For example, the word *experienced* may limit your applicants to older generations. The term *tech-savvy* may reduce your pool of older candidates. Instead, you could say, "has the knowhow" or "is familiar with Slack."

Diversity of Races and Ethnicities

More and more, throughout the United States, we are starting to see the importance of including more diversity in regards to race within the workplace. When people think of racial diversity, many think of a mix of African Americans and Caucasians. But a company might also hire Asians and Latinos, Arabs and Jews.

The future workforce needs to reflect the racial breakdown of the population in all places of work. There is still room for improvement, and it's imperative that we begin by identifying the problem and addressing it.

Although many companies and organizations are taking action to increase diversity, more needs to be done. "How to support Black colleagues," for example, has become a top-trending topic on LinkedIn and other platforms. CEOs have publicly addressed their own mistakes, and people are starting to engage with the issue.

Whether you are a manager or a CEO, there are strategies you can use to promote racial diversity and create a more equitable workplace. Additionally, you must make sure that the diversity you achieve is not done for the sake of meeting a diversity quota. Employees are very aware when this happens, and it can create a work environment that goes against all your goals for becoming a more inclusive team.

Employers must consider the specific challenges that specific racial minority employees face. In the United States, for example, Black women have long been overrepresented in precarious jobs.[80] Knowing this and actively attempting to change the system would involve ensuring that the jobs offered to Black women within your organization are intentionally nonprecarious.

Gender Diversity

Before we get into a discussion on gender diversity, it is crucial to explore what gender is. If you are unaware of the difference between sex and gender, don't worry. There's always more to learn. Throughout the past decade, trans people have helped increase awareness of the potential difference between the biological sex that people are born with and the gender that they identify with.

Although most of us are born as either biological males or females (with some individuals being born intersex), not every person is also born with the "matching" gender identity. For example, a person born with male biological sex characteristics may identify more with the attributes found in women according to the social constructs we have created as a society. Those who identify as the gender they were assigned at birth are considered "cisgender," and those who do not identify with the sex they were assigned at birth are "transgender."

Like other differences and diversities, transgender individuals face many inequalities that can intersect (refer to the beginning of this book for more on intersectionality). At the same time, they can struggle with parts of daily life at the workplace that cisgendered individuals do not deal with, such as having access to a bathroom that feels more comfortable to

---

[80] https://www.epi.org/blog/black-womens-labor-market-history-reveals-deep-seated-race-and-gender-discrimination/

them. To this end, more workplaces are beginning to incorporate unisex bathrooms in their buildings so as to alleviate these problems.

This being said, gender diversity usually refers to the ratio between people identified as men and people identified as women.

Many companies have embraced gender diversity in the workplace to increase their productivity and increase the number of talented employees they have. However, some employers still struggle with achieving true gender equality. These companies often have trouble eliminating the barriers that prevent women from advancing in the workplace or they are reluctant to hire female candidates because of familial expectations or childcare needs, for example. Top female candidates, in particular, care about gender-diverse work environments. A recent survey found that 61 percent of women look at the gender diversity of the employer's leadership team when deciding where to work.[81]

It's important to create a welcoming environment for all. Creating a gender-neutral workplace can help prevent workplace discrimination. Such a workplace can be accomplished by ensuring a safe working environment for all, writing better job descriptions that are not coded in gender terms, making sure your hiring team is diverse, offering fair compensation, taking exit interviews seriously, establishing an anti-bullying policy, and offering training against unconscious bias. Furthermore, it is important to empower underrepresented groups in the workplace so they can reach their full potential. Paying attention to the ratio of each gender in both the horizontal and vertical hierarchy of your company is also crucial: Even if you have a large quota of women or nonbinary individuals, if the people in positions of power are all men, you have not achieved diversity. By increasing the number of women in leadership positions, organizations can improve their profits. If women and men think differently and act differently, the difference is not a disadvantage. Women bring particular qualities to leadership positions, and having a solid mix of genders throughout the company and in positions of power helps your company by diversifying its set of skills and traits, too.

Ultimately, gender diversity increases employee confidence by showing that all employees, regardless of their gender, are considered equally valuable. When a meeting is made up mostly of men, for example, a woman may struggle to find the confidence to speak up. Likewise, she may be silenced or ignored or may even be expected to be the secretary.

_____

[81] https://www.pwc.com/gx/en/about/diversity/iwd/iwd-female-talent-report-web.pdf

Other times, she may be told to get coffee for others, even if she is the one leading the meeting.

Sexual Orientation Diversity

As the population continues to grow and society becomes increasingly more accepting, sexual orientation diversity continues to gain momentum. The modern gay rights movement started with the Stonewall Riots[82] in 1969, but public attitudes toward LGBTQIA+ (lesbian, gay, bisexual, trans, queer, intersex, asexual, and more) individuals have taken much longer to evolve. Individual U.S. states did not begin to make gay marriage legal until the 2000s, and it wasn't until 2015 that the U.S. Supreme Court prohibited states from banning gay marriage. Today, in many parts of the country people continue to try to pass laws intended to curb gay rights; for example, Florida in 2022 passed the Don't Say Gay Bill, prohibiting teachers from discussing gender identity or sexual orientation. To this day LGBTQIA+ individuals are the victims of violent and non-violent crimes. They are more susceptible to bullying, discrimination, and, very unfortunately, suicide. In many countries of the world, they are actively persecuted, and in some countries they are jailed and even executed.

Members of the LGBTQIA+ community continue to face unfair hurdles in employment and are more likely to deal with severe discrimination in the workplace. Many LGBTQIA+ individuals may struggle to find themselves feeling comfortable at work being open (or out).

A growing body of research supports the benefits of promoting sexual orientation diversity in the workplace, resulting in positive effects on job performance, creativity, and employee commitment as well as the alignment of employee and customer demographics.

Indeed, when a company is LGTBQIA+[83] friendly, customers who align with such values are more likely to go out of their way to support the company through their buying practices. Furthermore, sexual orientation diversity is accompanied by a host of individual benefits, including greater job satisfaction and organizational commitment, less stress, and improved relationships with coworkers and managers.

It is vital for companies to strive to foster an environment where LGBTQIA+ employees can be themselves and bring their full energy to work. When an employee feels comfortable and accepted, they can

---

[82] https://en.wikipedia.org/wiki/Stonewall_riots
[83] Lesbian, Gay, Bisexual, Transgender, Queer and/or Questioning, Intersex, Asexual, and "+," an acknowledgment that there are noncisgender and nonstraight identities that are not included in the acronym.

maximize their potential and energy. When an employee needs to hide their sexual orientation out of fear of being fired, for example, it can be difficult to feel loyal to the company or to give it their full performance.

It is your job to make sure that your company or organization is open about sexual orientation diversity and to make it clear to all employees that yours is an open and welcoming space that will not tolerate any kind of poor treatment.

In addition to supporting the diversity of the workforce, firms must make an effort to foster safe workplace environments. Likewise, by providing equal career opportunities for all employees free of unconscious (or conscious) bias, companies can create a more equitable workplace for their employees that fosters feelings of safety and belonging.

The right culture will improve the happiness of LGBTQIA+ workers, subsequently increasing their productivity and commitment to work. When workplaces are welcoming, everyone feels more confident and motivated to work. If the working environment is a safe space for LGBTQIA+ people, it benefits everyone.

Unconscious Bias

The term *unconscious bias* refers to a social stereotype. Everybody has unconscious beliefs about groups of people, and these are much more difficult to notice than conscious prejudices. Interestingly, unconscious bias is more prevalent than conscious prejudice. This is surprising given that unconscious attitudes are often incompatible with our values and ideals. Some situations activate these attitudes, such as watching movies in which certain genders, sexual orientations, or races are depicted in a way that we find irritating or uncomfortable.

The first step to avoiding unconscious bias is to be aware of the causes of bias. A diverse board of directors, for example, can improve the performance of all levels of an organization. Take a minute here to think: When you read the words "board of directors," did you picture a room full of White men? If you did not, congrats because this is the picture that most of us conjure.

The unconscious biases we carry with us throughout our lives can lead to inaccurate assessments based on incorrect rationales. This can limit the number of potential candidates we consider at a company, preventing innovation and hindering productivity.

Research shows that there are different ways to overcome these unconscious biases and create a more diverse workplace— training being the most efficient form. In other words, by pointing out the unconscious biases that we each have and placing these "on the table" rather than leaving them in the dark, we can become more aware of them.

Examples of unconscious bias in daily life include clenching your bag closer to your body when a nonwhite person walks near you or assuming that everyone in the world is straight until it is evident that a person is not.

In the workplace, an obvious example of unconscious bias is preferring a male over a female candidate even if their CV and personal skills are nearly identical.

Name bias is also a common form of unconscious bias in the workplace. Certain names are still preferred over others, such as Anglo-sounding names that tend to be associated with one being more qualified.[84]

Beauty bias is also common—it's often known as "pretty privilege." An example of this would be for a candidate to be hired on the basis of their looks while a candidate with more experience or who is more qualified is overlooked or simply not considered at all for a certain position.

A good strategy to combat unconscious bias is to expose team members to different perspectives. Although most companies don't admit it, middle managers and hiring managers are often the most susceptible to unconscious bias. By facilitating cross functional teams and training middle managers from diverse perspectives, you can improve company diversity and overcome unconscious bias, resulting in better decision-making that is representative of a variety of interests.

Category Two: Background, Status, and Beliefs

Education

If you have seen the TV show "Suits,"[85] you know that the law firm at the center of the show is notorious for only employing lawyers from Harvard. Although this made a great storyline for a show, in the real world this law firm would likely be condemned by most in the diversity and inclusion field.

As discussed, intersectional inequalities throughout the country make it very difficult for some to find employment in the face of a lot of competition. Maybe you're thinking, if I have a candidate from Harvard and one from a small community college, why would I not hire a person from Harvard? While you are right to a certain extent, this kind of logic lacks vision and understanding of why one person may have made it to

---

[84] https://asana.com/resources/unconscious-bias-examples
[85] https://www.imdb.com/title/tt1632701/

Harvard and why the other may have only been able to attend community college.

Let's have a go at a comparative case study. First, let's think about the pathway that the student at Harvard underwent in order to arrive at this position—let's call her Olivia. Perhaps Olivia was brought up in a loving home with two parents who also worked hard to provide their children with all the support that they needed. Throughout her entire life, Olivia always knew that she would go to college. Her parents checked her homework every night and made sure that she had all the support needed: She didn't need to clean anything in the house as her mother would take care of it while her dad went to work.

Olivia would take part in extracurriculars to boost her resume; the Model United Nations shines bright at the top of the resume she used to apply to Harvard. She was also on the student council, played sports, and volunteered at a nearby elderly people's home twice a week.

Of course, she enjoyed it, but most of her extracurriculars were done to embellish her resume in preparation for Harvard. Olivia would be busy from 6 a.m. to 10 p.m. every day. Once it was time to start applying to universities, Olivia spent countless hours working on her applications to all the Ivy League schools. Her parents, knowing how much it meant to her, made sure to pay for a tutor and for an SAT teacher. After weeks of hard work, Olivia made it in. Celebration time! Like her mom and dad, she would attend Harvard. All the hard work paid off.

Once at Harvard, Olivia fit in quickly. Her classmates were very competitive, so she often found herself struggling to get help. Nevertheless, having been brought up by parents who always pushed her and told her that she could do well, she knew that she would be able to get over any hurdle that she would ever face. So she got to work. Olivia scored highly and then she attended career meetings. She got herself internships through Harvard's career portal; as her professor knew the internship organizer, she did not have to apply directly.

For six months, Olivia worked, was paid for it, and then returned to class to finish up her degree. Once she finished the degree, her tuition fee was paid for and the letters of recommendation that she received from her many internship managers and professors—all from very respectable institutions—made it easy for her resume to make it to the top of the pile.

This pile is now on your desk, in front of you. Next to it is a different CV: that of Marc.

How did you picture Olivia in your mind? Can you find any unconscious bias in your thinking?

Marc comes from a different background. Marc lived with his five brothers and sisters, all in the same room. His primary school life was fun: He remembers running around the yard with all his friends and playing soccer and basketball after school. Then, as he started high school, things got a bit tougher. His dad passed away, leaving his mother alone with six kids to tend to.

Marc was the oldest of the six, which meant that he needed to help out a lot in the house. In the morning, when he wasn't out delivering newspapers, he would be helping his mom by getting his siblings ready and out the door to school at the right time.

After school, it was his responsibility to get the kids home, make them dinner, help them out with their homework, and tend to their hygienic needs before they went to sleep. Of course, that didn't leave much time for extracurriculars. At around 10 p.m., once he was done with all his responsibilities, he'd sit down and work on his own homework. His mom was working until around 6 a.m. on the graveyard shift as the janitor of a local hospital.

When it was time to start applying for university, Marc struggled to find the time to work on his applications. He had to take up another job because his mother's pay was reduced, so he would only have around two days a week to get all this schoolwork done. His grades weren't so good either—but what can a guy do about it if the decision is between caring for his family or studying biology?

Ultimately, he didn't bother applying to Harvard or any Ivy League university. Even if he had the grades, he wouldn't have the funds. Marc applied to a community college, the one down the street so he could still help his mom out with the kids and so he wouldn't have to find another job. He was accepted, qualified for a few high-interest loans to pay his tuition, and lowered his working hours.

Once community college began, he decided to give it his all. He focused on getting the top marks and building a relationship with his professors— someone in high school had told him that that's how you'd get all the good internships. As summer came around, he was offered an (unpaid) internship at a small law firm down the block, which meant he'd need to take out more loans. It's an investment, right? he thought. So he did it.

It wasn't the big firm up in the city, but it was an experience nonetheless. As the years went by, he climbed the echelons and got himself a leading position in the firm. His mom was receiving a large part of his salary so she finally could take two days off a week to rest and see her kids. And then Marc felt like he needed more as his job offered no prospects. He wanted to get out of the small town and, with his mom being more secure, he felt that now was the time. So he applied to your company.

Obviously, there are different levels of struggle that impact which school a person can go to and they have to do with more than a person's grades and intelligence. If you were to choose Olivia simply because she is from Harvard, you would be continuing the cycle in which those coming from backgrounds that are more difficult continue to be stuck, limited by their diplomas.

There is also another point to make here: Although Olivia and Marc have different degrees, the soft skills that each acquired—being a hard worker and having a strong work ethic—were developed through personal dedication to one's success. In addition, Olivia may have attributes that Marc does not have (for example, the perspective of a woman), and Marc may have much more resilience due to the many hurdles that he faced throughout his journey.

This is why ensuring that you cut educational bias and that you purposely hire individuals from all kinds of backgrounds is key—it gives a shot to everyone and it breaks the cycle in which only those from privileged backgrounds make it. It ensures that you can bring all sorts of perspectives and life skills into your company and that you do not restrict yourself solely to people who look good on paper. That's what true diversity is all about.

Marital and Parental Status

A different aspect of diversity includes what your workforce looks like in terms of their current family situations. It's important to be aware of the kinds of responsibilities that your employees have at home. For example, are some of your employees single parents? Are they married? Do you hire only single people, and do you think about whether a woman might have a child when you consider hiring her?

Your unconscious bias regarding familial status can affect the diversity of your office. For example, single parents are less likely to be hired in many cases because employers fear that the employee may need more sick leave or more time to tend to their kids.

Although this is a legitimate concern, remember that work should not be life: We work to live, not vice versa. As such, working environments should be adapted so that life can continue and allow the employee to live a balanced life.

Religious Beliefs

Religious beliefs are the third factor to consider in the second category of diversity. It is fair to say that the United States and many other countries have a wide variety of religions. But even to this day, religious bias and general antireligion rhetoric restrict some individuals' ability to find employment.

This unconscious bias changes the way HR hires people. It is no secret that anti-Muslim sentiment went through the roof after 9/11, and anti-Asian sentiment followed when the COVID-19 pandemic hit. Anti-Jewish rhetoric is often present.

Category Three: Work Experience

The workplace is the third category of diversity that should be measured. Earlier in this chapter, we briefly talked about horizontal and vertical positions, and this is a key point in the measurement of diversity. Although many organizations will tend to consider any kind of diversity as good diversity, diversity should not only characterize specific teams but run throughout the entire organization. Specifically, this means paying attention to more complex kinds of power imbalances.

For example, you will want to measure whether the diversity is concentrated within lower ranks, such as within entry-level jobs. Are most of your diverse employees in low-paid positions? Are they mainly in entry-level jobs or do you also have a very diverse board of directors? Although the quota of nonwhite applicants may be impressive in lower ranks, if most of the managers, leaders, and CEOs/CFOs, and so on are all very similar in terms of primary and secondary diversity, your organization has some work to do.

Look at the people in your company and ask yourself: Who has been here the longest? What is the turnover rate for individuals who fit the "diverse" category? Are they more likely to leave than the others? The answers to these questions may very well indicate that, while you have achieved horizontal diversity, vertical diversity is lacking.

This is crucial for many reasons, one of which is that those in positions of power are the ones making the decisions. If the decisions are only made by a group of individuals with similar interests and without the perspectives of diverse employees who could bring a panoply of views and interesting points to the table, you are missing out on a fantastic opportunity. Additionally, without their input, the extent to which your company is able to extend its diversity is limited.

Category Four: Work Style

The fourth and final category of diversity that should be measured is that of style—namely, your employees' work habits, their leadership styles, and the ways they communicate. Although you may not think that this is related to diversity, it is! If there is only one hegemonic way to "do things" at the office, this usually means that the various requirements and needs of individual employees are not being met.

For example, if the protocol to follow is strict hours (e.g., arrive at 8 a.m. every morning and stay until 5 p.m., no excuses), this lack of flexibility can make it difficult for some employees. For parents, it may not be possible to arrive at work at 8 if their children's school starts at 8. Hence, flexibility and understanding when it comes to work habits must be measured too.

It's important to acknowledge that certain individuals are much more productive when working from home. Leadership styles can also differ.

Finally, communication style refers to an organization's ability to match its communication to the way that the team and employees receive it best. Is communication done in a way that accounts for the employees who are not in the office for various reasons? Is communication done in a way that respects the expectations and responsibilities of employees (e.g., not expecting a response after hours)?

The Four Layers of Diversity

In order to create a well-rounded and inclusive workplace, businesses need to be aware of the different types of diversity that exist. While most people are familiar with racial and gender diversity, there are actually four layers of diversity that businesses need to be aware of.

This model is based on Lee Gardenswartz[86] and Anita Rowe[87] and provides a widely used method of identifying dimensions in diversity in organisations. The model correlates roughly with the legally protected areas of discrimination. The mentioned dimensions of diversity are not to be read as an exhaustive list. The shapes that diversity and discrimination take can vary according to context and change with time.

The Diversity Wheel model[88] gives an overview of the dimensions of diversity that are present and active in one's workplace or environment.

---

[86] https://www.linkedin.com/in/leegardenswartz/
[87] https://www.linkedin.com/in/anitarowe/
[88] https://www.gardenswartzrowe.com/why-g-r

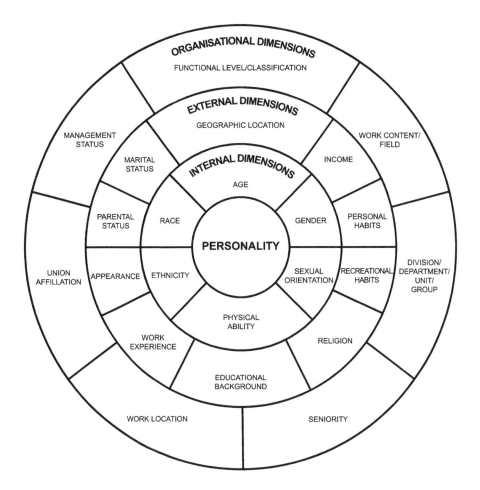

Personality dimensions

Personality, the dimension at the center of the model, encompasses all aspects of a person that can be described as personal style. Personality is shaped early in life and is both influenced by, and influences, the other three layers (internal, external and Organizational) throughout one's lifetime and career choices. This dimension includes an individual's likes and dislikes, values, and beliefs.

Internal dimensions

These include aspects of diversity over which we have no control (though "physical ability" can change over time due to choices we make to be active or not, or in cases of illness or accidents).

This dimension is the layer in which many divisions between and among people exist and which forms the core of many diversity efforts. These dimensions include the first things we see in other people, such as race or gender and on which we make many assumptions and base judgments.

The following areas belong to the internal dimensions[89]: age, gender, sexual orientation, physical ability, ethnicity, race, social origin.

External dimensions

These include aspects of our lives which we have some control over, which might change over time, and which usually form the basis for decisions on careers and work styles.

While external diversity can be heavily influenced by other people and their surroundings, even forcibly so, they ultimately are aspects that a person can change and often do over time.

The following areas belong to the external dimensions[90]: geographic location, income, personal habits, recreational habits, religion, educational background, work experience, appearance, parental status, marital status.

Organizational dimensions

This layer concerns the aspects of culture found in a work setting. While much attention of diversity efforts is focused on the internal dimensions, issues of preferential treatment and opportunities for development or promotion are impacted by the aspects of this layer.

The following areas belong to the organizational dimensions[91]: functional level/classification, work content/field, faculty/centre/department/degree programme/service unit, seniority/duration of study, work location/study location, research content/field, type of employment.

The model can be a useful framework for organizations seeking to foster a more diverse and inclusive environment. The model highlights the importance of not only individual characteristics (such as race, gender, and ethnicity) but also organizational factors (such as policies and practices) and external influences (such as social attitudes and institutional structures).

By taking all dimensions into account, organizations can more effectively address the challenges and opportunities posed by diversity. In particular,

---

[89] Gardenswartz, L., & Rowe, A. 2003
[90] Gardenswartz, L., & Rowe, A. 2003
[91] Gardenswartz, L., & Rowe, A. 2003

the model can help organizations to identify potential areas of bias and discrimination, develop targeted initiatives to promote inclusion, and measure the effectiveness of their efforts.

D&I Indicators

Measuring diversity can be difficult because people have different ways of perceiving and describing it. Start by looking at what your applicant pool looks like alongside other key indicators. Have a look at the differences among the people who are applying for the position you are looking to fill and compare them to the people you are currently employing. For example, establish the gender, age, and racial ratios of applicants in comparison to those of your current employees.

If you find that your applicants are very diverse and come from a wide selection of educational backgrounds, have varied gender identities and sexual orientations, and are from many different backgrounds, great! If you then realize that the pool of applicants you are looking at is drastically different from your current employees, this may be a sign that you need to implement more strategies to improve your organization's diversity.

This might show that the recruitment process is biased. You want to aim for an applicant pool that is similar to your employee diversity. However (and this is a big however!), if your team seriously lacks diversity, then you need to consider what you can do to attract more diverse applicants.

Second, consider the leadership teams. Are they diverse? Refer to our discussion on horizontal and vertical diversity for more on this.

Third, look at job satisfaction. Inclusion is especially evident when you consider job satisfaction. Employees who feel included and a part of the team tend to feel more satisfied. You can research this using surveys within your team or simply by asking your people how they feel. If you see that your team is generally satisfied but does not feel like they are very well-connected to others, you may need to incorporate more inclusion-centric activities and strategies.

Fourth, check the turnover rate. How is your job retention? Who leaves? Are your most diverse employees still there or have they all left? Are you constantly looking for new candidates to bring up diversity because new positions are opening rather frequently?

Although looking at metrics can help you pinpoint how you are doing in terms of numbers, this is usually not enough to truly establish whether your team is diverse. For this, you will need to take in qualitative data as well by asking your team for their opinions.

10. Measuring Hiring Practices

A diverse workforce does not result from hiring an average employee from an underrepresented group to fill a vacancy. Instead, it comes about when you bring in people with different backgrounds who are more likely to bring different ideas to the table. This can lead to employees with a wider range of skills and experience and eventually inspire creativity within the organization.

There are many debates surrounding diversity hiring initiatives and the way they should be carried out. Research has shown that people are starting to ask questions about what the new initiatives can do for them and how they can benefit from such programs. This is why organizations must pay careful attention to their hiring programs, measuring them as carefully as you measure workforce diversity.

How do you hire diverse candidates? There is no one-size-fits-all answer to the question. The approach that works best for each organization will vary depending on size, industry, and culture.

However, some basics of inclusive hiring include considering all candidates for a position regardless of their race, ethnicity, gender identity or expression, sexual orientation, age, disability status, or veteran status. Additionally, organizations should make sure to interview candidates in a variety of ways (in person and via video or Skype) and to provide opportunities for employees to provide feedback about the interview process.

An inclusive hiring strategy is a way to make sure that everyone who is qualified for the job can apply and be considered for the position. This means that the company will not only look for candidates who have the skills and experience required for the job, but it will also consider candidates who may be different from them, such as those with disabilities or different ethnic backgrounds.

Inclusive hiring practices are important to help locate talented employees who can fit into the team and contribute to the work environment. These practices focus on finding a diverse range of applicants, regardless of age, race, biological sex and gender identity, sexual orientation, or disability.

Steps to Achieve D&I Hiring

There are a number of steps that must be taken to ensure a successful hiring process for diverse candidates. For instance, it is important that the interviewer knows how best to interview and assess candidates' characteristics and skills as well as personality traits.

There are several steps to follow.

Define D&I for Your Organization

Define what diversity and inclusion mean for your organization. Remember that diversity includes intersectionality. There are many factors to consider when looking at diversity, including gender, race, generational status, neurodiversity, ability, and more. The experiences of a Black woman will differ from the experiences of a White woman even though they are both women and may have held similar roles.

Conduct a Diversity Hiring Audit

Organizations must take time to assess their current hiring process to see if it can be improved to ensure a more diverse and inclusive workforce.

This assessment should include looking at the types of candidates who are being interviewed, how many candidates are being interviewed, and what criteria are used to determine whether a candidate is chosen. After the assessment is completed, changes may need to be made in order to increase diversity within the organization.

If the organization is already diverse, then it will need to determine how best to integrate a diverse candidate into the organization. This will ensure that employees have ample opportunities to grow and excel within the company.

Adopt Inclusive Hiring Metrics

When you are assessing your D&I, make sure you are using inclusive hiring metrics, like the percentage of employees who are from underrepresented groups, the number of women in leadership roles, or the percentage of employees who have disabilities. By using inclusive hiring metrics, employers can make sure that their workplace is welcoming and comfortable for everyone.

Make Sure Your Career Website Is Accessible to All Candidates

Dyslexia is a reading disability that affects the ability to decode written words. Individuals with dyslexia may have difficulty recognizing certain letter shapes and may have trouble with reading quickly. A font that is easy to read can help individuals with dyslexia navigate through a job application or resume. Additionally, using fonts that are not too large or small can help reduce the amount of time needed to read through a document. You can also utilize different types of content such as videos and downloadable information sheets.

When creating a career website, it is important to adhere to Web Content Accessibility Guidelines[92] (WCAG). These guidelines include providing transcripts and closed captions for video and audio files as well as alternative texts for images. Additionally, color contrast standards should be adhered to when developing your website.

Also, instead of using stock photos that trivialize diversity, use authentic images of your team and photos from company events.

Make Inclusion Part of Your Brand

Inclusion should be a part of every employer's brand. When it comes to hiring, it's important to make sure that your company is communicating its commitment to inclusion. You can share externally the percentage of employees with diverse backgrounds working for you.

Share your inclusion efforts internally too, including several metrics such as the number of minority candidates interviewed or hired, the number of employees with disabilities, or the percentage of women in management. By tracking these numbers over time and making changes where necessary, companies can show that they are taking steps to ensure that everyone in their workforce is treated fairly and equally.

Use a Structured Interview Process

When it comes to conducting interviews, use an interview guide and prepare a script with questions specifically about the position. This will help remove unconscious bias from the interviews.

Establish Diverse Interview Panels

This effort can help your hiring team form a more complete view of each candidate and assess their qualities in greater detail. A diverse interview panel can help reduce bias. By having a panel that includes people from different backgrounds, organizations can better understand the different ways candidates think and approach problems. This can help them find the best candidates for the job, regardless of race, gender, or ethnicity.

Use Recruitment Technology

Use recruitment technology to help you find the best candidates for your job.

Recruiting technology can support more diverse hiring practices by providing employers with a way to identify potential candidates quickly and easily. Additionally, by tracking the progress of applicants through the hiring process, companies can ensure that they are considering

---

[92] https://www.w3.org/WAI/standards-guidelines/

qualified candidates and making sure that everyone who is interviewed is given an opportunity to be considered for the position.

Several applicant tracking systems also have built-in functionality to help reduce bias and assist you in making objective decisions. These tools will allow you to assess candidates objectively and compare them against criteria that are relevant to your organization. By using these metrics, you can ensure that your hiring process is fair and unbiased.

How to Apply Predictive Analytics in Recruitment

Despite the impact of the pandemic on global unemployment, we are already seeing signs of a much tighter labor market in many countries.[93] This labor shortage has made attracting and retaining talented candidates more and more difficult. It's even tougher when organizations don't utilize technological advances to their benefit.

Without analyzing data and making the right predictions, the hiring process for most organizations just becomes a guessing game.

More now than ever, we have access to workforce data for studying and analyzing candidate compatibility. Yet only 21 percent of HR managers[94] believe that their companies are using that data to make better business decisions.

Recruitment analytics refer to the act of using data to help make decisions in the recruitment process. These data are analyzed carefully and connections are made among the different data points, which helps improve the hiring process of an organization:

- For executives, a recruitment analysis provides a deep level of insight into the organization's hiring performance. With the analysis they are able to drive efforts to align recruitment strategies with the company's overall goals.
- Recruitment analysis gives recruitment teams a much-needed tool to monitor the efficiency of their talent pipeline, identify any potential recruitment risks, and avoid them.
- Line managers use recruitment analytics to reveal insights that they can act upon and use to measure the success of their processes.

The benefits of recruitment analytics include the following:

- They provide visibility into the effectiveness of your recruitment strategies.

---

[93] https://go.manpowergroup.com/talent-shortage
[94] https://www.gartner.com/en/human-resources/insights/talent-analytics

- They help you improve your hiring processes.
- They aid in keeping track of high-potential candidates for future hiring purposes.
- They allow you to build a robust talent pool or a record of all candidates that you keep coming back to.
- They help you predict which candidates will be high achievers and which ones are not the optimal choice for the company.

The Four Levels of Recruitment Analytics

Recruitment analytics include four different foci or levels.

1. Descriptive Analytics: What Happened?

Descriptive analytics focus on examining past data to assess something that has happened in the recruiting process and highlight any potential worrisome trends. Descriptive analytics can help companies understand what candidates want, how they apply, and what marketing campaigns are most effective.

2. Diagnostic Analytics: Why Did it Happen?

In recruitment, diagnostic analytics can be used to identify factors that may be impacting a candidate's decision-making process and help to improve the recruitment process. This type of recruitment analytics is more about what caused the worrying trends in the recruiting process to occur.

For instance, if the number of applicants in a certain role is declining, diagnostic analytics would determine the potential reasons for that falling number. By understanding how candidates are thinking and behaving, recruiters can target their messaging more effectively and ensure they are reaching the right people.

3. Predictive Analytics: What Will Happen?

Predictive analytics is about what could happen in the future. It uses a mix of machine-learning tactics and statistical data to create a predictive model. This predictive model then provides the likelihood of different outcomes.

Having this data in hand, recruitment teams are able to make decisions based on facts rather than mere assumptions.

4. Prescriptive Analytics: How Can We Make It Happen?

Prescriptive analytics concentrates on what to do next. It gives managers the ability to find out the best course of action to take in a certain situation.

The way it does this is by providing multiple future outcomes for different decisions based on potential elements.

Predictive Analytics

We're going to focus on *predictive analytics,* which can provide meaningful insights into the efficiency of your company's recruitment efforts. It can also be used for a variety of purposes, including marketing, product development, and customer service. For example, predictive analytics can be used to identify potential customers who are likely to respond to a marketing campaign or to develop new products that are likely to be successful in the market. In recruitment, it creates an avenue for managers to hire intelligently through the use of data. It can be used to identify job candidates who are likely to be successful in a given role.

Predictive analytics follows a set pattern. These steps are part of what is known as the "predictive analytics lifecycle."

1. Collect Data

In the first stage of the predictive analytics lifecycle, you collect data from varying sources. Where you collect this data from depends on what you want to know. A data source can be anything.

When it comes to collecting data, a general rule of thumb is that the more data sources you pick, the better your predictions will be.

2. Pre-Process the Data

Phase 2 involves the pre-processing of data. This is the most time-consuming step of the whole predictive cycle as you have to clean the data, format it, combine it, and then sample it.

Put simply, the data is processed in such a way that it becomes ready to use for the predictive model.

3. Choose the Type of Analysis to Run

In this step, you have to establish the type of analysis you want to run. You do that based on knowledge from the previous step.

Once you pick an analysis, you can then choose a predictive model based on your needs. There are many options in terms of picking a predictive model, such as neural networks and decision trees.

You don't have to do the heavy lifting yourself. Your data analytics expert would know what the right choice is for your use.

4. Train the Predictive Model

Next comes the training phase.

Your predictive model needs to be trained in order to make accurate predictions. This means that you will have to take your model on a test drive with a large chunk of data to see how it reacts to it.

Your predictive model trains itself based on the data provided to it. The more quality data you provide it with, the better predictions it is going to make for the future.

5. Predict the Future

After all the pre-processing, analysis establishing, and training has been done, it's time for your predictive model to do what it's been learning to do all along: predict the future.

6. Optimize Your Process

Once the predictions have been made, the process does not stop there. You have got your scores, percentages, graphs, and all the other numbers you can think of. Now you need to learn from the process so that you can do it even better next time.

Ways to Use Predictive Analytics in Hiring

It is now time to use those insights and act on them. Use them to optimize your recruiting process and see where and how you can make positive changes.

Predictive analytics is no crystal ball that will fix all your talent acquisition problems, but it does let leaders and decision-makers of an organization pinpoint specific trends with a very high degree of certainty. This then assists them in optimizing their decisions to get better results.

If companies want the best candidates to work for them, they need to snatch up the right talent as soon as it's available. According to a Robert Half survey,[95] skilled candidates only stay on the job market for an average of ten days before they end up getting a job.

Not only that, but candidates are job-hopping more now than ever. This means that your organization needs to optimize its hiring processes to land the best candidates and retain them.

Predictive analytics is important because it provides managers with insightful data that then helps them:

- identify strong hires for job vacancies,
- make faster and better offers to skilled candidates, and

---

[95] https://rh-us.mediaroom.com/2018-04-05-Does-Job-Hopping-Help-Or-Hurt-Your-Career

- give candidates a better experience.

Recruiters use a number of tech tools, such as applicant tracking systems (ATS),[96] performance management solutions,[97] and HR platforms to help optimize their hiring process. In addition, more and more recruiters are turning toward collecting data almost every day. But even while collecting so much data, recruiters hardly know how to use it to make the right predictions.

Let's take a look at some of the most effective ways organizations can use predictive analytics in their hiring and recruitment processes.

Predictive Hiring

An area where companies can greatly benefit from applying predictive analytics is hiring. By analyzing data, they can assess their talent pool, which helps them make better hiring decisions.

Recruiters and hiring managers in many companies still rely on resume screening and traditional interviewing techniques to narrow down a list of candidates and make their hiring decisions. Companies can instead use people data from their existing employees. This type of data helps predictive algorithms narrow down skilled candidates before they even make it to the hiring manager. In essence, the algorithm recommends only the best-fit applicants.

There are a number of predictive hiring tools on the market that use attrition, employee engagement, and performance data to shortlist the best possible candidates.

Predicting Employee Turnover and Facilitating Retention

Employee turnover costs businesses big money. In fact, according to Gallup,[98] employee turnover can cost companies around 150 percent of an employee's annual salary, due to the time and money spent in finding a replacement. Further research[99] shows that 75 percent of employee turnover causes are preventable.

Predictive analytics allow organizations to recognize the employees who are at a higher risk of leaving. It also helps companies assess the financial impact of these employees leaving.

---

[96] https://www.jobvite.com/blog/recruiting-process/what-is-an-applicant-tracking-system/
[97] https://www.hrhelpboard.com/performance-management/performance-management-system.htm
[98] https://www.gallup.com/workplace/236294/millennials-job-hoppers-not.aspx
[99] https://www.benefitnews.com/news/avoidable-turnover-costing-employers-big

It further details the workforce aspects that may cause an employee to resign. By eliminating these factors, organizations are better able to retain their existing talent and optimize their future hiring plans.

Talent Sourcing

Making sure that you are hiring the right employee is more important than ever because of the soaring talent acquisition costs across all industries. These increasing costs along with a talent shortage and an ever-more competitive job environment mean that companies need to rely on agile methods of talent acquisition.

Predictive analytics tools can be of enormous help here. They can aid the talent acquisition processes of organizations by filling talent pipelines with candidates who have a higher probability of switching jobs in the future and maybe coming your way.

These data can be analyzed by a number of sources, such as a candidate's social media profiles, their company health information, and any stock fluctuations that may take place. The analysis also considers company turnover rates and tenure.

Final Thoughts

It is important to understand that data alone can only do so much. Any data utilized by predictive analytics are useless if there is not a human to make the final decisions on hiring.

For an organization to use predictive analytics effectively, it must begin with an evaluation of the predictive analytics tools in light of its goals. Any tool can only provide a solution if you know what the problem is first.

Once you've got that down, you can then use advanced technological tools, such as predictive analytics, to save time and money by making faster hiring decisions and choosing and retaining the best candidates for your organization.

11. Diversity Recruitment Marketing Best Practices

Diversity has gradually become a priority for hiring managers, with employers making changes to advance diversity in their workplace. We can also attribute this growing interest to increased immigration, growing diversity, and globalization of the corporate sector.

In addition, a rising need has developed for employers to target their products and services to specific segments of the market, causing them to recognize the importance of building and maintaining a diverse and inclusive workplace.

According to research[100] conducted by LinkedIn, 37 percent of recruiters chose attracting more diverse candidates as the number-one trend to focus on in the coming years.

Unfortunately, many organizations still struggle with diversity, equity, and inclusion (DEI) as part of their recruitment pipeline; only 35 percent of companies[101] feel as if they are moving in the right direction with their DEI practices.

If your talent acquisition team is finding it challenging to make diversity recruitment a central part of its process, consider how to use recruitment marketing to get the ball rolling and make the right changes.

What Is Recruitment Marketing?

For many organizations, recruitment marketing can be a bit of a minefield. Increased competition among employers for the best candidates combined with the demand to increase diversity makes the process seem daunting. One of the initial stages of talent acquisition, *recruitment marketing* refers to the process of attracting talent to your organization.

In traditional marketing, you promote a product or service to your target buyer. In recruitment marketing, you essentially promote yourself as an employer to potential candidates.

Recruitment marketing is essentially how employers spread the word about their company culture and the open vacancies. It includes factors such as your brand, target candidate characteristics, and budget. By taking these factors into account, you can create a plan that will help you attract the best candidates for your open positions. To diversify your

---

[100] https://zety.com/blog/hr-statistics
[101] https://www.lever.co/blog/2021-report-highlights-the-state-of-diversity-equity-and-inclusion-efforts/

business as well, your marketing efforts should be geared toward a wider population and be as inclusive as possible.

There are many ways to eliminate conscious or unconscious biases from your company. One way is to use diversity recruitment marketing. Diversity recruitment marketing helps organizations identify and recruit a diverse workforce by focusing on the unique needs of underrepresented groups. This approach can help organizations build a more inclusive and diverse workforce, which can lead to improved productivity and innovation.

To make diversity recruitment marketing work for you, follow the steps outlined in the rest of the chapter.

Assess the Effectiveness of the Current Recruitment Process

Before you go about developing a diversity recruitment marketing campaign, it is imperative to evaluate where you currently stand and what is and isn't working for you. How effective is your current recruitment marketing process?

Conduct an analysis of the current advertisements you use for the purpose of targeting underrepresented groups. In addition, review the media outlets and platforms you use.

Determine which platforms are working the best at attracting diverse talent. Measure response rates and the actual number of hires. The outlets that exhibit the best results should then be reviewed to determine what aspects of their recruitment marketing content are working and leading to success.

Take what you learn from this process and apply it in your diversity recruitment marketing processes for the future. In this step, it can help to be as comprehensive as possible because that can have a long-lasting impact on the success of your future staffing efforts.

Set the Right Goals

Thousands of talent teams aim to improve workplace diversity through a more inclusive hiring process. Many of them, however, often fail at the very first step. The biggest reason behind a failure to implement the right strategies is unrealistic diversity goals.

Let's say you want to hire web developers who are well-versed in a certain type of tech stack, hold a specific academic qualification, and reside anywhere within fifty miles of your office.

If 85 percent of the people who meet this criterion are straight White males between the ages of 30 and 50, what comes next would be rather unsurprising: About 85 percent of your applicant pool will be straight White males between the ages of 30 and 50. This is a problem that no amount of diversity recruitment marketing will fix.

So what can we do here?

1. **Consider the long-term impact of your actions today.** Realize how your actions today can have a long-lasting impact on the promotion of diversity in your organizational structure. When you hire for junior positions, provide the employees with training and educational opportunities that route them toward creating a culture that is diverse.
2. **Make sure your recruitment marketing attracts a wider applicant pool.** Establish the fact that your recruitment marketing should not only attract straight White males in the ideal age range in the current recruiting round. You can do so by creating a robust hiring process with a diverse recruitment strategy at its very base.
3. **Take proactive steps to back initiatives that promote diversity.** Recruitment marketing can only take you so far. Go the extra mile and support programs that work to improve and promote diversification of workplaces. Recognize what you can do to take the idea forward. Create networks with diversified talent. Reach out to them and nurture relationships with them. Before you reach out, though, it is good practice to recognize where the gap exists in your organization. For example, if you feel that your organization is predominantly male, network with more female candidates.

In the end, it is important to make sure that the goals you are setting on diversity make sense for your organization and its long-term goals. You need to align your recruitment marketing with your organizational goals and the demographics of the talent pool you are hiring from.

Employ Methods to Attract a Diverse Talent Pool

People can only apply for a position if they know about it. If the majority of your workforce is made up of privileged groups of individuals, such as White males, there is a high chance that you are advertising for job roles in places where there is a dominant White male population.

Consider Where You Are Implementing Your Diversity Recruitment Marketing

If you want to attract underrepresented groups or minorities, you should probably widen your horizon and start looking somewhere else.

For the purpose of hiring from a specific demographic, you can look at specialized diversity job boards. Consider social media platforms to reach a wider candidate pool and target a larger demographic.

You can also use automation in your pursuit. Applicant tracking systems include recruitment marketing tools that are automated to make the entire process easier for you. Through these tools, you can create and post a job advertisement across a range of platforms, including diversity employment boards and social media.

Represent Your Company's Diversity Through Its Web Platforms

Work on your employer brand by showcasing what candidates can expect from your company, both from the recruitment process and once they are hired. If you already have individuals from varying backgrounds on your team, use their pictures and videos to represent them on your business's website.

If, however, there is not much in the way of diversity in your teams currently, be transparent and open about it. Let applicants know what you are doing to improve diversity and inclusivity at your workplace.

Think about the brand image you want to cultivate. From your official website to the job boards and social media platforms that you post content on, let the audience know that you are a DEI-centric company.

Here is how you can leverage recruitment marketing to drive a diverse candidate pool and further your employer brand:

- Let your internal subject matter experts (SMEs) share their stories and personal experience with the company with your candidates.
- Add your genuine intentions to diversify to important web pages, such as your company's *About* or *Careers* pages.
- Attract and nurture candidates by giving them insight into your company policies directed toward tackling the lack of diversity and improving inclusivity.
- Increase awareness by posting open applications where candidates get to choose how they can shine within your organization, no matter who they are and where they come from.
- Garner interest in your organization by sharing DEI-centric content and initiatives.

Look at Your Language

The language you use in your job postings can be greatly influential to your diversity and talent acquisition efforts. More now than ever, people are aware of and recognize if the right kind of language is being used to address them.

Some words and phrases can quickly prompt adverse reactions in certain people, especially those who come from underrepresented groups.

Even if you are taking steps to improve diversity in your organization, the language that is involved in and around your recruitment marketing can come off as biased if you don't use inclusive phrases.

One of the biggest areas of impact of language is gender diversity. Men and women traditionally respond very differently to different job descriptions.

In addition, you need to understand the varying phrases that different communities use to represent and define themselves. Not doing so can make your job ads unsearchable and make many individuals feel excluded.

The wrong wording choices can make your organization come off as a place that sustains inequality and imbalance.

Use Data to Identify Your Biggest Roadblocks

Today, data is king. And rightfully so! The right data can help you optimize your diversity recruitment marketing efforts by helping you recognize your weak points and overcome the roadblocks that you face when it comes to inclusive hiring.

Questionnaires to Monitor Equality

You can add an equality monitoring questionnaire to your job application process. This will allow you to collect data based on the demographics of candidates. Ideally, this questionnaire should be optional for candidates to fill out.

Reports on Equality Performance

Based on the data received as a result of the equality monitoring questionnaire, the applicant tracking system you use is going to provide you with a detailed report on the performance of your diversity initiatives.

The report will help you identify how diverse your applicant pool is. Moreover, it will tell you how that diversity changes as candidates progress through the recruitment process at each stage.

By comparing these data points across different teams and locations, you will be able to identify areas of your business that need immediate attention along with parts that are acting as the biggest roadblocks in your inclusion efforts.

For example, if the diversity of your applicant pool is not in line with the diversity of candidates getting to the interview, ask yourself why. You can use the method of blind hiring to reduce—if not altogether mitigate—this bias.

Going a step further, if the diversity of the candidates getting hired does not reflect the diversity of the candidates that get to the interview stage, consider using interview scorecards to make sure your interview process is fair and free from stereotypical presumptions.

Make Efforts to Eliminate Conscious or Unconscious Biases

In order to eliminate any unconscious biases, it is important to be open to new perspectives and to learning about different cultures and to be aware of the ways in which our own biases might affect our decisions.

Use Blind Hiring

Blind recruitment[102] is gaining popularity among employers and for good reason. By redacting all personal information (such as name, age, photos, race, ethnicity, and gender pronouns) from resumes and applications, a blind hiring process enables companies to reduce the risk of practicing conscious and unconscious biases during the selection process.

Most modern applicant tracking systems come with blind hiring software. With the blind hiring tool added, employers have an easier time incorporating it in their existing process. You won't have to manually redact information from resumes.

Train Employees to Recognize, Address, and Mitigate Their Biases

More and more research[103] shows that hiring procedures are actually pretty highly biased.[104]

When it comes to hiring, recruitment managers need to be able to think broadly. They should be able to standardize the process by understanding what hiring prejudices are and how they operate.

Managers and employers should look into training and educating their teams on the topic of biases.

---

[102] https://www.forbes.com/sites/forbeshumanresourcescouncil/2022/06/01/blind-recruiting-what-is-it-and-how-do-you-do-it/

[103] https://hbr.org/2016/04/if-theres-only-one-woman-in-your-candidate-pool-theres-statistically-no-chance-shell-be-hired

[104] https://hbr.org/2017/05/study-employers-are-less-likely-to-hire-a-woman-who-wears-a-headscarf

Provide awareness training so that your employees can recognize and identify their biases. Once the recognition is made, encourage organizational conversations about what can be done to mitigate those prejudices in their entirety.

Measure the Effectiveness of Your Diversity Recruitment Initiatives

Marketers across the board use key performance indicators (KPIs) and other metrics to measure the efficacy of their campaigns and efforts. Similarly, to measure how effective your current diversity recruitment marketing pipeline is, your hiring team can create their own diversity KPIs that help increase the efficiency of the entire process. These KPIs are bound to look different for every company.

One thing to note here is that your KPIs do not necessarily need to be set in stone. Rather, there should be some sort of wiggle room for changes as your team progresses through the process and you gather more data and insights.

As your teams grow and your objectives change, your recruitment goals will pivot as well to accommodate for future talent acquisition needs.

Realize That Recruitment Is Only the Beginning

In the tech industry alone, only 26 percent of companies[105] have a DEI policy in action. Although awareness of the topic of inclusion is clearly growing, we still have a long way to go. Focusing on recruitment is a great first step in the right direction. But relying on it completely for your diversity efforts is not enough.

Once a candidate is hired at your workplace, they want to know what you can do for them going forward and what efforts you will make to help them feel like a part of a community. Company culture, even before you hire the candidate, will inadvertently affect your diversity efforts.

Here are seven simple and straightforward ways you can foster a company environment that provides people from all backgrounds and experiences with a place of belonging:

- During onboarding, introduce the new employee as a whole person, going beyond their professional responsibilities and duties in the job role.

---

[105] https://employers.builtin.com/report-state-of-dei-in-tech/

- Be open to feedback from your staff. Ask them how they feel and whether they feel like a part of the organization. Genuinely listen while they voice their concerns as there is almost always room for improvement. Limit any distractions.
- Solicit input from your employees whenever possible during meetings instead of speaking over them. It is okay to let them guide the conversation at times.
- Delegate tasks without any sense of inequality or bias. Professional trust should be shown to employees based on merit.
- Do not hesitate to share stories and encourage others to do the same. This makes people feel at ease.
- Promote a culture of psychological safety.
- Encourage your teams to build employee resource groups (ERGs).

Final Thoughts

Building a diverse company culture takes time, but it's worth the effort. There will be times when you make mistakes, but with patience and perseverance you can eventually succeed.

People may find something in a job description that doesn't sit right with them or you may be inadvertently showcasing only male-dominated success stories on your social media. The best way to ensure that you remain a proponent of professional equality and inclusivity is to ensure your recruitment marketing campaign itself is inclusive of your entire team, where everyone's opinions count.

12. How to Write Job Adverts with Diversity in Mind

Diversity and inclusion are the name of the game nowadays. Standard job descriptions no longer cut it in the eyes of candidates. Creating Inclusive job descriptions can help organizations attract a more diverse pool of applicants. Job descriptions should be tailored to the specific position. They should not include any possible aspect that could exclude certain groups of people.

A run-of-the-mill job listing that relies on traditional phrasings and wordings is unrelatable, unexciting, and inaccessible for many.

With the professional market becoming increasingly open to including a wider talent pool, companies need to assess whether their new vacancies are being promoted by using inclusive job adverts.

Why Your Current Job Description Criteria May Be Turning Away Diverse Talent

Through the years, we have realized that language is not simple and can have a long-lasting impact on individuals, especially those who belong to underrepresented groups in our society.

Oftentimes, even the words and phrases we use in our daily routine are "gendered." In recent research carried out by LinkedIn,[106] it was found that, although men and women both used the same methods to browse jobs online, the way they applied was vastly different. They found that despite viewing the same number of jobs as male users on the platform, women were

- less likely to apply for positions they had viewed on the website and
- less likely to apply for positions that were more senior than their current position (what LinkedIn calls "stretch roles").

In other words, LinkedIn's research shows that women on average apply for fewer positions and in particular for less senior positions.[107]

If you make your job advertisements more inclusive, you are likely to attract more women applicants. According to a LinkedIn report, when women do apply to a job, they are 16 percent more likely than men to get

---

[106] https://www.linkedin.com/business/talent/blog/talent-acquisition/how-women-find-jobs-gender-report
[107] https://www.bi.team/blogs/women-only-apply-for-jobs-when-100-qualified-factor-fake-news

hired. If the role is more senior than their current position, that number goes up to 18 percent.[108]

The problem with candidate self-screening is especially important to consider when we talk about fresh graduate recruitment. Most new graduates simply do not meet all the requirements that are outlined in the job description. This, however, does not translate to them being absolutely useless and incompetent in a job role. But it does translate into most of them never bothering to apply.

Many of these new graduates can, in fact, do the job effectively with some training and mentorship. The same applies to women who also choose not to apply unless they meet all the requirements. Employers and hiring managers must make sure that female job seekers do not screen themselves out of the process as that could mean that companies are missing out on diverse talent.

Another study[109] conducted by Duke University and the University of Waterloo revealed that people are less inclined to apply for job adverts that contain biased phrasing and gendered language, whether they realize it or not.

This bias in language is more prominent in job listings for positions in technology and engineering professions—fields that are typically more male-dominated. More masculine-associated words, such as "leader" and "dominant" are utilized in these job ads. These words were not included in job descriptions for roles and professions in female-dominated fields, such as human resources.

Although these subtleties in language may seem unimportant, they certainly should not be underestimated.

Aside from including gender-biased language that can put off viable talent, the content in your job descriptions might be unengaging. The boilerplate approach of creating bullet points and list of perks hardly ever works anymore to attract diverse talent.

People also want to know what your company is doing in the way of inclusivity and diversity. Make sure to include such information in your job postings.

---

[108] https://www.linkedin.com/business/talent/blog/talent-acquisition/how-women-find-jobs-gender-report
[109] http://www.fortefoundation.org/site/DocServer/gendered_wording_JPSP.pdf?docID=16121

So, even if diverse candidates do come across your company's job descriptions, they may not engage with them due to the corporate jargon, gendered phrasing, unengaging content, and a lack of information about D&I.

Tips for Writing Job Descriptions That Attract a Diverse Talent Pool

If you are looking to make your workplace more diverse, it helps to be thoughtful about what you include in and omit from your job adverts.

It is always a good practice to paint a picture of what it's like to work at your organization. Try to sell and promote the story of your workplace culture, the dynamics of teamwork in it, and what you stand for.

Combine the following tips to write job descriptions that overcome the hurdles in attracting a diverse talent pool.

Start by Using the Right Language

Using the wrong type of language does not always mean failing to employ gender-neutral words. It goes beyond that.

Often, employers focus on producing a job ad in the language of the market that they want to hire for. However, meanings can often get lost in translation.

A good practice is to apply an element of localization to your job descriptions and adverts.

Write your job ads in the language and for the culture that you are advertising for. Localize the text to the applicant pool that you intend to target. You should remember to

- make sure that you understand the language of the place that you want to hire people from and create content that will be easily understandable and relatable for them and
- create the job ad in a language that the target talent pool has access to, as well as in the variety of the language that people speak in the area.

Avoid Racial Bias

Job descriptions with racial bias can make people feel like the company isn't interested in hiring them. Job descriptions should have no racial bias whatsoever to get the best person for a job.

Most companies are aware that race-specific terms are to be avoided. But not all employers are aware of all the words that can alienate certain underrepresented groups, terms like *blacklisting, native English speaker, migrants, illegals,* and *top school.*

Furthermore, while writing job descriptions, organizations should make sure they don't add a requirement (unless necessary) to keep a group of people away, like wearing any particular kind of dress, not covering one's head, or shaving facial hair. These things can create problems for people who are members of certain cultures.

Avoid mentioning race or nationality at all costs. Avoid including phrases such as "strong English-language skills" unless the job warrants it. This discourages nonnative speakers from applying.

Whenever possible, opt for blind recruiting by removing all identifying information from the resume application. Look beyond your referral network. Subject everyone to the same standards of interviewing and screening. Challenge any biases that occur due to locations, schools, and names.

Avoid Gender Bias

Gender biases in language are one of the biggest culprits in turning diverse candidates away. Job seekers should see themselves in a job description, and that can't happen when your descriptions are gender-biased. Job descriptions should not use words such as he, she, his, or hers, as these words do not add anything specific to the role. Job descriptions should use gender-neutral words such as he/she, you, staff, salesperson, parental leave, or employee.

Although gender binary is still a core concept in many societies, the world is gradually moving toward a much more gender-diverse society. Many languages, such as English, have pronouns that do not cover the entirety of this gender diversification.

This means that it is not just women who can find your job descriptions exclusionary.

Go for phrases and pronouns that are not specific to any gender.

Remove Gender-Coded Words

The language used in job descriptions matters a lot. Organizations should avoid using any words that immediately signal gender. Job titles like mailman or fireman are gender-specific. They tend to favor one gender over the other, so they should be avoided. Also, avoid using words like superhero, ninja, hacker, or guru. Instead, use words like developer, engineer, and project manager.

Moreover, gender-coded words don't reflect the modern workforce well anymore and aren't inclusive. Job seekers who identify as female might not apply for the job if they see these words in the description. Job descriptions should use inclusive words rather than traditional, gender-coded words. This way, job seekers will feel like they're applying for something that is meant for them.

The following list includes some common variations in the English language that tend to represent one gender over the other.

Feminine-Coded Words[110]	Masculine-Coded Words
• support • share • responsible • understand (or understanding) • together • committed • interpersonal • feel • collaborate (or collaboration) • connect	• strong • lead — includes leader(s) • analysis — includes analyze and analytical • individual(s) • decisions(s) • driven • competitive • expert • objectives • principles

Reduce Age and Experience Bias

Age and experience bias is a real problem in today's workplace. Too often, employers discriminate against older workers, assuming that they don't know how to use technology. This is not only unfair, but it's also bad for business. After all, there are plenty of people over the age of fifty who are perfectly capable of using new technologies. The bottom line is that when it comes to hiring, don't let age or experience bias cloud your judgment. Instead, focus on finding the best person for the job, regardless of their age or technological expertise.

Use Software to Analyze Language

Job descriptions serve as a gateway for the right applicants to reach you.

If you are not sure whether the text that you have created for a vacancy is gender-neutral and checks all the right boxes, you can use software and tools to help you fight the subtle bias that you may have missed in your job ad.

---

[110] https://blog.ongig.com/diversity-and-inclusion/list-of-gender-coded-words/

A great tool for this purpose is Gender Decoder.[111] It's completely free and all you have to do is copy and paste your job advert text into the evaluation window. Another useful tool is Textio.[112] This is a much more versatile tool that analyzes job descriptions in real-time.

As you write, any text that could come across as gender biased is highlighted. Textio then suggests alternate words.

This may seem like a small change, but automation can go a long way in achieving positive results. In fact, software company Atlassian saw an 80 percent increase[113] in their recruitment of women in tech-related roles after using Textio to structure their job adverts and several other communication pieces.

You can also find many alternative software programs by using the search phrase "Textio alternatives" in Google.

Be Mindful of Literacy Inclusion

Literacy inclusion means making sure that your written communications are accessible by all potential applicants, including readers with special needs, such as the visually impaired, and readers with varying literacy skills. Even something as simple as completing the alt tag box for images on your website can make a difference to some of your audience; the alt tag helps the visually impaired know what an image shows when their text to speech software reads it to them.

Literacy inclusion also includes *readability,* which is the level of reading difficulty of your written content. Using shorter words and shorter sentences, for example, can increase readability. So can word choice: Try to use more widely understood words.

Furthermore, you should always keep your paragraphs short with enough white space between them to reduce visual "noise."

You can use Hemingway Editor[114] and Grammarly[115] to improve fluency and sentence structure in order to help your writing read better.

---

[111] http://gender-decoder.katmatfield.com/
[112] https://textio.com/
[113] https://review.firstround.com/atlassian-boosted-its-female-technical-hires-by-80-percent-heres-how
[114] https://hemingwayapp.com/
[115] http://grammarly.com/

Make Your Job Descriptions Communicate Accessibility

Write the content of your job vacancy in a way that welcomes individuals of all abilities. Let the applicants know that your workplace values the contribution of every employee.

Showcase the accommodations your business makes to individuals with disabilities. This could be anything from work-from-home opportunities to flexible hours to accommodating software.

For instance, instead of writing, "Must be able to lift 60 pounds," write, "Moves equipment weighing up to 60 pounds." Avoid phrases like "able-bodied individual."

Exclude the Jargon

Don't use jargon or industry-specific terms when communicating with potential candidates. When it comes to finding the right words to use in your job descriptions, plain speech is always going to be your best friend. Avoiding ambiguous phrases such as *leverage, metrics,* and *KPIs* will make you more appealing. Even if jargon is important for the specific role, the applicant can learn it later on in the job.

There will be candidates who have the right skills and may fit in the vacancy pretty well even if they don't fully understand the industry lingo.

Needlessly complex language also discourages fresh graduates from applying to jobs as they feel they don't have the technical skills required. In fact, 64 percent of new graduates believe that they should not apply for a job role if they don't understand every single part of the description. Nearly half (47 percent) said they had gone to an interview without fully understanding what the job entailed.[116]

Removing jargon from your job advert is not going to damage its SEO as algorithms nowadays are much smarter than that.

You can use Jargon Decoder[117] tool to eliminate jargon from your job description text.

Make a Conscious Effort to Improve D&I

It can be difficult to develop language that gets your intentions across to readers and lets them know about your efforts to improve diversity and inclusion.

---

[116] https://www.milkround.com/insights/job-ad-jargon-decoder/#/
[117] https://www.milkround.com/insights/job-ad-jargon-decoder/#/decoder

Try to state what you stand for specifically and clearly. For instance, you might include a section that tells the candidate that you welcome applicants from diverse backgrounds.

If you want to go a step further, remove phrases and keywords that might segment a certain set of the population, such as "top-tier university."

If you want to make a conscious effort to improve your workplace's diversity, you need to become aware of the language you use every step of the way and not just in the beginning of the process or toward the end of it.

Take a lesson from your previous job descriptions and see where you can improve. Look at historical data and ask yourself:

- Did this particular job description attract a certain kind of candidate only?
- Did advertisements heavy with gendered language attract a certain gender only?
- Did a jargon-heavy description result in more skilled candidates?
- How long did it take for the job advertisement to result in a hire?
- Did it result in confusion between the candidates and recruitment managers in any way?

Welcome Disabled Workers

Those of us who have done well in our careers without any significant glitches or serious challenges might not understand the issues people face when entering and navigating the job market. Job hunters with disabilities can have a hard time finding employment opportunities simply because employers aren't familiar with the accommodations they might need. Job hunters can get frustrated, feeling they are fighting an uphill battle to find the proper gig. For those with disabilities, finding a job can be even more difficult.

When you're writing a job description, whether for an opening you have right now or just for future reference, consider best practices for including applicants with disabilities. Focus on creating job descriptions that welcome all aspirants.

In the job description itself, it's important to mention that you are open to hiring people with disabilities to make sure everyone feels welcome. Such a simple but powerful statement can help disabled workers find your company and apply for your available roles. After all, people who have a disability represent a significant consumer market. About 56.7 million people—19 percent of the population—had a disability in 2010, according to a broad definition of *disability*, with more than half of them reporting the disability was severe, according to a comprehensive report on this population released by the U.S. Census Bureau.[118]

The job description will mention accommodations that can be made for applicants throughout the selection process. This could include things like particular communication methods or assistance with on-the-job tasks. Providing a range of accommodations will help to create a sense of comfort and trust between employees and applicants.

Don't Be Afraid to Incorporate Storytelling in Your Job Descriptions

Storytelling is immersive. Try to leverage your personal and memorable experiences or employee stories in your job description to invoke a positive response from your candidates.

According to a survey[119] of 1,000 candidates from all over the world, 54 percent said that they thought a company was more inclusive and cared about diversity if they showcased real-life stories of the company's employees. It showed them that they cared about their workers.

A popular technique is to include a list of the benefits, requirements, and other information about the job. A list, however, does not compel the candidate in any way. It doesn't show them where you stand in terms of diversity.

Instead of using the conventional approach, tell a short story about what the benefits look like in practice. Show the applicant how workers have benefitted in the past and how they can aid in the future. Even a short video featuring your diverse employees will have a positive impact.

Write Impact Descriptions Rather Than Lists of Requirements

More and more companies are ditching the traditional job description in favor of "impact descriptions." These descriptions dive into the details of the vacancy and provide a breakdown of the key milestones that a worker is expected to achieve within a specific time at the company.

Use Technology to Connect Diverse Talent and Employees

Technology can help bridge connections between diverse candidates and existing employees. This is done by appointing diverse employees who currently work in a company to address the concerns and questions of diverse applicants through social media and other platforms.

---

[118] https://www.census.gov/newsroom/releases/archives/miscellaneous/cb12-134.html
[119] https://pathmotion.com/resources/diversity-recruiting-whats-on-candidates-minds/

Companies can also leverage the power of technology and social media to deliver the day-to-day experiences of their diverse employees in the workplace.

Through the use of technology, employees and applicants are able to hang out virtually before applications are underway. This promotes the employer brand as well as engages the applicants.

Highlight Benefits for People Requiring Flexibility

Along with including your intent to diversify your workplace and create an inclusive environment, your job ad should explain the kind of benefits diverse candidates can experience.

In essence, highlight your inclusive benefits, diversity commitment, and values. Don't make people ask you about flexible working hours or health insurance. Include these details in your job ads in plain sight for candidates to see.

Final Thoughts

There are plenty of reasons companies should make an effort to be more inclusive in their hiring practices. For one thing, it's simply the right thing to do. Overlooked and underestimated communities have been struggling for far too long, and it's time for businesses to step up and give them a fair chance.

But aside from the moral argument, there are also plenty of socioeconomic benefits that come from inclusive hiring. A more diverse workforce leads to a wider range of perspectives, which can lead to more creativity and innovation. It can also help build better relationships with the broader community, which can benefit the company in many ways. Ultimately, there's no downside to being more inclusive in your hiring practices. It's good for business, and it's good for society as a whole.

But in order for that to happen effectively, you need to attract the right people by showing how your organization can benefit them and the accommodations that can support them.

General Rules for Job Descriptions

Job descriptions are an important tool for any company. They help to identify the tasks that are expected of employees and the skills that are required for the job. By following the general rules in this chapter, you can create effective job descriptions that will help your company function more efficiently.

Humanize Your Ad

Remember that you are creating an ad for people, not machines. So it should give them a reason to apply. Replace the phrases "ideal candidate" or "perfect candidate" with "you" or with any words that will connect with your target audience.

Set realistic expectations. Research the keywords relevant to the role and ask people who are already working in the position. Let them describe the role in their own words. Think of your ad as an "employee testimonial."

Be Clear About the Job Requirements

When it comes to qualifications, it's important to be clear about the necessary skills required for a job. Job descriptions might include generic experience, but that doesn't mean everyone has that same experience. Job descriptions should be specific about the educational requirements or any other kind of necessary qualifications. This way applicants will know if they fit the job requirements, and only qualified people will apply.

Job descriptions should also specify whether relocation is required. Job seekers should know this type of information before going to the trouble of applying for a job.

Highlight Company Culture

When it comes to job postings, one way to stand out from the competition is to highlight the company culture in your job postings. This can help potential employees see how they would fit into the company and what their future with the company might look like.

Writing a job description can help set the tone for an organization. A good job description should be positive, indicating that the individual filling the position will be able to achieve goals and objectives. Additionally, it should be specific, detailing what the individual will need to do and how they will contribute to the organization.

Don't Go Too Short or Too Long

Your job descriptions need to be clear, concise, and easy to understand. They should also provide context for the position and how it relates to the company's goals. Two short sentences are not going to entice anybody to actually apply to your company, so make sure your descriptions are full and detailed.

But job descriptions that are too long can also discourage job seekers from applying for a role. You need to keep in mind that candidates' attention is limited. They are not going to read a ten-page description of your job. Most people visit LinkedIn and job boards through mobile devices. If they need to scroll more than four times on a mobile screen, then your advert is too long, and you should create a shorter version.

Before you post a new ad, ask yourself if you feel that it is appealing. If you have doubts, invest more time in rewriting it.

The company The Muse did a test on how the length of a job advertisement influences the number of clicks they get. They found that, in general, job posts containing fewer than 250 words got about the same number of clicks as those with more than 1,000 words. But in certain job categories, like social media, jobs under 750 words got about 2.8 times more application clicks. For legal and education jobs, the trend was the opposite—job posts with more than 750 words got about 2 times as many clicks.[120]

Write for Mobile

The length of a job ad is also going to play a role when people are checking adverts on their cell phones. More and more people are using their mobile devices for job searching. During 2021, 67% of job applications were completed on mobile devices, according to a report by Appcast. In 2019, only 51% of job applications were completed that way, the company said.[121] If your advertisement is long on a computer screen, imagine how long it will look on a cell phone screen. People will forget what they read at the beginning before they even finish reading it.

---

[120] https://www.themuse.com/advice/we-used-data-to-prove-just-how-long-a-job-description-should-be-to-attract-candidates
[121] https://recruitingdaily.com/news/almost-70-of-2021-job-applications-were-made-from-mobile-devices/

Don't Recycle Job Descriptions

Since your company is evolving, the information in your ads should change too. Don't use the same ad for years. Candidates who see the recycled ads for months or years could get the impression that something is wrong with your company.

Job descriptions should reflect the current needs of the organization. Organizations that are willing to revise their job descriptions make applicants feel optimistic about the company's culture.

Target the Location

If you are entering into a completely new market, check out the competitors. Are you the only company using "Associate Developer" as a title for your role? If the whole local market is using "Junior Developer," update your ad. Always try to reflect the language and culture of the location where you are hiring.

Share Your Values

When it comes to diversity and inclusion, it is important to mention them in your job description. Additionally, it is important to make sure that your company culture supports D&I values. Additionally, ensure your company handbook outlines the values, how they are supported, and how employees may raise questions or concerns about them. Also show what organizations and events your company supports.

Provide Contact Details and Recruiter's Name

Most recruiters don't want their contact details shared in a job description. The reason is simple: They don't wat to be flooded by calls from candidates who are not right for the role. But contact details will raise the number of candidates and improve the candidate experience—most people want to speak with another person and not simply launch their resumes into a black hole.

Final Thoughts

Drafting a good job description is key to hiring the best candidate. The job description is the first thing applicants read about the organization and as such it can make or break their trust. Make your job descriptions inclusive and accessible to applicants from all backgrounds. In addition, job seekers should feel reassured by job descriptions that the organization will focus on them as individuals rather than merely as members of an underrepresented group.

Your description should stand out to be the best asset for your company or team.

Finally, remember that to write the perfect job description you must aim to strike a balance between providing enough detail while staying focused.

14. The Legal Side of Diverse Hiring

Before the U.S. Supreme Court decision in *Brown v. Board of Education*,[122] most businesses and entities blatantly discriminated against those who were disabled or had special needs status. However, after the Supreme Court ruled against school segregation in 1954 with this landmark decision, schools and businesses around the country had to become more sensitive toward race and other issues in hiring practices.

In recent years a number of high-profile lawsuits allege that employees have been the victims of discrimination by their employers. These lawsuits have often resulted in large legal fees and settlements as well as class-action status for the plaintiffs. The most common types of discrimination that are alleged in these lawsuits include race, gender, and age discrimination.[123] Other cases have alleged religious discrimination and disability discrimination.

Legal Implications

As more and more companies strive for a diverse workforce, it's important to understand the legal implications of hiring employees from diverse backgrounds and underrepresented groups. In the United States, laws prohibit discrimination based on factors like race, religion, and national origin. These laws generally cover three areas:

- Employers cannot refuse to hire someone simply for being a member of a protected class.
- Additionally, employers must provide equal opportunities to all employees. This includes ensuring that all employees have the same access to training and development opportunities.
- Finally, employers must take steps to prevent harassment or discrimination against employees of underrepresented groups.

By understanding the legal implications of hiring a diverse workforce, employers can create a workplace that is both fair and inclusive. These implications are both complex and extensive, especially for employers with multiple business locations—because the law as applied to each location may mean different things. For example, an employer with a business located in a predominantly White neighborhood may be sued for discrimination if they only hire Black employees.

---

[122] https://en.wikipedia.org/wiki/Brown_v._Board_of_Education
[123] https://www.npr.org/2022/04/14/1092804493/telsa-racial-discrimination-lawsuit-15-million

The best way to avoid legal problems is to develop a comprehensive diversity policy that takes into account the unique needs of your business. By taking the time to create a policy that is tailored to your company, you can help to ensure compliance with the law and avoid any potential legal problems. When developing your policy, you will have to study Equal Employment Opportunity Commission guidelines and discuss the policy with your HR and legal teams.

If you know you have problems with your hiring practices, start by contacting an employment law specialist. Get help before problems become legal ones. Additionally, consider implementing training on unconscious bias to help your team make better hiring decisions.

The ADA

The ADA (Americans with Disabilities Act) requires employers to accept the essential job limitations of employees who are disabled, regardless of any costs that might be involved in helping them attain their peak function. It is now illegal for an employer to refuse to hire a disabled person if he or she can perform the essential functions of the position. The employer must also provide reasonable accommodation during the hiring process so that disabled applicants or employees can remain competitive in their fields.

Disparate Impact

Disparate impact and disparate treatment are both discriminatory. *Disparate treatment* is intentionally discriminating against a group of people. *Disparate impact* refers to the results of policies or actions that affect different groups of people differently. For example, if you regularly promote men to managerial positions but never promote women, that is disparate treatment. If your job description lists the ability to lift 150 pounds, many women won't even apply, so the ad will have disparate impact, favoring male candidates.

Disparate impact cases are much harder to prove.

Federal Laws

Comprehension of the legal implications of diverse hiring is essential for the protection of both employers and employees. An employer should know about the ADA (Americans with Disabilities Act)[124], EEO (Equal

---

[124] https://www.ada.gov/

Employment Opportunity Act)[125], FMLA (Family Medical Leave Act)[126], and OSHA (Occupational Safety and Health Act)[127].

The Equal Employment Opportunity Commission (EEOC) is responsible for enforcing federal laws that make it illegal to discriminate against a job applicant or employee because of the person's race, color, religion, sex (including pregnancy), national origin, age (forty or older), disability, or genetic information. It is also illegal to discriminate against a person because they complained about discrimination, filed a charge of discrimination, or participated in an employment discrimination lawsuit or investigation.[128]

The EEOC has published guidance on the types of questions that employers should not ask job applicants during interviews. Some of these prohibited questions relate to an applicant's diversity, such as his or her race, color, religion, national origin, ethnicity, or country of birth. Asking these types of questions could lead to a claim of discrimination if the employer ultimately decides not to hire the applicant. Asking about an applicant's citizenship status is also generally prohibited. However, there are some limited circumstances under which an employer can ask about an applicant's citizenship status, such as if the employer is required by law only to hire U.S. citizens. In addition, certain jobs with the federal government may require applicants to be U.S. citizens.

According to the EEOC, it is important for employers to establish clear employment policies that comply with federal antidiscrimination laws. For example, if an employer knows that they will be hiring diverse employees, then it is critical for them to know whether hiring diverse employees is essential to their success.

It is difficult to manage all of the regulations that surround diversity hiring. Nonetheless, it is essential for an employer to be aware of these laws in order to learn how to protect their business from lawsuits. The following laws are the most common ones in the United States pertaining to diverse hiring:

- **Title VII of the Civil Rights Act of 1964**[129]**:** This law prohibits workplace discrimination based on race, gender, religion, and national origin. It also prohibits retaliation against an employee for reporting discrimination or filing a complaint. It is important to note that this

---

[125] https://www.eeoc.gov/

[126] https://www.dol.gov/agencies/whd/fmla

[127] https://www.osha.gov/laws-regs/oshact/completeoshact

[128] https://askjan.org/resources/U-S-Equal-Employment-Opportunity-Commission.cfm

[129] https://www.eeoc.gov/statutes/title-vii-civil-rights-act-1964

act only applies to employers with fifteen or more employees, but there are different acts that can apply if the employer has fewer than fifteen employees.

- **The Rehabilitation Act of 1973**[130]**:** This law prohibits federal contractors and subcontractors from discriminating against disabled individuals who apply to work for them as well as current employees. Federal agencies and departments are also prohibited from discriminating against individuals with disabilities. The EEOC also stated that this act applies to employment agencies.
- **The Age Discrimination in Employment Act**[131]**:** The Age Discrimination in Employment Act (ADEA) forbids age discrimination against people who are age forty or older. It does not protect workers under the age of forty, although some states have laws that protect younger workers from age discrimination.
- **The Civil Rights Act of 1991**[132]**:** This law prohibits discrimination and retaliation based on race, color, religion, sex, and national origin.
- **Employee Polygraph Protection Act**[133]**:** This law protects employees from being required to take polygraph examinations in order to be hired or remain employed.
- **Equal Pay Act of 1963**[134]**:** This law prohibits wage discrimination based on gender. It also prohibits retaliation because an employee filed a complaint about equal pay for men and women.
- **Overtime Pay Act of 1963:** This law ensures that all employees receive the same amount of overtime pay.
- **Wage and Hour Law**[135]**:** This law protects employees from being discriminated against based on their pay. It also prohibits employers from allowing child labor and unsafe work conditions.
- **Employee Retirement Income Security Act (ERISA)**[136]**:** This act protects employees from employer violations of Medicare or Social Security laws.

Complexities of Diversity Hiring Law

The laws, as stated, seem fairly straightforward. But for every argument made on one side of an issue, there's been an equally successful one made on the other side, making diversity hiring law even more challenging to

---

[130] https://www.eeoc.gov/statutes/rehabilitation-act-1973
[131] https://www.eeoc.gov/age-discrimination
[132] https://en.wikipedia.org/wiki/Civil_Rights_Act_of_1991
[133] https://www.dol.gov/agencies/whd/polygraph
[134] https://www.eeoc.gov/statutes/equal-pay-act-1963
[135] https://www.dol.gov/agencies/whd/flsa
[136] https://www.dol.gov/general/topic/retirement/erisa

manage. For example, all of the laws regarding diversity hiring stipulate that employers cannot use criminal records as a way to discriminate against workers. However, it is still very difficult for a person with a criminal record to get hired, so employers are finding ways around the law, perhaps by stressing other ways the applicant with a criminal record doesn't measure up. Another example is age rules set by employers. For example, companies may require commercial drivers to be younger than a certain age because of data showing that older people have more accidents. *Hodgson v. Greyhound Lines, Inc.*, established the legality of that specific discrimination.

It is also possible for an employer to discriminate against an applicant if the specific type of discrimination has not yet been outlawed. For example, in most states you can be fired for your weight. If your employer thinks you're too over- or underweight, they can let you go.

Another complexity is known as *reverse discrimination.* If my efforts to be inclusive and hire diversely mean that you get overlooked for the job, you might be able to sue me for reverse discrimination, arguing that the only reason you weren't hired is that you weren't a member of an underrepresented group.

Diversity Hiring Laws in Canada and India

In other countries, laws governing diversity hiring often take a different route. For instance, in Canada, the Employment Equity Act of Canada[137] sets out parameters within which employers can work to ensure that they hire employees who represent a wide range of demographics. Canadian employers must also meet certain tests to show their compliance with the law.

In India, the Indian Code of Conduct, Equal Remuneration Act, and Prevention of Discrimination Act[138] are comprehensive pieces of legislation pertaining to diverse hiring. India also incorporates an Equal Remuneration Act that prohibits employment discrimination on the basis of religion, language, and caste. In 2018, India's Minimum Wage Act[139] aimed to eliminate discriminatory wages by making it illegal for employers to offer fixed wages based on an employee's caste, religion, and region.

---

[137] https://laws-lois.justice.gc.ca/eng/acts/e-5.401/
[138] https://www.indiacode.nic.in/handle/123456789/1494
[139] https://clc.gov.in/clc/node/572

15. Job Interviews

Job interviews are a necessary evil in the world of employment. They give employers a chance to size up a potential employee and see if they would be a good fit for their company. However, job interviews can be problematic for certain minority groups.

Neurodivergent[140] people, for example, may have more difficulty with social communication, resulting in anxiety during the interview process. Women tend to underestimate and undersell themselves more than men do in an interview,[141] which can result in them being passed over for the job. Non-native speakers may also have more difficulty expressing themselves compared to native speakers, which could put them at a disadvantage.

That is why is important to design your interview process to be more inclusive.

Interviewing Neurodivergent People

The best way to learn about something is to experience it firsthand, but when it comes to autism and other neurodiversities, that's not always possible. If you want to hire neurodiverse employees, you need to access some of the many resources available to help you learn about the autistic community and how to best support them. One great way to start is by reading books or articles written by autistic people.

This will give you a better understanding of what it's like to live with autism and how it can impact every aspect of life. You can also look for webinars or podcasts created by autistic individuals or organizations that focus on employment Issues. This type of research will not only educate you about the challenges faced by autistic people in the workplace, but it will also give you some ideas about how to create a more inclusive and supportive work environment for all your employees.

Bear in mind that traditional interview styles are not always a good fit for neurodivergent people. Many of them experience language and social communication issues, which might make it challenging to obtain

---

[140] *Neurodivergent* is a nonmedical term that describes people whose brain develop or work differently for some reason. Neurodivergent people have different strengths and struggles than do people whose brains develop or work more typically (https://my.clevelandclinic.org/health/symptoms/23154-neurodivergent).
[141] https://news.harvard.edu/gazette/story/2020/02/men-better-than-women-at-self-promotion-on-job-leading-to-inequities/

relevant information from them. When interviewing neurodivergent candidates, it is important to remember that they might not make eye contact, and they might speak in a monotone or not show much emotion.

This doesn't mean they're not interested in the job or not paying attention to the interviewer—it's just how they communicate. To put them at ease, let them know beforehand that there is no need to shake hands or make small talk. Instead, focus on the questions and give them time to think about their answers. Give candidates in advance a detailed outline of what the interview will involve. It can also be helpful to provide candidates with the questions in advance.

During the interview offer alternative interview modes or venues. Depending on the applicant's needs, a phone, video, or email interview may be preferred. If you can, find out which they're most comfortable with.[142]

Asking questions is a key part of any conversation, but sometimes it can be difficult to get the information you're looking for. In these cases, it's important to be flexible in your questioning. If the person you're speaking to hesitates before answering, give them a moment to collect their thoughts. You might also need to reword or re-ask your question in a different way. Ask more open-ended questions, avoiding questions that can be answered with a "yes" or "no.".[143] By being flexible in your questioning, you'll be more likely to gather the information you need.

Gender Bias During Interviews

Women often face different challenges than men do when it comes to job interviews. Studies show that women are far much more likely to be judged on their appearance at interviews than men are, which increases the pressure for female job-hunters.[144]

They also might be interrupted more often, asked different (and sometimes personal) questions, or treated with less respect. To combat this inequality, it is important to have a diverse team of interviewers, including both men and women. This way, all candidates will be given an equal opportunity to shine. In addition, avoid asking personal questions and focus on the candidate's qualifications for the position.

---

[142] https://www.spectroomz.com/blog/interviewing-autistic-candidates
[143] https://www.hireautism.org/resource-center/interviewing-your-applicant-with-autism/
[144] https://www.welcometothejungle.com/en/articles/women-vs-men-job-interviews

Interviewing Minority Candidates

As companies strive to create a more diverse workforce, it's important to make sure that minority candidates are well represented in the interview process. That is why it is important to make sure that your interview panel is not just full of Caucasian men and that it reflects your diverse company.

But you also don't want to put undue pressure on the minority candidates by making them feel like they're being examined under a microscope. The key is to strike a balance between making the panel diverse and making all the candidates feel comfortable. One way to do this is to have a few different people on the panel, each with their own strengths and weaknesses. This way, the candidate can relate to at least one person on the panel, and they'll feel like they're being judged on their merits, not on their skin color or gender.

Another way to strike this balance is to have a mix of people from different departments on the panel. This way, the candidates can get a sense of the company as a whole, and they'll be able to see that there are opportunities for everyone, regardless of race or gender.

By following these tips, you can ensure that your interview panel is both diverse and effective.

Interviewing Non-Native Speakers

When interviewing non-native English speakers, it is important to remember that they might need extra time to think about their answers or may use different words than you are expecting. Avoid interrupting them and be patient—you might be surprised by the eloquence of their responses once they have had a chance to finish thinking about what they want to say.

That being said, there are a few things you can do to help facilitate communication. First, try to use simple language and avoid jargon. Second, ask open-ended questions that encourage elaboration. And finally, be prepared to repeat or rephrase your questions if necessary. By following these tips, you can ensure that you obtain the information you need from your interviewee while also respecting their ability to communicate in a second language.

Final Thoughts

Creating an interview process that is more inclusive will not only help you find the best candidate for the job but also show your commitment to diversity and inclusion in the workplace. A more inclusive interview process will take into account the unique challenges that neurodivergent people, women, and non-native speakers face.

For example, questions can be worded in a way that is less likely to trip up neurodivergent candidates, and interviewer bias can be mitigated by using blind screening methods or using a structured interview format, which has been shown to reduce bias in hiring. You can also provide training for your interviewers on how to recognize and avoid bias.

Providing multiple avenues for candidates to apply (e.g., online, in person, by phone) can also help to accommodate the needs of a broader pool of qualified applicants. By making small changes to your interview process, you can send a strong message that you are an inclusive employer.

16. Cognitive Biases in the Workplace

In the 1970s, Amos Tversky and Daniel Kahneman,[145] two Israeli psychologists, defined *cognitive bias* as "a tendency to perceive a situation in a manner that favors a particular response." In layman's terms, this means that we see the world through our own filters and perceive it in such a way that it makes us feel good about our decisions. Even when we are aware of these biases, we still fall prey to their effects.

How many times when your team wins the baseball game, do you swear that you knew it was going to win all along? No one actually believes that you have the ability to make 100 percent accurate predictions, but no one really cares. Everyone's happy the team won.

But what happens when a cognitive bias isn't so innocent? Imagine, for example, that three people walk out of a store right before the owner yells that she's been burgled. Two of the three people are women, and one is a man. One of them is Black, and two are White. And two of them are dressed well, and one is dirty and disheveled. One witness may only pay attention to the race of the people and tell the police that she saw the thief, the Black person. Another witness may focus on gender, concluding that the thief has to be the only man. Still a third witness may focus only on the appearance of the three people and tell the cops that the thief was the dirty, disheveled one.

A stereotype is an idea that we have about a person or group of people that is generally inaccurate. If one person ever acts the way we expect the entire group of people to behave, then our stereotype is affirmed, strengthening it even further.

We'll now examine twenty different types of bias you might encounter in the workplace and ways to confront each one.

Gender Bias

Studies show that women are paid less than men in most jobs. In 2016, a woman earned 82 cents[146] for every dollar a man made. Some of this disparity can be attributed to the fact that women tend to gravitate toward lower-paying professions, which have less potential for pay increases. Some female professionals receive higher salaries than their male counterparts do, despite the wage gap. Still, we cannot deny that there

---

[145] https://www.sciencedirect.com/topics/neuroscience/cognitive-bias
[146] https://www.bls.gov/cps/earnings.htm

is a wage gap. What's interesting about this disparity is that it exists even among religious or racial minorities and across different fields.

What is behind this disparity? *Gender bias* refers to our tendency to believe that men are better than women at most jobs but women are better than men at domestic work and work involving some types of nurturing, like nursing and teaching young children. Unconscious gender biases have been studied extensively in the workplace. They can cause us to deny women opportunities in the workplace or to promote them at a slower rate than their male counterparts even if they're doing an equally good job.

How to Fight Gender Bias in the Workplace

- **Break Stereotypes.** The idea that men and women are better at certain jobs because of their genders is a stereotype. These stereotypes should be broken by hiring people who don't fit the stereotypical molds for the specific jobs.
- **Become Aware of Your Unconscious Biases.** Most gender biases happen unconsciously, which is why we need to try to become conscious of them.
- **Set Gender-Neutral Standards.** This method can be used in organizations that are afraid that they might be unconsciously discriminating against women.
- **Document Biases.** Companies can document their unconscious biases and share the data with their employees to help raise awareness.
- **Promote Diversity in the Workplace.** Diversity is a great way to achieve equality at the workplace. Diversity also improves innovation, which is essential in every field of work.

Ageism Bias

- *Ageism* refers to prejudice against people because of their age. It can be directed against people who are young as well as at people who are forty and older. Ageism generally involves one or more of the following stereotypes:
- Young people are rebellious and immature.
- Teenagers are more likely to be late for work and make mistakes.
- Young workers lack experience.
- People forty or older are out of touch with new technology.
- People forty or older are set in their ways and resist change.

How to Fight Age Discrimination

Performance matters more than age. In most cases, hiring and keeping older people in a company is an investment; they've already proven themselves and they have years of experience under their belts. If a company has employees who are older than the average age but are great workers, the managers should keep them. They should also promote diversity in their staff because this helps companies recruit the best employees from all walks of life.

- Avoid stereotyping candidates over forty-five by assuming that they're less innovative, resistant to change, or less committed to their work.
- Separate experience from age.
- Follow the rules of retirement when recruiting.
- Don't assume that older people will be less reliable or less committed to their work.

Name Bias

- People stereotype names, assigning certain names with particular qualities. Some White people upon hearing what they assume is a Latinx or Black-American name, will assume the bearer of the name won't be as good of a worker.

How to Fight Name Discrimination

- Use a blind recruiting process that removes names and addresses from an applicant's profile.
- Develop a larger candidate pool with many candidates from many backgrounds.

Beauty Bias

Anjola Fagbemi,[147] a Chicago-based beauty blogger, posted a viral video of the freebies she received over a summer for being really good looking. Pretty people often get treated better than the rest of us, and this bias, called *beauty bias,* happens in the workplace too. Sometimes it means that the better-looking people get promoted faster or get raises other people don't. It even applies to the recruitment and hiring process, meaning that when there are two candidates similarly qualified, the better-looking one will often be the one hired.

In 1974, Landy and Sigall conducted research[148] in which they had sixty male undergraduate students read an essay that they thought was written by a female freshman. Participants were given higher quality and lower quality essays, and, through the attachment of an author photo, some were led to believe she was physically attractive and some were led

---

[147] https://nypost.com/2022/01/05/attractive-women-reveal-benefits-of-pretty-privilege/
[148] https://www.simplypsychology.org/halo-effect.html

to believe that she was not. Still others were given no photo and no information about her appearance. The men who read the better essay ranked it higher than did those who read the poorer essay. The men ranked the essay higher when they believed the author was attractive, lowest when she was unattractive, and in the middle when they didn't know about her appearance. Researchers found the greatest impact of the writer's attractiveness on evaluation of the lower-quality essay.

Although this research focused on men reading an essay by a woman (with no data collected about the men's sexuality), the beauty bias has been found to apply to both men and women. However, it does not apply equally. For example, men and women deemed unattractive typically earn less than their attractive counterparts; but unattractive men take the greater hit. A University of Wisconsin-Madison study[149] found that the unattractive woman earns only 4 percent less than the female average, and the attractive woman earns 4 percent more than the average. But an unattractive man earns 9 percent less than the male average per hour, and their attractive counterparts earn 5 percent more.

Weight and height affect the genders differently at work too. A University of Iowa study[150] found that, among women earning $70,000 or more, a unit of body weight increase or decrease correlates directly to either lower or higher income, respectively. The study also found that, among men in that $70,000+ wage bracket, a unit of height increase correlates directly with a higher wage.

But what do we even mean by *attractive?* Is there one standard that applies universally within a society? No—these standards vary by sexual identity, race, and geographic region, among other factors. For example, a White person considered attractive by generally accepted White beauty standards will likely be favored in a workplace that predominantly features White managers. But a Black person considered attractive by generally accepted Black beauty standards won't necessarily do better in that same environment. In fact, that person may even be discriminated against because of their appearance. A 2020 study[151] showed that Black women with natural hair were more likely to be deemed "less professional, less competent, and less likely to be recommended for a job interview" than were Black women with straightened hair or White

---

[149] https://www.ncbi.nlm.nih.gov/pmc/articles/PMC6261420/
[150] https://www.psypost.org/2021/08/deep-machine-learning-study-finds-that-body-shape-is-associated-with-income-61683
[151] https://journals.sagepub.com/doi/abs/10.1177/1948550620937937?journalCode=sppa

women. Darkness of skin color also affects Black people's chances of getting hired, according to research at the University of Georgia.[152]

There's no direct connection between beauty and competence, but there's a link between how we value beautiful people and how we value the work they do. We often assume that beautiful people are more competent, and this can negatively affect people whose physical appearance doesn't fit into the norm of what is considered attractive.

How to Fight Beauty Bias

- Use an anonymous recruitment processes where there's no way of knowing what candidates look like.
- Create inclusive environments in which all employees feel welcome at work.
- Omit faces from resumes when presenting candidates. This will encourage hiring managers to focus on the candidate's profile, skills, and experience.
- Use a structured interview process that focuses on experience and skills.
- Conduct phone screenings before face-to-face interviews.

Halo Effect

The halo effect is a phenomenon in which people with certain positive traits are automatically thought to be better at their jobs overall. For example, people who are outgoing, fun, and friendly are perceived to be more competent than people who are introverted, serious, and professional.

The halo effect is often reinforced by the experiences we have. So, if you previously worked well with someone who happened to have a direct communication style, then when it's time to hire, you may be looking for more people with that style. Or if you grew up with a father who loved to make jokes, you might feel more comfortable around joke-making men and so you may be drawn unconsciously to that type of job candidate.

The halo effect and the beauty bias can overlap. As the study by Landy and Sigall demonstrated, men equate more attractive physical appearance in women with higher ability (the study did not differentiate between gay and straight men). When women don't conform to the female stereotype of being beautiful, friendly, and nurturing, they are often judged negatively at work.

---

[152] https://www.businessbecause.com/news/insights/7902/beauty-bias-workplace

How to Fight the Halo Effect

- Measure competence by the quality of work instead of by physical or personality traits.
- Hire people whom you know will add to your team's culture.
- Conduct multiple rounds of interviews and have different people leading the different rounds.

Horns Effect

- The horns effect is the reverse of the halo effect. It involves judging people negatively because of a single personality trait. For example, because your uncle is an activist who is opinionated and judgmental, if a candidate tells you she is an activist, you might decide she must also be opinionated and judgmental.

How to Fight the Horns Effect

- Remember that first impressions aren't always reliable.
- Take time to get to know someone; don't rely on a first impression.
- Remember that everyone is multidimensional. A single negative trait doesn't make someone a bad person.
- Try to focus on a person's skills and not their negative traits.
- Try to distance yourself from what you perceive as a negative trait; it could be a reflection of how you see yourself.

Confirmation Bias

Confirmation bias is the tendency of people to favor information that confirms their beliefs and avoid information that challenges them. The term is also used in medical situations in which it describes the tendency of experts to pay more attention to confirming evidence and to overlook contradictory evidence.

Confirmation bias is often applied to judgments of creditworthiness and risk. One example happens in the insurance industry in which insurance companies pay out on claims they have already received more often than they do on claims they haven't received before.

During an interview, confirmation bias may cause problems for both candidates and employers. For example, if a candidate believes that tech companies operate very casual environments, then when one person walks by the interview room wearing a T-shirt, she may take that as evidence of that casualness, even if ten other people walk by wearing suits. If the interviewer believes that women don't tend to like data-driven roles, he may warn the candidate that the job will require lots of computer time. When the candidate says that she likes that, the employer may assume that she's merely exhibiting her general willingness to fit in socially and not expressing her actual preference.

How to Fight Confirmation Bias

- Use more than one source of information to evaluate people; look past confirmation bias to try to uncover the facts.
- Use a standardized set of questions that are used with everyone.
- Use multiple-choice questions instead of asking applicants what they would do when faced with specific situations.
- Look for ways to challenge people's beliefs.

Conformity Bias

Groupthink is the name for the phenomenon of seeking out and developing groups that reinforce the beliefs you already have. The resulting conformity bias is the tendency for like ideas to reinforce like ideas. Instead of thinking through our ideas, we simply take our cues about what to think from one another. In conformity bias, people ignore or deny information that isn't consistent with the ideas they and other group members already have.

It can help when everyone at a workplace shares similar values in the sense that people will get along with less conflict. But groupthink isn't going to generate any useful problem solving or creative ideas. The more alike people are, the more they will hold each other in thrall to those similar and more rigid ideas.

How to Fight Conformity Bias

- Try to encourage staff who may be quieter or hold back from sharing their ideas to speak up more, so that the group is not too homogenous.
- Use brainstorming techniques to encourage free development of ideas.
- Bring people together. Try to push people in existing friendships and who are colleagues to work in teams with others. Encourage new alliances.
- Take your time when making decisions; do your own research and consult people who are experts in their fields before making a final decision.
- Don't dismiss or ignore ideas that aren't the same as your own or those of your team.

Affinity Bias

We tend to favor those who are like us. The affinity bias is a tendency to value people who are similar to us over those who are dissimilar.

Affinity bias may be unconscious. During recruiting, the hiring manager may choose a candidate who is similar to him; for example, if the hiring manager is a golfer, he may be more likely to hire another golfer than someone who doesn't play golf at all.

When a hiring manager keeps hiring people who are like him, the employees become less and less diverse. It will then become more and more difficult for anyone different to work well with the team.

How to Fight Affinity Bias

- Try to learn from different types of people; someone who isn't a member of your immediate circle will bring different elements to your workplace that you may have overlooked.
- Make a point of learning about other cultures and perspectives; this way you can broaden your skillsets and gain an understanding of what other groups are like.

Contrast Effect

If your view of something is suddenly distorted when you start comparing it to something else, you're experiencing the contrast effect. Let's say that you took a test, and the passing mark was 75 percent. You scored 80 percent and were initially very happy with the result. Then you noticed that your friend scored a 95 percent. Suddenly, the 80 percent stops feeling so good, even though it's great and all you needed.

How to Fight the Contrast Effect

- Try not to take things personally if someone reacts negatively toward you.
- Understand how constructive and destructive competition is; it's important to know when to challenge your co-workers and when not to.
- Encourage healthy debate rather than instigate conflict.
- Set benchmarks for yourself and others.

Status Quo Bias

We're naturally resistant to change. This means we all suffer from the status quo bias. We take comfort in predictability.

When management tries to introduce new ideas and promote change, workers often react with resistance, simply because it's something new, even if it might represent improvement.

Recruiters may be resistant to change when they fail to experiment with new hiring practices like diversifying the sourcing of candidates.

The status quo bias is related to *spent cost fallacy;* we tend to value what we've already done and invested effort in.

How to Fight the Status Quo Bias

- Try not to fall into the trap of the recency effect, discounting older data because you've only seen recent information.
- Use SWOT analysis when weighing new strategies and ideas.
- Gather a group of people with different backgrounds and viewpoints and work on a new idea together; that way you will have a mix of inputs from different perspectives to create better ideas.

Anchoring Bias

Anchoring bias is an unconscious tendency to base our decisions on the first and most obvious piece of information that we have. Our brains are constantly trying to save time and make decisions by relying on the first or easiest-to-access piece of information.

Imagine that a recruitment team, for example, gives an assessment to all applicants, and the first person to take it happens to score a ten out of ten and is the only one to do so. Even if other applicants are better than the first in other ways, the team may feel like no one measures up to that first person.

How to Fight Anchoring Bias

- Try to present your ideas in a way that gives an objective overview of the situation; you can try using statistical data or surveys to back up your ideas.
- Remember that one factor does not make a decision; don't place too much weight on one particular aspect.
- Compare and contrast your ideas with others and think about what would work best for the situation.
- Use data while making decisions; look at your business as numbers rather than focusing on how one interviewee answered a particular question.
- Be open to trying new techniques and strategies; don't be afraid of something new just because it's unfamiliar.

Authority Bias

This bias makes us more likely to think that someone who has more status and authority is right. Authority bias is evident in the recruiting process where companies choose people they know or have worked with before, even when they are not the best fit for a job.

Authority bias is also at play when team members blindly follow their manager's instructions without challenging them.

How to Fight Authority Bias

- It's important to trust your instincts when there's something you don't agree with; trust that voice in your head that tells you something isn't right.
- Do not be afraid to challenge someone just because they are older, more experienced, or a senior member of your team.
- Look for people who challenge the status quo, think independently, and say things like, "I don't know" or "Let me check on that."
- Encourage healthy debate and collaboration among team members; they will then be more likely to think outside the box.
- If a higher-up makes a decision that you don't agree with, voice your concerns without being disrespectful.

Overconfidence Bias

Overconfidence bias is a tendency to put a lot of weight on our own skills, ideas, and beliefs. How else can we explain the fact that 73 percent of American drivers[153] think they're better than the "average driver"?

When it comes to choosing a candidate, managers and recruiters often rely on their gut feelings or on their instincts about a particular candidate or person, assuming that they have some sort of intuition about who will make a good employee.

This is often the most dangerous bias and can cause people to commit several major mistakes, including underestimating the negative effects of a decision, assuming a high probability of success, and believing that they have more control than they do over what happens to them.

Remember that past successes don't predict future ones.

How to Fight Overconfidence Bias

- Analyze your experiences and look for patterns that show some repeated behaviors so you can learn from them.

---

[153] https://newsroom.aaa.com/2018/01/americans-willing-ride-fully-self-driving-cars/

- Be more willing to seek perfection instead of settling for good enough; you don't always have to be the best, but you need to strive toward it often.
- Accept constructive feedback from others and learn from your mistakes.
- Ask for feedback from other people.

Perception Bias

Perception bias is the process of generalizing beliefs about a group on the basis of superficial or stereotyped traits. For example, if someone is obese, we assume they eat junk food all the time.

At the workplace, people with perception bias may assume that employees of Asian origin are quiet, hardworking, and diligent and that Black employees are lazy or irresponsible.

How to Fight Perception Bias

- Recognize that stereotypes are not always true.
- Challenge other people's perception biases.
- Examine your beliefs about others before jumping to conclusions; it may be that there's more to their behaviors than you think.
- When making decisions, look beyond the stereotype and try your best to understand individuals on their own terms.
- Don't assume things about another person without getting to know them.
- Be careful with blanket thoughts such as "All women are . . ." or "All recruiters are. . ." .

Illusory Correlation

We will often link two events together that have nothing to do with each other in a phenomenon called *illusory correlation.* It is often paired with *illusory association bias.* If you're presenting a candidate to an interviewer and you mention that the candidate is an Iron Woman, the interviewer may assume the candidate approaches work the same way she approaches competition, with determination and focus and lots of preparation. But that, in fact, may not be the case. Maybe the candidate saves all her drive for competition and she approaches work much more causally.

Illusory correlation can also happen when we do not distinguish between coincidences and reality.

How to Fight Illusory Correlation

- When you're making decisions based on data or statistics, look beyond the numbers to see patterns and trends.
- Keep two events separate even if they seem to be related; work on isolating each factor from other factors that might influence your decision.
- See things for what they are; avoid making assumptions and keep an open mind about everything.
- Learn to think like a statistician. This helps you to be more objective in your decisions, especially when you're looking for patterns in data.

Affect Heuristic

The affect heuristic, also called *emotional reasoning,* involves emphasizing our own feelings, emotions, and gut reactions when evaluating others. For example, if a man with a goatee yells at you about your dog being off leash in the park in the morning and that afternoon you interview a candidate who also has a goatee, you might be inclined to reject him because he reminds you of your emotional morning encounter.

The affect heuristic also comes into play if you care too much about what people think about you. That may cause you to have trouble separating your desire to please from your ability to make a good decision. For example, if the son of your boss's best friend interviews, you may be inclined to hire him even if he is not the best candidate.

How to Fight the Affect Heuristic

- Recognize the importance of analyzing the entire situation instead of relying on your feelings alone.
- Ensure that you've considered all possible explanations for events before making a decision; this will help you avoid attaching too much importance to your feelings.

Recency Bias

This is a form of memory bias in which we tend to focus on the most recent events, instead of what's most relevant. Recency bias is the opposite of postponement effect or selective reminding in which we may be more likely to remember distant memories than recent experiences.

To a recruiting manager processing a hundred applications every week, recency bias is a common problem; the person who just applied for a job only hours ago may seem more qualified than someone who applied for the same job months ago. Recency bias is also called the *recent events overweighting principle,* because recent events tend to be more significant to us than older events.

How to Fight Recency Bias

- Keep track of your own decisions and see if they were influenced by recent events or information.
- To overcome recency bias, make a careful review of all the information you have before making a decision or taking an action.
- Give equal importance to each piece of information.
- Be open-minded when it comes to your decision-making process; it's important not to rely too much on your feelings or recent events.

Idiosyncratic Rater Bias

Idiosyncratic rater bias is a form of halo effect bias in which we judge others based on our own interpretations of their behavior. Managers rate their subordinates on their own interpretation of "success," which is subjective. If the manager is a workaholic, they may prefer any subordinate who works long hours. This can often leave the company with employees who are all similar, and it takes away from their individual talents and strengths.

A hiring manager can be biased by placing extra importance on cultural fit, for example. If they have less experience in managing a diverse team, they may define cultural fit as being like the manager or looking like the manager. Recruiters can also overvalue certain traits in potential candidates. If a recruiter has a good sense of humor and enjoys joking around with people, they may only look for other candidates who have similar senses of humor.

How to Fight Idiosyncratic Rater Bias

- Think about things as they are; don't let your own biases affect your judgment.
- Keep an open mind about all candidates; it's okay to leave some of them out. You can always come back to them later when you have a chance to better evaluate them. The bigger picture is more important than any single trait or characteristic in job applicants.
- Always use objective assessments in your decisions; avoid using "personality tests" to evaluate your candidates.

Outgroup Homogeneity Bias

The tendency to perceive members of our own groups as being more different from each other than members of other groups is known as *outgroup homogeneity bias.* Another way of thinking of this bias is as a tendency to see others as all the same: *Women are all . . . Black people are all . . . .*

How to Fight Outgroup Homogeneity Bias

- Be open to the fact that the uniqueness of your own group is probably similar to that of other groups.
- Try to consider your own actions, attitudes, and behaviors within the context of the people around you—not just within your own groups.
- Pay attention to the level of diversity within all groups; if it's low, then increase it.

17. Getting Buy-in for Your D&I Efforts

A diverse workforce brings a wealth of perspectives and experiences to the table, which can help businesses innovate and stay ahead of the competition. However, implementing D&I initiatives can be challenging, as it requires buy-in from everyone in the organization.

Without buy-in, D&I efforts are likely to stall or fail altogether. So why is buy-in so important? One reason is that it helps ensure that everyone in the organization is invested in the initiative. Buy-in also helps to build support for D&I initiatives within the wider community, which can make it easier to attract talent and win new customers. Finally, buy-in ensures that D&I efforts are sustainable over the long term. With so much at stake, it's clear that business leaders need to work hard to get buy-in for their D&I efforts.

It's also important to reach out to find the right people for your D&I efforts. Not all of those who are underrepresented in tech will want or need their time spent on diversity-related issues, so don't assume that a woman software engineer is interested in recruiting other females into engineering jobs.

A co-worker in a wheelchair might also be better suited to working toward improvements around workplace accessibility instead of other co-workers. But you should not expect that because this is important to you, it will also be important to them.

The aim of diversity is not just to have more people from underrepresented minorities in your company, but also to ensure they are spending their time working on important issues. The best way for you as a manager or founder to get the most out these partnerships is by understanding what exactly they mean and where to start—don't assume.

How to Get Buy-In

When it comes to diversity and inclusion, the onus is often on employees to "just get along." But the truth is, D&I is everyone's responsibility.

There's no question that companies need to do more when it comes to diversity and inclusion. But getting buy-in for your D&I efforts can be a challenge. Following are a few tips to help you get started.

1. Educate Yourself and Others on the Business Case for D&I

Countless studies show the positive impact of diversity on businesses. Whether it's improving innovation or attracting top talent, there are plenty of reasons to make D&I a priority. Be sure to educate yourself on the business case for D&I so you can effectively communicate the benefits to others.

2. Get Executive Buy-in

The most effective way to get buy-in for your D&I efforts is to secure support from upper management. If you can show executives how D&I will benefit the company as a whole, they are more likely to get on board with your initiatives.

It's no secret that D&I efforts can be a hard sell to company leadership. Often, these initiatives are seen as costly and time-consuming, with little guarantee of return on investment. However, there are several good reasons to invest in D&I programs.

For one thing, they can help attract and retain top talent. In today's competitive job market, employees are increasingly looking for companies that value diversity and inclusion. Furthermore, D&I programs can foster a more creative and innovative work environment. When people of different backgrounds and perspectives are brought together, they can challenge each other's assumptions and come up with new and better ideas.

When pitching D&I initiatives to execs or HR, make sure to frame them in terms of business objectives. For example, if you want to start a mentorship program, explain how it will improve employee retention or help develop future leaders within the company.

3. Cultivate Allies

Find people who share your passion for D&I and enlist their help in promoting your efforts within the company. These allies can be invaluable in providing support and helping to carry out your initiatives.

By having like-minded individuals on your team, you can more effectively raise awareness and bring about positive change within the organization. Furthermore, these allies can also help dispel any misconceptions or resistance that may exist among employees.

4. Foster an Environment of Open Dialogue

Discussing D&I can be difficult, but it's essential for making progress. Create an open and inclusive environment where everyone feels comfortable sharing their thoughts and experiences. Encourage candid conversations about the challenges and opportunities of diversity in the workplace.

The words matter, too, which is why you should try to avoid terms like "preference" or "celebrate differences." Stick with more neutral phrases like "valuing diverse perspectives" or "including different voices." By using less loaded language, you can create an environment where people feel more comfortable discussing the issues.

5. Focus on Common Goals

As we all know, D&I initiatives are important for creating a respectful and productive workplace. However, these initiatives can sometimes be controversial, with different people having different opinions on what needs to be done.

In these cases, it's important to remember that we all have the same goal: to work in a respectful and productive environment. By focusing on our shared goal, we can build consensus around D&I initiatives.

Final Thoughts

As our workforce becomes increasingly diverse, it's more important than ever for companies to invest in D&I initiatives. A recent study by McKinsey found that companies in the top quartile for racial and ethnic diversity are 35 percent more likely to have financial returns above their respective national industry medians. Additionally, another study found that gender-diverse companies are 15 percent more likely to outperform their peers.[154]

Not only is there a moral case to be made for D&I programs, but there's also a strong business case. When making your case to company leaders, be sure to emphasize both the moral and business arguments for investing in D&I initiatives. By doing so, you'll increase the chances of getting buy-in for your efforts.

---

[154] https://www.mckinsey.com/~/media/McKinsey/Email/Classics/2020/2020-02-classic.html

18. Sourcing

As recruiters, we are constantly striving to increase the diversity of our organizations. We want to ensure that our workplaces are representative of the communities we serve. But, sometimes, our desire to increase diversity can conflict with our duty to hire the best candidate for the job.

On the one hand, we want to hire the most qualified candidates who will help our organizations prosper. On the other hand, we want to make sure that our workplaces are diverse and inclusive. Sometimes the most qualified (in terms of skills and experience) individual happens to be from an underrepresented group. Sometimes this is *not* the case. How can we reconcile our two goals when they appear to be in conflict?

The answer lies in changing our definition of "the best candidate." Too often, **we fall into the trap of thinking that the best candidate is simply the most skilled and experienced person for the job**. But this isn't always true. **Sometimes, the best candidate is somebody who brings a different perspective or life experience to the table**. After all, what we ultimately want from our employees is help improving and increasing quality or productivity. This kind of change is often the result of seeing things in a new light and thinking differently and more effectively. And those kinds of changes come about when we expand the diversity of our employees.

In order to find skilled, diverse candidates, we need to cast a wider net. We need to reach out to a wider variety of people and encourage them to apply for positions at our organizations. And when we do receive applications from a diverse pool of candidates, we need to be open-minded about what "the best candidate" looks like. Only then can we truly create workplaces that are diverse and inclusive–and that thrive.

The goal of a recruiter is to present more diverse candidates to their company. With their help, the company will build more diverse teams and a more inclusive environment.

Diverse talent can be found in many places, and there is no single place to look for it. When diversity hiring, if you are unsure about any aspect, educate yourself. Do not make assumptions.

There are some pitfalls to diversity hiring. First, companies need to be careful not to tokenize diversity by hiring individuals based solely on their race or gender rather than considering their skills and abilities. Second, it's important for companies to make sure that any diversity training they provide is actually effective in promoting inclusion and reducing bias.

The best way to access a wide range of talent is to create a flexible and inclusive work culture that takes into account the needs and potential of all employees. This means developing opportunities for everyone, regardless of their background or ability. In recent years, there has been a growing trend toward such inclusion in the workplace. This is driven by a recognition that diversity helps bring about new perspectives and ideas, which can lead to increased innovation. By creating an inclusive workplace culture, we can not only tap into an underutilized talent pool, but also send a strong message that everyone is welcome and valued. Ultimately, inclusive workplace culture is good for business, and it's the right thing to do.

Gender Diversity Sourcing

If you're looking for female applicants, one approach is to target associations and sororities. You can also start your online search with very general keywords.

Search string examples:

> woman OR women OR "women's" OR female

Or search with female pronouns:

> women OR "women's" OR female OR she OR her OR lady OR ladies OR Miss OR Mrs

Too many keywords will make your search too wide!

Examples of diversity searches that are too general:

> she OR her OR woman OR female OR women OR female OR girl OR girls

> he OR him OR male OR man OR men OR boy OR boys

To create a more specific search string, specify a site and combine it with keywords:

> site:linkedin.com/in (she OR her OR female OR woman) "finance manager"

This will give you many results, especially for people who are using pronouns (she/her) on their profiles.

You can also implement other phrases like "she is" or "she's" into your search string. This will help you find people with these phrases in their LinkedIn bios or in their profiles, as it is common for people to speak about themselves in the third person:

- "As an experienced and professional finance manager, Olivia is able to lead and motivate **her** team."

- "**She is** a talent acquisition leader."
- "**She's** an experienced sales manager."

Example search string:

> site:linkedin.com/in ("she is" OR "she's") "finance manager"

To narrow your search, use the phrase ***intitle:*** operator as this will help you target job titles in the title of the web page:

> site:linkedin.com/in intitle:"finance manager" ("she is" OR "she's")

> (intitle:"my bio" OR intitle:"about me") "finance manager" ("she is" OR "she's" OR "I am" or "I'm")

> site:linkedin.com/in intitle:"finance manager" "she is"

You can even target specific phrases in recommendations:

- "she is"/"he is"
- "she was"/"he was"
- "she led"/"he led"
- "she managed"/"he managed"
- "she is my manager"/"he is my manager"
- "she is my leader"/"he is my leader"
- "she was my manager"/"he was my manager"
- "she is my boss"/"he is my boss"
- "she is my supervisor"/"he is my supervisor"
- "she was my boss"/"he was my boss"
- "she was my supervisor"/"he was my supervisor"
- "she worked"/"he worked"
- "they worked"
- "I worked with her on"
- "I worked with him on"
- "I worked with them on"
- "I recommend her"
- "I recommend him"
- "I recommend them"

Example:

> site:twitter.com "she is my leader"

> site:linkedin.com/in "she is a leader" "finance manager"

Gender-Affiliated Groups

During your search, you can also target groups that are organized around gender. Simply use targeted keywords: group, member, membership, club, association, organization, society etc.

(group OR member OR membership OR club OR association OR organization OR society)

The best way is to target gender-specific phrases:

("for women" OR "women for" OR "women in" OR "women who" OR "woman at" OR "women at")

Simply refine your phrase as needed:

- "woman in science"
- "women in tech"
- "women in stem"

Example:

site:linkedin.com/in ("for women" OR "women in" OR "women who" OR "women for")

site:linkedin.com/in ("for women" OR "women in" OR "women who" OR "women for") (group OR member OR membership OR club OR association OR organization OR society)

site:linkedin.com/in ("for women" OR "women in" OR "women who" OR "women for") (group OR member OR membership OR club OR association OR organization OR society) "Finance Manager"

By running this string, you will find millions of LinkedIn profiles and groups, such as "By Women, for Women, an international nonprofit organization. And by using the name of the organization in your search phrase, you will find all the profiles that are associated with it:

site:linkedin.com/in "By Women, for Women"

You can refine your search by adding more keywords:

site:linkedin.com/in "By Women, for Women" "Finance Manager"

Of course, you can also use the **intitle:** operator:

site:linkedin.com/in intitle:"Finance Manager" ("By Women, for Women")

site:linkedin.com/in intitle:"Finance Manager" ("for women" OR "women in" OR "women who" OR "women for") (group OR member OR membership OR club OR association OR organization OR society)

You can also try to target a list of users in affinity groups by using the intitle: operator with the specific names of the groups:

site:linkedin.com/in intitle:Members ("By Women, for Women")

Try replacing *members* with other words, like *directory, member list, find a member,* and *search for members.*

Many groups are also on Twitter. They use their own specific hashtags:

- #WomenWhoCode
- #shecoded
- #femaleengineer
- #womenintech
- #WomeninSTEM
- #womeninSCIENCE
- #womenwhocode

You can search via Twitter for those keywords or use applications like Followerwonk[155] by searching in the Twitter bios.

Learn more about targeted search strings in *Full Stack Recruiter: The Ultimate Edition.*[156]

LGBT Sourcing

The LGBT community (also known as the LGBTQ+ community, LGBTQIA+ community, GLBT community, or gay community) is a loosely defined grouping of lesbian, gay, bisexual, transgender, and other queer individuals united by a common culture and social movements.[157] In the United States, 3.5 percent of adults identify as LGB and 0.3 percent identify as transgender.[158] The numbers of actual LGBTQ+ people are likely much higher because many LGBTQ people still don't publicly identify as such given persistent bias and stigma against them.

Nearly half[159] of LGBTQ employees in the U.S. stated that they remain closeted at work, and 75% reported[160] experiencing negative day-to-day workplace interactions related to their LGBTQ identity in the past year.

Like all diversity initiatives, achieving equality in your recruitment process for LGBTQ talent starts with taking the steps to support existing LGBTQ employees and improve inclusion efforts within the workplace.[161]

---

[155] https://followerwonk.com/
[156] https://www.fullstackrecruiter.net
[157] https://en.wikipedia.org/wiki/LGBT_community
[158] https://williamsinstitute.law.ucla.edu/publications/how-many-people-lgbt/
[159] https://www.hrc.org/news/hrc-report-startling-data-reveals-half-of-lgbtq-employees-in-us-remain-clos
[160] https://www.bcg.com/publications/2020/inclusive-cultures-must-follow-new-lgbtq-workforce
[161] https://info.recruitics.com/blog/10-ways-to-ensure-your-recruitment-process-is-lgbtq-friendly

Because people will often state in their bios that they are lesbian, gay, bisexual, or transgender, anyone is able to find these diverse talents with simple search queries:

site:twitter.com (lgbtq OR lgbt OR lgbtqia OR trans OR bisexual OR queer)

You can also use the intitle: operator for your search:

site:linkedin.com/in intitle:(lgbtq OR lgbt OR lgbtqia OR queer)

Consider these additional acronyms:

- **LGBTQIA**—Lesbian, Gay, Bisexual, Transgender, Intersex, Queer and/ or Questioning, and Asexual and/or Ally
- **LGBTQIAPD**—Lesbian, Gay, Bisexual, Transgender, Queer and/ or Questioning, Intersex, Asexual and/or Ally, Pansexual, and Demisexual
- **LGBTIQA+/LGBTQ+**—Adding a "+" to the acronym is an acknowledgment that there are noncisgender and nonstraight identities that are not included in the acronym.
- **Nonbinary**—If you want to target nonbinary people, you can use their pronouns and nonbinary keywords in your search string.

Example:

site:twitter.com ("ux engineer" OR "product engineer" OR "product designer" OR "product design") ("they/them" OR "non-binary" OR nonbinary) -inurl:status -inurl:statuses -intitle:replies

This string will help you target people on Twitter who have those keywords on their profile together with nonbinary pronouns.

X-Ray Search via Emoji

Irina Shamaeva[162] shared with the sourcing community how to find people via emojis. Many people who support or are part of the LGBT community use emojis like the rainbow, rainbow flag, two women, two men, or the transgender flag with pink, blue, and white stripes):

- site:linkedin.com/in intitle: 🌈 "UX Designer"
- site:linkedin.com/in "UX Designer" 🏳️
- intitle:🏳️ site:linkedin.com/in
- intitle:🌈 site:linkedin.com/in (finds 🏳️s too!)
- intitle:👭 site:linkedin.com/in
- intitle:👬 site:linkedin.com/in
- intitle:🏳️‍⚧️ site:linkedin.com/in

---

[162] https://www.linkedin.com/in/irinashamaeva/

You can of course replace linkedin.com with twitter.com or any other website that has bios of people or member profiles.

As **sexual identity is none of your business**, you should not be reaching out to this talent group by saying you found them through keywords!

In order to attract top talent (regardless of gender or sexual identity), and be on the right side of history, it's imperative that recruiters and hiring managers take deliberate measures to advocate for LGBTQ equality. Ensuring that lesbian, gay, bisexual, transgender, and queer job seekers feel safe and inclined to apply to a company does not have to be a complicated undertaking.[163]

Personal Pronouns

Words are powerful. They are some of what binds humans together. One part of speech that is especially important in terms of identity is the pronoun.

Pronouns are words that stand in for proper and common nouns in conversation. For example, instead of having to say your name when talking about anything related to yourself (Xavier likes sandwiches; give Xavier a ham sandwich), you can use a pronoun (I like sandwiches; give me a ham sandwich). The pronouns *I* and *me* are easy to make sense of; problems can arise when we are talking about someone in the third person: He likes sandwiches; give her a sandwich. In that case, we need to know if the person goes by him, her, or something else altogether.

There has possibly never been another time in history when pronouns have been so important in terms of signaling identity. Millennials are twice[164] as likely to identify as LGBTQ than are previous generations, and many LGBTQ+ people choose their own pronouns.

Whether in the workplace or in personal life, it is crucial to recognize the importance of pronouns for the LGBTQ community and explore proper solutions to address their concerns. Organizations and businesses should encourage their employees to put their correct pronouns in their email signatures or portfolios. You can include your pronouns, typically in the format of "X/X" or "X/X/X" (e.g., "he/his" or "she/her/hers") in written communication where they're easy to see.

Employees can also specify their pronouns in their name tags or before a meeting begins. These actions may seem trivial, but they help make our

---

[163] https://hwest.ca/blog/lgbtq-equality-in-recruitment
[164] https://lp.bigeyeagency.com/hubfs/Gender_BeyondtheBinary.pdf

workplaces more inclusive of gender nonconforming, transgender, and gender nonbinary individuals.

Using the appropriate pronouns is a first step toward respecting people's gender identities and creating a space where they feel safe enough to express them.

Because pronouns don't have to align with the person's biological sex, you have to know what pronouns a person likes to use, and you can't assume. There are many choices, which makes the issue even more confusing:

- he/him/his (masculine pronouns)
- she/her/hers (feminine pronouns)
- they/them/theirs (neutral pronouns)
- ze/zir/zirs (neutral pronouns)
- ze/hir/hirs (neutral pronouns)
- xe/xem/xyr (neutral pronouns)
- co/cos (neutral pronouns)
- hy/hym/hys (neutral pronouns)
- ey/em/eirs (neutral pronouns)

Others prefer that you use their name instead of any pronoun.[165]

Just as it can be offensive to call someone by a nickname that they don't like, it can be offensive to use the wrong pronouns. It is even more offensive to ignore the person's wishes once they have called them to your attention.

Some people are irritated by using "they/them" to refer to a single person, arguing that it is grammatically incorrect or has no place in language. But language is continually evolving. Merriam-Webster recently added "they" as a gender pronoun that can be used to refer to a nonbinary individual.

Using someone's correct gender pronouns is a way to respect their sense of identity. It is a way to value their emotional and psychological sense of gender.

X-Ray Search Strings

If you read *Full Stack Recruiter: The Ultimate Edition,*[166] you know that for X-ray search strings you will primarily need **site:** operator and relevant keywords:

    site:linkedin.com/in "Account Executive" "New York" "she/her"

---

[165] https://agis.interligne.co/en/19197/
[166] https://fullstackrecruiter.net/

```
site:linkedin.com/in "Account Executive" "New York" ("she/her" OR "they/them")
```

If you want to narrow your results, the **intitle:** operator allows you to get more accurate results by including only websites with these keywords in their page title:

```
site:linkedin.com/in intitle:"she/her" "Account Executive" "New York"
```

```
site:linkedin.com/in intitle:"they/them" "Account Executive" "New York"
```

Even though some people may hyphenate their they-them pronouns, Google will identify them as they/them.

When you use nonbinary pronouns (they/them, zie/zim, etc.), your search results will show you the profiles of gender-nonconforming talent. Include pronouns in your search string with relevant keywords:

```
site:dribble.com intitle:Bio "she/her"
```

```
site:linkedin.com/in intitle:"she/her"
```

For nonbinary people, use they/them or both other keywords "nonbinary" and "nonbinary":

```
site:linkedin.com/in intitle:"they/them" OR intitle:"non-binary" OR intitle:non-binary
```

And you can even combine them and target more people who use pronouns in page titles:

```
site:linkedin.com/in intitle:"she/her" OR intitle:"they/them"
```

Don't forget that some people still use the traditional pronouns he/them, she/them, etc. A person who uses multiple pronouns (either interchangeably or in different contexts) may list both subject pronouns: "she/they" or "they/he."[167]

Note: *Even if the majority of the people use English pronouns, some people will use the pronouns of their native language. If you are searching in markets where English is not a primary language, you should consider using local pronouns. This will help you find talent that no one else is able to find.*

Inanchor Operator

Google's search engine is world-renowned for its ability to turn up relevant results for even the most specific of queries. However, many users are unaware of the full range of options available to them.

---

[167] https://en.wikipedia.org/wiki/Preferred_gender_pronoun

One powerful tool is the **inanchor:** command, which allows you to use the anchor text of links to narrow your results. This can be especially useful when you are looking for pages on a particular topic that may not be using the exact same terminology in their own content.

For example, a search for books **inanchor:sourcing** will return pages in which the anchor text on links to the pages contains the word *"sourcing"* and the page contains the word *book*.

The reason the **inanchor:** operator is so powerful is that it targets anchor text, the visible characters and words that hyperlinks display when linking to another document or location on the web. These clickable words used to link one web page to another can help you find hidden gems among the millions of web pages out there. So next time you're stuck on a Google search, remember to try out the "inanchor:" operator to see what you can find.

You can also use the **inanchor:** operator while Google X-raying:

```
(inanchor:"them/they" OR inanchor:"they/any" OR inanchor:"she/he/they"
OR inanchor:"they/them" OR inanchor:"he/they" OR inanchor:"she/they"
OR inanchor:"he/she/they" OR inanchor:"they/she" OR inanchor:"they/he"
OR inanchor:"he/him/they" OR inanchor:"they/she/he")
```

You can also replace OR with the pipe symbol | to shorten your search query as you can see here:

```
(inanchor:"them/they"|inanchor:"they/any"|inanchor:"she/he/
they"|inanchor:"they/them")
```

Sourcing via Languages

When searching for candidates who are proficient in multiple languages, try using phrases like "native Mandarin" or "fluent French." This will help you find candidates who are native speakers of the language. However, this method is not very accurate as there are many people who would rate themselves fluent in a language that is not their native tongue.

When searching for speakers of a particular language, it can be helpful to search for both the spelled-out name of the language as well as its common abbreviation. For example, when searching for Chinese speakers, you are likely to find people who mention Chinese as the main language they know on their LinkedIn profile and others who use Mandarin. Mandarin is the only official language of China, and children in China are taught Mandarin in school.

As a result, fluency in Mandarin is rapidly increasing. There are many more speakers of Mandarin than there are of Cantonese. Therefore, if you're looking for Chinese speakers, your best bet is to search for those who list Mandarin as their main language. But you should always add common abbreviations and other similar type of languages into your search string.

If you're looking to hire someone who is truly fluent in a language, it's important to use the native spelling of the language in your search keywords as well. For example, if you're looking for someone who knows Czech, use "Čeština" rather than "Czech Language." This will help you find candidates who know the ins and outs of the language and who can communicate effectively with native speakers.

Additionally, make sure to use local words when searching for candidates. This will help you narrow down your results to those who are familiar with the local dialect and culture. Taking these steps will ensure that you find the best possible candidates for the job.

Sourcing Personal Names

Personal names are a useful tool when diversity sourcing. As Glen Cathey[168] mentioned in his blog,[169] you can find a huge number of people by searching by first name. However, he also added that this approach is severely limited when using Internet search engines—searching for ten to twenty names isn't a very effective way to search the Internet for diversity, as it excludes more people than it includes due to the search-term limitations. It is most valuable and inclusive when searching systems that allow for very long or unlimited search strings (LinkedIn Recruiter being a good example).

My recommendation is to use this method to identify what candidates have in common so you can add that information to your search string. For example, you might discover that a high percentage of candidates belong to a particular organization that you can then use as a keyword in your search. To use a first name search most effectively, try to target the most common and popular names for each diversity group. This will help you to find more suitable candidates quicker:

(Abigail OR Adriana OR Adrienne OR Aimee OR Alejandra OR Alexa OR Alexandra)

---

[168] https://www.linkedin.com/in/glencathey/
[169] http://booleanblackbelt.com/2010/06/how-to-search-linkedin-for-diversity-sourcing/

(Aaron OR Abdul OR Abel OR Abraham OR Abram OR Adalberto OR Adam OR Adan)

You can include first names in any search string:

site:linkedin.com/in intitle:"Finance Manager" (Abigail OR Adriana OR Adrienne OR Aimee OR Alejandra OR Alexa OR Alexandra)

This last string will help you target people on LinkedIn with the role of finance manager and any of the listed first names.

First Names

Most parents choose gender-specific names for their babies. In a recent survey, 98 percent of names given to female babies were gender specific, and 95 percent of names given to male babies were gender specific. **Only 2 percent of names given to baby girls and 5 percent of names given to baby boys were unisex.**[170]

Following are the most popular first names for Black and Hispanic babies, based on various sources. Bear in mind that the popularity of names changes each year, and parents are starting to give more gender-neutral names to their kids, so if you are planning to search for diverse candidates this way, you will miss many of them.

Most Popular Hispanic American First Names

Male[171]

1. José	2. Luis	3. Carlos
4. Juan	5. Jorge	6. Pedro
7. Jesús	8. Manuel	9. Santiago
10. Sebastián	11. Matías	12. Nicolás
13. Samuel	14. Alejandro	15. Mateo
16. Diego	17. Benjamín	18. Daniel
19. Joaquín	20. Tomás	21. Gabriel
22. Lucas	23. Martín	24. Emmanuel
25. Alexander	26. David	27. Emiliano
28. Juan José	29. Andrés	30. Felipe
31. Ignacio	32. Leonardo	33. Adrián

---

[170] https://cdn.sisense.com/wp-content/uploads/What-Baby-Names-Tell-Us-About-Ethnic-and-Gender-Trends.pdf
[171] https://www.1happybirthday.com/popular_names_latino.php

34. Francisco	35. Rodrigo	36. Ángel
37. Miguel Ángel	38. Fernando	39. Santino
40. Bautista	41. Agustín	42. Juan Pablo
43. Vicente	44. Thiago	45. Maximiliano
46. Pablo	47. Eduardo	48. Christopher
49. Kevin	50. Isaac	

Female[172]

1. Sofía	2. Valentina	3. Isabella
4. Camila	5. Valeria	6. Mariana
7. Gabriela	8. Sara	9. Daniella
10. María José	11. Victoria	12. Martina
13. Luciana	14. Ximena	15. María Fernanda
16. Lucía	17. Natalia	18. Catalina
19. Mía	20. Fernanda	21. Nicole
22. Julieta	23. Abril	24. Samantha
25. Andrea	26. Antonella	27. Emily
28. Emilia	29. Paula	30. Alessandra
31. Juana	32. Antonia	33. Juliana
34. Alejandra	35. Guadalupe	36. Emma
37. Regina	38. Danna	39. Abigail
40. Agustina	41. Renata	42. Allison
43. Brianna	44. Valery	45. Florencia
46. Constanza	47. Josefina	48. Ashley
49. Laura	50. Manuela	

Most Popular Black American First Names
Male[173]

1. Deion	2. Deiondre	3. Dele
4. Denzel	5. Dewayne	6. Dikembe
7. Duante	8. Jamar	9. Jevonte

---

[172] https://www.1happybirthday.com/popular_names_latino.php
[173] https://www.familyeducation.com/baby-names/first-name/origin/african-american

10. Kadeem
11. Kendis
12. Kentay
13. Keshawn
14. Khalon
15. Kofi
16. Kwamin
17. Kyan
18. Kyrone
19. La Vonn
20. Lado
21. Laken
22. Lakista
23. Lamech
24. Lavaughn
25. LeBron
26. Lisimba
27. Ludacris
28. Mablevi
29. Marques
30. Mashawn
31. Montraie
32. Mykelti
33. Nabulung
34. Naeem
35. Napoleon
36. Obiajulu
37. Quaashie
38. Quaddus
39. Quadrees
40. Quannell
41. Quarren
42. Quashawn
43. Quintavius
44. Quoitrel
45. Raimy
46. Rashon
47. Razi
48. Roshaun
49. Runako
50. Salim

Female[174]

1. Beyonce
2. Cassietta
3. Cleotha
4. Deiondre
5. Dericia
6. Gaynelle
7. Kacondra
8. Kanesha
9. Keilantra
10. Kendis
11. Keshon
12. Lachelle
13. Lakin
14. Lanelle
15. Laquanna
16. Laqueta
17. Laquinta
18. Lashawn
19. Latanya
20. Latonya
21. Latoya
22. Mekell
23. Moesha
24. Muncel
25. Najwa
26. Nakeisha
27. Nichelle
28. Niesha
29. Quanella
30. Quanesha
31. Quisha
32. Ranielle
33. Ronnell
34. Shandra
35. Shaquana
36. Shateque
37. Sidone
38. Talaitha
39. Talisa
40. Talisha
41. Tamika
42. Tamira
43. Tamyra
44. Tanasha
45. Tandice
46. Tanginika
47. Taniel
48. Tanisha
49. Tariana
50. Temima

---

[174] https://www.familyeducation.com/baby-names/first-name/origin/african-american

Most Popular Asian American First Names

Male[175]

1. Ryder	2. Abdullah	3. Abdul
4. Kim	5. Aran	6. Cai
7. Van	8. Arjun	9. Cam
10. Arun	11. Jin	12. Tai
13. Rui	14. Akio	15. Yoshi
16. Takeshi	17. Maeko	18. Akira
19. Katsumi	20. Akihiro	21. Hyun-Ki
22. Hikaru	23. Ryou	24. Makoto
25. Jung	26. Maemi	27. Kuuya
28. Li	29. Niran	30. Ping
31. Eiri	32. Jung Hee	33. Kamol
34. Adisa	35. Aja	36. Ehan
37. Takashi	38. Tuan	39. Virote
40. Pheakdei	41. Young Min	42. Benjirou
43. Akiyoshi	44. Kazuma	45. Jing
46. Ami	47. De	48. Ichiro
49. Osamu	50. Peng	

Female[176]

1. Anna	2. Tara	3. Alisha
4. Kim	5. Gia	6. Asia
7. Shreya	8. Aya	9. Reina
10. Mei	11. Jaya	12. Karin
13. Indira	14. Emi	15. Nisha
16. Mali	17. Ami	18. Akira
19. Kiyomi	20. Miyuki	21. Tora
22. Tai	23. Kimiko	24. Yuna
25. Lamara	26. Rui	27. Mai
28. Eun Ae	29. Jin	30. Kimi
31. Kanae	32. Aiko	33. Minh

[175] https://www.randomnames.com/all-asian-boy-names
[176] https://www.randomnames.com/all-asian-girl-names

34. Mai Ly	35. Koyuki	36. Lei
37. Azami	38. Hyun-Ae	39. Hachi
40. Mari	41. Yun Hee	42. Zuleika
43. Namiko	44. Misaki	45. Nari
46. Yasuko	47. Eun Mi	48. Moriyo
49. Mayumi	50. Chika	

Surnames

Another way to search for diverse candidates is to use surnames in your search strings. There are many ways to find out which surnames are the most common. One way is to use Google and search for phrases like "Most common surnames" or "Most common Asian Surnames," "Most Common Black Last Names," "Common African-American Last Names," or "Most Common Black American Surnames."

Bear in mind that in locations where English is not a primary language you will need to add location as a keyword into your search string. For example, instead of typing "most common Czech surnames," search for "most common surnames in Czech Republic."[177]

Most Common Hispanic Surnames in the United States[178]

1. García	2. Rodriguez	3. Hernández
4. Martinez	5. Lopez	6. Gonzalez
7. Pérez	8. Sánchez	9. Ramírez
10. Torres	11. Flores	12. Rivera
13. Gomez	14. Díaz	15. Cruz
16. Morales	17. Reyes	18. Gutiérrez
19. Ortiz	20. Chavez	21. Ramos
22. Ruiz	23. Mendoza	24. Alvarez
25. Jiménez	26. Castillo	27. Vasquez
28. Romero	29. Moreno	30. Gonzalez
31. Herrera	32. Aguilar	33. Medina
34. Vargas	35. Castro	36. Guzmán
37. Mendez	38. Fernández	39. Muñoz

---

[177] https://en.wikipedia.org/wiki/Czech_Republic
[178] https://namecensus.com/last-names/common-hispanic-surnames/

40. Salazar	41. Garza	42. Soto
43. Vazquez	44. Alvarado	45. Contreras
46. Delgado	47. Peña	48. Rios
49. Guerrero	50. Sandoval	

Most Common Black Last Names in the United States[179]

1. Williams	2. Johnson	3. Smith
4. Jones	5. Brown	6. Jackson
7. Davis	8. Thomas	9. Harris
10. Robinson	11. Taylor	12. Wilson
13. Moore	14. White	15. Lewis
16. Walker	17. Green	18. Thompson
19. Washington	20. Anderson	21. Scott
22. Carter	23. Wright	24. Hill
25. Allen	26. Miller	27. Mitchell
28. Young	29. Lee	30. Martin
31. Clark	32. King	33. Edwards
34. Turner	35. Coleman	36. James
37. Evans	38. Hall	39. Richardson
40. Adams	41. Brooks	42. Parker
43. Jenkins	44. Stewart	45. Campbell
46. Howard	47. Simmons	48. Sanders
49. Henderson	50. Collins	

Most Common Chinese Last Names in the United States[180]

1. Wong	2. Chen	3. Chan
4. Wang	5. Chang	6. Lin
7. Wu	8. Liu	9. Huang
10. Li	11. Ng	12. Yu
13. Cheng	14. Yee	15. Yang
16. Chu	17. Chin	18. Ho

---

[179] https://namecensus.com/last-names/common-hispanic-surnames/
[180] https://www.statewidedatabase.org/info/metadata/asian_american_ethnic_id_by_surname.pdf

19. Lam	20. Hsu	21. Lau
22. Fong	23. Leung	24. Chow
25. Cheung	26. Tang	27. Lu
28. Sun	29. Ma	30. Zhang
31. Chiu	32. Lai	33. Tam
34. Lo	35. Tsai	36. Liang
37. Woo	38. Chou	39. Hu
40. Chiang	41. Yuen	42. Chao
43. Kwan	44. Tong	45. Shen
46. Kuo	47. Louie	48. Moy
49. Eng	50. Kwong	

Most Common Japanese Last Names in the United States[181]

1. Suzuki	2. Sato	3. Tanaka
4. Takahashi	5. Watanabe	6. Nakamura
7. Yamamoto	8. Kobayashi	9. Ito
10. Saito	11. Yamada	12. Yoshida
13. Kato	14. Kimura	15. Matsumoto
16. Hayashi	17. Sasaki	18. Yamaguchi
19. Mori	20. Shimizu	21. Abe
22. Ikeda	23. Inoue	24. Hashimoto
25. Ogawa	26. Ono	27. Ishikawa
28. Okada	29. Sakamoto	30. Maeda
31. Murakami	32. Ishii	33. Yamashita
34. Nishimura	35. Kondo	36. Fujita
37. Nakagawa	38. Sakai	39. Nakajima
40. Hasegawa	41. Harada	42. Takeuchi
43. Fujii	44. Aoki	45. Matsuda
46. Okamoto	47. Goto	48. Tamura
49. Arai	50. Takeda	

---

[181] https://www.statewidedatabase.org/info/metadata/asian_american_ethnic_id_by_surname.pdf

Most Common Korean Last Names in the United States[182]

1. Park	2. Kim	3. Choi
4. Cho	5. Chung	6. Kang
7. Yi	8. Han	9. Pak
10. Hong	11. Song	12. Shin
13. Oh	14. Yoon	15. Hwang
16. Yoo	17. Choe	18. Kwon
19. Ahn	20. Chun	21. Yun
22. Suh	23. Son	24. An
25. Cha	26. Min	27. Nam
28. Bae	29. Im	30. Chon
31. Rhee	32. Won	33. Yim
34. Kwak	35. Shim	36. Jun
37. Sin	38. Paik	39. Seo
40. Bang	41. Jang	42. Hyun
43. Whang	44. Huh	45. Chae
46. Mun	47. No	48. Sim
49. Sohn	50. O	

Most Common Indian Last Names in the United States[183]

1. Singh	2. Shah	3. Khan
4. Patel	5. Ali	6. Desai
7. Mehta	8. Rao	9. Sharma
10. Gupta	11. Ahmed	12. Parikh
13. Hussain	14. Joshi	15. Amin
16. Bhatt	17. Gandhi	18. Ram
19. Ahmad	20. Mathew	21. Chacko
22. Dave	23. Varghese	24. Sheth
25. Jain	26. Lal	27. Mathai
28. Husain	29. Bhakta	30. John

---

[182] https://www.statewidedatabase.org/info/metadata/asian_american_ethnic_id_by_surname.pdf
[183] https://www.statewidedatabase.org/info/metadata/asian_american_ethnic_id_by_surname.pdf

31. Trivedi	32. Das	33. Pandya
34. Sandhu	35. Iyer	36. Siddiqui
37. Kumar	38. Parekh	39. Sidhu
40. Prasad	41. Vyas	42. Fernandes
43. Grewal	44. Qureshi	45. Chand
46. Dhillon	47. Ullah	48. Mistry
49. Nair	50. Hasan	

Most Common Filipino Last Names in the United States[184]

1. Reyes	2. Santos	3. Garcia
4. Cruz	5. Ramos	6. Delacruz
7. Mendoza	8. Bautista	9. Deguzman
10. Fernandez	11. Flores	12. Gonzales
13. Villanueva	14. Lopez	15. Deleon
16. Castillo	17. Aquino	18. Rivera
19. Domingo	20. Perez	21. Castro
22. Santiago	23. Tolentino	24. Delrosario
25. Torres	26. Soriano	27. Sanchez
28. Martinez	29. Rodriguez	30. Dizon
31. Hernandez	32. Valdez	33. Pascual
34. Ramirez	35. Francisco	36. Corpuz
37. Mercado	38. Navarro	39. Javier
40. Ocampo	41. Diaz	42. Pascua
43. Gutierrez	44. Velasco	45. Antonio
46. Angeles	47. Morales	48. Dejesus
49. Manuel	50. Mariano	

Most Common Vietnamese Last Names in the United States[185]

1. Nguyen	2. Tran	3. Le
4. Pham	5. Huynh	6. Vu
7. Phan	8. Truong	9. Hoang

---

[184] https://www.statewidedatabase.org/info/metadata/asian_american_ethnic_id_by_surname.pdf
[185] https://www.statewidedatabase.org/info/metadata/asian_american_ethnic_id_by_surname.pdf

10. Ngo	11. Dang	12. Do
13. Bui	14. Vo	15. Ly
16. Duong	17. Luong	18. Dinh
19. Trinh	20. Luu	21. Doan
22. Dao	23. Thai	24. Mai
25. Van	26. Cao	27. Vuong
28. Phung	29. Quach	30. Ta
31. Diep	32. Ton	33. La
34. Thach	35. Thi	36. Thanh
37. Dam	38. Vong	39. Trieu
40. Buu	41. Phu	42. Vinh
43. Quang	44. Tieu	45. Hoa
46. Trang	47. Giang	48. Luc
49. Banh	50. Nghiem	

Most Common Hawaiian Last Names

1. Alana	2. Hale	3. Hekekia
4. Iona	5. Iosua	6. Kahale
7. Kahananui	8. Kahele	9. Kahue
10. Kalama	11. Kalawaiʻa	12. Kalili
13. Kalua	14. Kama	15. Kamaka
16. Kameāloha	17. Kapule	18. Kawai
19. Kaʻanāʻanā	20. Kaʻaukai	21. Kaʻuhane
22. Keahi	23. Kealoha	24. Keawe
25. Kekoa	26. Keliʻi	27. Mahelona
28. Mahiʻai	29. Māhoe	30. ʻAkamu

Most Common Native American & Alaskan Native Last Names

The most popular Native American and Alaskan Native last name in America is Smith, with a total count of 21,742 people who have the surname. Targeting just this surname will not give you lots of relevant results as this surname is common across the whole USA. That is why you will need to add more relevant keywords to your string to get more accurate results.

1. Smith	2. Johnson	3. Begay
4. Locklear	5. Jones	6. Yazzie
7. Williams	8. Brown	9. Davis
10. Wilson	11. Thompson	12. Thomas
13. Miller	14. Jackson	15. White
16. Martin	17. Lee	18. Hunt
19. James	20. Lewis	21. Anderson
22. Taylor	23. Clark	24. Garcia
25. Martinez	26. Benally	27. Scott
28. Tsosie	29. Nelson	30. Moore
31. King	32. Walker	33. Oxendine
34. Jacobs	35. Nez	36. Hill
37. Harris	38. Allen	39. Mitchell
40. Young	41. John	42. Phillips
43. Baker	44. Morgan	45. Chavis
46. Adams	47. Lopez	48. Roberts
49. Henry	50. Wright	

You can also target specific surnames of Indigenous peoples of North America. There are many tribes of indigenous peoples including Cherokee, Navajo, and Apache.

Most Common Cherokee Last Names

The Cherokee tribe are one of the indigenous peoples of the Southeastern Woodlands of the United States. Prior to the 18th century, they were concentrated in their homelands, in towns along river valleys of what is now southwestern North Carolina, southeastern Tennessee, edges of western South Carolina, northern Georgia, and northeastern Alabama.[186]

---

[186] https://en.wikipedia.org/wiki/Cherokee

Awiakta	Catawnee	Colagnee
Culstee	Ghigau	Kanoska
Lisenbe	Nelowie	Onelasa
Sequoyah	Sullicooie	Tesarkee
Watike	Yargee	

Most Common Navajo Last Names

The Navajo are a Native American people of the Southwestern United States. The Navajo people are the second most populous Native American group in the United States, with around 300,000 individuals as of the early 21st century. Most of them live in New Mexico, Arizona, and Utah.[187]

Acothley	Adakai	Begay
Bylilly	Claw	Hatahle
Lapahie	Tabaaha	Todicheene
Tsinajinnie		

Most Common Apache Last Names

The Apache are a group of culturally related Native American tribes in the Southwestern United States, which include the Chiricahua, Jicarilla, Lipan, Mescalero, Mimbreño, Ndendahe (Bedonkohe or Mogollon and Nednhi or Carrizaleño and Janero), Salinero, Plains (Kataka or Semat or "Kiowa-Apache"), and Western Apache (Aravaipa, Pinaleño, Coyotero, Tonto). Distant cousins of the Apache are the Navajo, with whom they share the Southern Athabaskan languages. There are Apache communities in Oklahoma and Texas and reservations in Arizona and New Mexico. Apache people have moved throughout the United States and elsewhere, including to urban centers. The Apache Nations are politically autonomous, speak several different languages, and have distinct cultures.[188]

Altaha	Chatto	Chino
Dosela	Goseyun	Mescal
Shanta	Tessay	

Most Common Native Hawaiian and Other Pacific Islander Last Names

Indigenous peoples of the United States who are not Native American or Alaskan Native include Native Hawaiians, Samoans, and Chamorros.

---

[187] https://en.wikipedia.org/wiki/Navajo
[188] https://en.wikipedia.org/wiki/Apache

The U.S. Census groups these peoples as "Native Hawaiian and other Pacific Islander."[189]

Most Common Alaskan Natives Last Names

Adjuk	Aglukak	Chiklak
Chimeralrea	Echalook	Eegeesiak
Etuangat	Ikkidluat	Illchuk
Ishulutak	Kannak	Karetak
Kasaluak	Lucassie	Maksagak
Marniq	Meyok	Nangmalik
Napayok	Nashalook	Ohaituk
Olanna	Omilgoitok	Palluq
Pigalak	Qanatsiaq	Qarpik
Sammortuk	Saunik	Takirak
Takumjenak	Ugyuk	Ullulaq
Unatweenuk	Ussak	Waska

Popular Hawaiian Last Names[190]

Aka	Akamai	Akamu
Akana	Alama	Alana
Alika	Anela	Aukai
Hale	Halia	Haoa
Haukea	Havika	Hekekia
Ikaika	Inoa	Iokua
Ka'ana'ana	Ka'aukai	Kahale
Kahananui	Kahele	Kahue
Kai	Kalama	Kalawai'a
Kalili	Kalua	Kama
Kamealoha	Kane	Kapule
Ka'uhane	Kawai	Keahi
Keaka	Kealani	Kealoha
Keawe	Kekoa	Keli'i
Keona	Konani	Leilani

[189] https://en.wikipedia.org/wiki/Native_Americans_in_the_United_States
[190] https://parenting.firstcry.com/articles/60-hawaiian-last-names-or-surnames/

Leimomi	Likeke	Lui
Mahelona	Mahi'ai	Makali
Maliah	Mana	Manu
Moana	Noelani	Peleke
Pualani	Urima	Wailani

Global Last Names

There are many surnames in the world. Some surnames are derived from place names, and others are derived from professions or trades. Some surnames are common, and others are rare. Some surnames have been passed down through the family for many generations, and others were recently created.

Several countries in the world use a different variant of surnames for men and women.

Czech Republic

Most Czech women's surnames are formed by taking the surname of their father or husband and adding the ová suffix at the end. For example, if the husband has the surname Novák, the wife will have Novák**ová**. They can only circumvent this rule in limited circumstances, including when their partner is a foreigner, if they have temporary residence in another country, or if they possess another foreign nationality.

Not attaching the -ová suffix to Czech woman's name could lead to confusion and would be incoherent from a linguistic point of view. And that is why it is easy for you to search for women in the Czech Republic as you need target only the -ová:

> site:linkedin.com/in intitle:*ová (Praha OR Prague)

This string will help you target people on LinkedIn in Prague with a surname ending in ová.

> site:linkedin.com/in intitle:Accountant intitle:*ová (Praha OR Prague)

This string will help you target accountants on LinkedIn in Prague with a surname ending in ová.

Most Common Czech Last Names For Women[191]

1. Nováková	2. Svobodová	3. Novotná
4. Dvořáková	5. Černá	6. Procházková

---

[191] https://surnam.es/czech-republic

7. Veselá	8. Horáková	9. Pokorná
10. Marková	11. Benešová	12. Králová
13. Fialová	14. Zemanová	15. Doležalová
16. Hájková	17. Navrátilová	18. Urbanová
19. Kopecká	20. Blažková	21. Malá
22. Bartošová	23. Musilová	24. Šimková
25. Machová	26. Němcová	27. Holubová
28. Kadlecová	29. Blahová	30. Štěpánková

Slovakia

In Slovak there are even fewer exceptions regarding suffixes for women's names.

Most Common Slovak Last Names For Women

1.Kováčová	2.Vargová	3.Nagyová
4.Tóthová	5.Horváthová	6.Molnárová
7.Balážová	8.Nováková	9.Lukáčová
10.Hudáková	11.Kollárová	12.Poláková
13.Szabóová	14.Kovácsová	15.Gajdošová
16.Šimková	17.Szabová	18.Némethová
19.Oravcová	20.Kováčiková	21.Urbanová
22.Hudecová	23.Pavlíková	24.Beňová
25.Sedláková	26.Takáčová	27.Lacková
28.Marková	29.Mikulová	30.Farkašová

Poland[192]

In Polish, surnames are created in a similar way as in Czech, but surnames of *unmarried* women are treated differently. Nowadays, the renaming rule for unmarried women is being abandoned, and in addition married women often use untranslated surnames or add a man's untranslated surname to their original surname.

Male surnames that are adjectives (Czarny, Farny) are turned into female surnames by changing grammatical gender: Czarna, Farna. This is also true for the most common surnames ending in the suffixes -ski and -cki,

---

[192] https://cs.m.wikipedia.org/wiki/P%C5%99echylov%C3%A1n%C3%AD_p%C5%99%C3%ADjmen%C3%AD

which become -ska and -cka: Bujnicki, Bujnicka, Ciszewski, Ciszewska. If the husband's surname ends with a consonant, the suffix -owa is usually added for the female surname: Kupisz, Kupiszowa, Michalak, Michalakowa. Sometimes the suffix -ówna is used.

In these cases, the woman's surname adds the suffix -ówna [read: -uvna] to the father's surname: Pawlak, Pawlakówna, Kupisz, Kupiszówna. If the husband's surname ends with the vowel -a, then it takes the suffix ina: Zaręba, Zarębina, Kulesza, Kuleszyna. The suffix -ianka is also used: Zaręba, Zarębianka, Kulesza, Kuleszanka.

Lusatia[193]

In Lower Sorbian, the language of Lusatia, which is a province in Germany, surnames are different for married and unmarried women. Names of married women most often have the suffix -owa (Nowak, Nowakowa), similar to Czech. Some female surnames take the suffix -ka; these are formed mostly from male surnames of foreign origin (Budarka, Urbanka). Lower Sorbian also includes the suffix -ina/-yna (Markula, Markulina, Nowka, Nowcyna), which is not known in Czech.

Lithuania

In Lithuanian, surnames are created differently for married women and unmarried girls. Male surnames end in -as, -is, -ius, or -us. Girls' suffixes are -aitė, -ytė, -iūtė, and -utė. The suffix for married women is -ien.

Latvia[194]

Latvian uses suffixes for surnames for women. Usually the suffix is -a, but often -e is used for names of foreign origin (Ozoliņš, Ozoliņa). Surnames that already end in -a or -e do not change.

Iceland[195]

In Icelandic, classical surnames are very rare; most often a patronymic or matronymic name is used instead of a surname. The child takes the *first* name of the father and then a gender-based suffix is added: -son in the case of a boy and -dóttir in the case of a girl (Garðarsson, Garðarsdóttir). If the father is not known, the name is taken from the mother's *first* name and the usual suffixes are added. Surnames do not later change, even with marriage.

---

[193] https://cs.m.wikipedia.org/wiki/P%C5%99echylov%C3%A1n%C3%AD_p%C5%99%C3%ADjmen%C3%AD
[194] https://en.wikipedia.org/wiki/Latvian_name
[195] https://cs.m.wikipedia.org/wiki/P%C5%99echylov%C3%A1n%C3%AD_p%C5%99%C3%ADjmen%C3%AD

Here's an example: A man named *Jón Einarsson* has a son named Ólafur. Ólafur's last name will not be *Einarsson* like his father's; it will become *Jónsson*, indicating that Ólafur is the son of *Jón* (Jóns + son). The same practice is used for daughters. Jón Einarsson's daughter *Sigríður's* last name would not be *Einarsson* but *Jónsdóttir*.

Icelanders who are officially registered as nonbinary are permitted to use the patro/matronymic suffix -bur ("child of") instead of -son or -dóttir.[196]

Other Countries

There are many naming conventions throughout the world. It would be prohibitive to list them all here. But you can easily look them up on the Internet and then create suitable search strings. For example in Arabic, a son might be called Ali ibn Hussein, but his sister might be called Aisha bint Hussein.

The difference is between **bin** or **ibn**, which means "son of", or **bint**, which means "daughter of".[197] Your search string for women might look like this:

    site:linkedin.com/in intitle:bint Dubai

Final Thoughts

You will get many false positives when running a search on names. There are no guarantees that a name equals an underrepresented candidate. Remember that the search tips included in this chapter are meant only to point you in the right direction.

Sourcing by Ethnicity and Race

The U.S. Census Bureau[198] defines *race* as a person's biological, physical, and usually visible traits, which are inherited from parents, that can be used to self-identify with one or more general categories of humans. An individual can report on the Census as White, Black or African American, Asian, Native American and Alaska Native, Native Hawaiian and Other Pacific Islander, or some other race. Some Census survey respondents may report multiple races. *Ethnicity* is a broader term than *race*. The term is used to categorize groups of people according to their cultural expression and identification. Commonalities such as racial, national,

---

[196] https://www.icelandreview.com/news/icelandic-names-will-no-longer-be-gendered/
[197] https://www.councilscienceeditors.org/wp-content/uploads/v28n1p020-021.pdf
[198] https://www.cosb.us/home/showpublisheddocument/5935/637356700118370000

tribal, religious, linguistic, or cultural origins may be used to describe someone's ethnicity.[199]

Race

Let's look at some of the different races of potential candidates.

White

This category includes all individuals who identify with one or more nationalities or ethnic groups originating from Europe, the Middle East, or North Africa.

Black or African American

This category includes all individuals who identify with one or more nationalities or ethnic groups originating in any of the Black racial groups of Africa, Oceania, or Australia or, more recently, from the Caribbean.

Native American or Alaska Native

This category includes all individuals who identify with any of the original peoples of North and South America, including Central America, and who maintain tribal affiliation or community attachment.

Asian

This category includes all individuals who identify with one or more nationalities or ethnic groups originating in the Far East, Southeast Asia, or the Indian subcontinent.

Native Hawaiian and Pacific Islander

This category includes all individuals who identify with one or more nationalities or ethnic groups originating in Hawaii, Samoa, Guam, or other Pacific Islands.

Some Other Race

If you do not identify with any of the above groups, you can simply choose the "Some Other Race" category on the Census and then clarify how you identify yourself.

Although organizations like the Census Bureau may want to collect race and ethnicity data, people don't always fit into simple categories.

---

[199] https://www.verywellmind.com/difference-between-race-and-ethnicity-5074205

Ethnicity

Latinx/Latino/Latina/Hispanic

In the United States the terms *Hispanic* and *Latino* (or *Latina* for a woman or sometimes written as *Latinx* to be gender-neutral) were adopted in an attempt to loosely group immigrants and their descendants who hail from Central or South America.[200] The word *Hispanic* was first introduced by the Nixon administration on the 1970 Census. *Hispanic* is a term that generally includes people from Spanish-speaking Latin America, including those countries/territories of the Caribbean, or even from Spain.

People of Latin American descent tend to identify first with their specific country of heritage and then second as "Latino/Latina/Latinx" or "Hispanic," according to Dr. Rubén Martinez, director of the Julian Samora Research Institute at Michigan State University. For example, a person whose family is from Mexico will typically identify as "Mexican-American" before identifying as "Latino/Latina/Latinx" or "Hispanic."[201]

Latinx is a gender-neutral term used in place of *Latino* or *Latina* to refer to all people of Latin American descent, regardless of their sexual orientation or gender identity. This term has become more common among members of the LGBTQ community and their advocates who see it as an inclusive way to identify.

When sourcing for candidates from this group you will be targeting several keywords:

Hispanic OR Latino OR Latina OR Latinx

You might consider Spanish or Portuguese as keywords too:

Hispanic OR Latino OR Latina OR Latinx OR Spanish OR Portuguese

You can add these keywords to any other search string. For example, if you want to target pages with the keywords *Resume, CV,* and *BIO* in the title, you will need to create this string:

(intitle:resume OR intitle:CV OR intitle:bio) AND (Hispanic OR Latino OR Latina OR Latinx)

Targeting LinkedIn is easy too; simply use the **site:** operator together with keywords:

---

[200] https://www.britannica.com/story/whats-the-difference-between-hispanic-and-latino
[201] https://eu.usatoday.com/story/news/nation/2019/06/29/latina-latino-latinx-hispanic-what-do-they-mean/1596501001/

site:linkedin.com/in intitle:Manager (Hispanic OR Latino OR Latina OR Latinx)

This string will help you find LinkedIn profiles that have *Manager* in their page titles and include one of the keywords in brackets.

Black People/African Americans

African Americans (also referred to as Black Americans and formerly Afro-Americans) are an ethnic group consisting of Americans with partial or total ancestry from any of the Black racial groups of Africa.[202] But Black Americans can also include people with ancestry from countries with Black populations not in Africa, such as Cuba, Haiti, the Dominican Republic, Brazil, Colombia, Ecuador, and Venezuela.

Your search string will be

"African American" OR Black

Capitalize Black when referring to race, ethnicity, or culture since, for many people, *Black* reflects a shared sense of identity and community.[203]

Native Americans

Native Americans, the early indigenous occupants of North America, are also known as American Indians, First Americans, and Indigenous Americans. Your search string will be

"Native American" OR "Indigenous American" OR "Alaska Native" OR "American Indian."

Combine More Keywords

You can combine more keywords into your search strings for X-ray search:

(Hispanic OR Latinx OR "African American" OR Black OR "Native American" OR "Alaska Native")

Combine these keywords with other keywords like job titles:

(Hispanic OR Latinx OR "African American" OR "Native American" OR Black OR "Alaska Native" OR "American Indian") AND "Senior Director"

Use the **site:** operator and site to find relevant profiles:

site:linkedin.com/in (Hispanic OR Latinx OR "African American" OR "Native American" OR Black OR "Alaska Native" OR "American Indian") AND "Senior Director"

---

[202] https://en.wikipedia.org/wiki/African_Americans
[203] https://www.nytimes.com/2020/07/05/insider/capitalized-black.html

Organizational Searches

At some point during the recruitment process, as you attempt to diversify your company, you will turn to organizational searches. The organizations you will search include universities, alumni groups, sororities and fraternities, business and professional affiliations, health care groups, and interest groups.

Universities

Use the "schools" filter in LinkedIn Recruiter to search for Historically Black Colleges and Universities (HBCUs), Hispanic Serving Institutions (HSIs), tribal colleges, and women's colleges. Or take a look at Campus Ethnic Diversity Rankings and choose schools that rank well and have departments for the role you're looking to fill.

Hispanic-Serving Institutions

HSIs are defined as accredited, degree-granting public or private nonprofit institutions of higher education with 25 percent or more total undergraduate Hispanic full-time equivalent (FTE) student enrollment. You will find the full list of HSIs at the end of this book.

When you target universities, don't forget to search for "Universidad" as this Spanish word for University could be included on the profile of your potential candidates.

You have several options for targeting those universities. Most people will do this:

("Allan Hancock College" OR "Alliant International University" OR "Barstow Community College" OR "Bakersfield College")

But you can create better strings like this:

("Allan Hancock" OR "Alliant International" OR "Barstow Community" OR Bakersfield AND College OR University OR Universidad)

If you want to target all colleges you do not need to list them all in one long search string:

"Casa Loma College" OR "CBD College" OR "Cerritos College" OR "Chaffey College" OR "Citrus College"

Instead, turn it into a simpler string:

("Casa Loma" OR CBD OR Cerritos OR Chaffey OR Citrus) AND College

You should always add also a location to narrow your search:

("Casa Loma" OR CBD OR Cerritos OR Chaffey OR Citrus) AND College
AND California

If you want to target profiles on LinkedIn you will need to run this string:

site:linkedin.com/in (("Casa Loma" OR CBD OR Cerritos OR Chaffey OR
Citrus) College)) AND California

Historically Black Colleges and Universities (HBCUs)

There are many Historically Black Colleges and Universities (HBCUs)
located in nineteen states, the District of Columbia, and the U.S. Virgin
Islands. You can find a full list of HBCUs at the end of this book.

The search strings will be similar to the one you saw HSIs:

"Albany State University" OR "Clark Atlanta University" OR "Fort Valley
State University."

You can create a more efficient string:

("Albany State" OR "Clark Atlanta" OR "Fort Valley State") AND University

Tribal Colleges and Universities (TCUs)

Use the same principles here as for HIS and HBCUs:

"Bay Mills Community College" OR "Chief Dull Knife College" OR "Fort
Peck Community College" OR "Little Big Horn College"

You can also use these keywords:

(Tribal OR "Native American" OR "American Indian" OR "Alaska Native")
AND (School OR University OR College)

Alumni Groups

Alumni are people who previously attended or graduated from a
particular school, college, or university.[204]

To get the best results you should use **intitle:** and **inurl:** operators together
with the right keywords:

alumni, alum, graduates, grads, directory, members

To target Harvard, for example, run this string to get to their Alumni
website[205]:

intitle:Alumni Harvard

intitle:"Alumni Harvard"

---

[204] https://www.yourdictionary.com/alumni
[205] https://alumni.harvard.edu/

Or more complex search string

> ((intitle:"Alumni Harvard" OR (intitle:Alumni Harvard))

You will learn that their alumni group has a name that you can immediately use in your next string:

> inurl:bio "Harvard Alumni"

This will help you to find any page that has the keyword *bio* and phrase *Harvard Alumni.* You can add more phrases like "About me" and any others you learn from the book *Full Stack Recruiter: The Ultimate Edition.*[206]

Sorority/Fraternities Searches

You can target sororities and fraternities to identify more diverse candidates. For example, if you are looking for Hispanic candidates, you can target Hispanic sororities by using their names.

First, you need to find a list of those sororities:

> ("La Hermandad de Oe Me Te" OR "Gamma Alpha Omega" OR "Omega Delta Phi" OR "Kappa Delta Chi")

You can combine this with other strings, like this one:

> site:linkedin.com/in intitle:"Finance Manager" ("La Hermandad de Oe Me Te" OR "Gamma Alpha Omega" OR "Omega Delta Phi" OR "Kappa Delta Chi")

This string will find all people working as finance managers who are from those sororities or connected with them.

Search for African-American fraternities and sororities:

> ("Sigma Pi Phi" OR "Alpha Phi Alpha" OR "Kappa Alpha Psi" OR "Omega Psi Phi" OR "Phi Beta Sigma" OR "Sigma Rhomeo" OR "Wine Psi Phi")

Then focus the search further:

> site:linkedin.com/in intitle:"Finance Manager" ("Sigma Pi Phi" OR "Alpha Phi Alpha" OR "Kappa Alpha Psi" OR "Omega Psi Phi" OR "Phi Beta Sigma" OR "Sigma Rhomeo" OR "Wine Psi Phi")

You can find a list of sororities and fraternities at the end of the book.

Associations & Organizations

There are many reasons you might need to find a list of organizations or associations connected with a particular ethnicity, gender, or other

---

[206] https://fullstackrecruiter.net/

underrepresented group. There are a few simple steps you can follow to find the information you need.

First, try searching for the term on a search engine such as Google or Bing. If that doesn't yield any results, try adding the word *directory* to your search query. This should bring up a list of websites that provide directory services for the relevant group. If you still can't find what you're looking for, try contacting the group directly and asking for help. With a little patience and effort, you should be able to find the information you need.

For example, imagine you are looking for Asian associations or organizations. The easiest way to start your search is to Google the phrase "Asian Professional Associations and Organizations." Add the keyword "list" at the beginning to yield more refined results:

List Asian Professional Associations and Organizations

When you find several organizations you can add them all into one string that will help you to find all sites that have these groups on their pages. To refine further, add keywords:

List Asian Technology Professional Associations and Organizations

When you find several organizations, you can add them all into one string that will help you find all sites that have these groups on their pages:

"Asian American Journalists Association" OR "Asian American Professional Association" OR "Asian American Hotel Owners Association"

You can also combine the keyword "Asian" with other keywords to find societies, clubs, and groups:

Asian (Member OR Membership OR Group OR Society or Club)

If you want to narrow the results further, use the intitle: operator together with the keyword "Asian":

intitle:Asian (Member OR Membership OR Group OR Society or Club)

By combining all the keywords with operators like intitle: or inurl:, you will achieve your goals much faster.

To recruit diverse applicants, search for a variety of organizations:

- People of color
- African-American (with and without the hyphen)
- Asian-American (with and without the hyphen)
- Hispanic
- Latino
- Native American

- Pacific Islander
- Other ethnicities
- Minority
- Veterans
- Disabled
- Working mothers (on maternity leave)
- Military
- Gay and lesbian
- LGBT

You can find an organization for just about anything. For example, if you are looking for female candidates who are tech experts, start by identifying the groups building communities of women in technology:

> ("Women in Technology International" OR "Society of Women Engineers" OR "American Association of University Women" OR "Women in Science International Trust" OR "Women Techmakers" OR WITI OR "Women in Technology International" OR "Women Who Tech")

You can combine keywords with other search strings. For example, to find LinkedIn profiles of finance managers who are members of a women in tech community, use this string:

> site:linkedin.com/in intitle:"Finance Manager" ("Women in Technology International" OR "Society of Women Engineers" OR "American Association of University Women" OR "Women in Science International Trust" OR "Women Techmakers" OR WITI OR "Women in Technology International" OR "Women Who Tech")

Partial List of Women in Tech Organizations

Ada Developers Academy	Ladies Get Paid
Ada's List	Ladies that UX
Black Girls Code	Ladies, Wine, & Design
Change Catalyst	League of Women Coders
Elpha	MotherCoders
Girl Develop It	National Center for Women & Information Technology (NCWIT)
Girlboss	
Girls in Tech	org/Anita Borg Institute
Girls Who Code	PowerToFly
Hexagon UX	Project Include

Switch

TechLadies

TechWomen

The Next IT Girl

UX HER

Women Hack

Women in America

Women in Innovation

Women in STEM

Women in Technology International (WITI)

Organizations Fighting for Gender Equality

Abaad MENA

Amnesty International

Association for Women's Rights in Development

Center for Reproductive Rights

Equality Now

European Institute for Gender Equality

European Women's Lobby

Gender at Work

Gender Equality Resource Center

Global Fund for Women

Human Rights Watch

International Alliance of Women

International Center for Research on Women

International Women's Development Agency

MATCH International Women's Fund

Men Engage Alliance

Plan International

PROMUNDO

Rise Up

Save the Children

Time's Up

UN Women

Womankind Worldwide

Women for Women International

Women's Environment and Development Organization

Hispanic Associations & Organizations

You can use the same method for looking for members of Hispanic organizations:

"National Council of Hispanic Women" OR NSHMBA OR MAES OR "National Council of La Raza" OR NCLR OR "Hispanic Women's Corporation"

Refine with keywords:

site:linkedin.com/in (intitle:"Finance Manager") ("National Council of Hispanic Women" OR NSHMBA OR MAES OR "National Council of La Raza" OR NCLR OR "Hispanic Women's Corporation")

Business and Finance

Association of Latino Professionals in Finance and Accounting

Latin Business Association

National Society of Hispanic MBAs

US Hispanic Chamber of Commerce

Educational & Cultural Associations

American Association of Teachers of Spanish and Portuguese

ASPIRA Association

Association of Hispanic Arts

Hispanic Educational Telecommunications System

National Association of Latino Arts and Culture

Political & Labor Associations

Congressional Hispanic Caucus

National Association of Hispanic Federal Executives

Hispanic Elected Local Officials

Labor Council for Latin American Advancement

Cuban American National Foundation

Engineering

Society for the Advancement of Chicanos and Native Americans in Science

Society of Hispanic Professional Engineers

Society of Latino Engineers and Scientists

Healthcare

Interamerican College of Physicians and Surgeons

National Association of Hispanic Nurses

National Hispanic Medical Association

Law and Criminal Justice

Hispanic National Bar Association

Media

National Association of Hispanic Journalists

Real Estate

National Association of Hispanic Real Estate Professionals

Social Work

National Association of Puerto Rican and Hispanic Social Workers

African American Associations & Organizations

This string targets members of African-American organizations:

> NSBE OR NSMBA OR AAWIT OR "African American women in technology" OR NAACP OR "African American chamber"

Refine your search with keywords:

> site:linkedin.com/in intitle:"Finance Manager" (NSBE OR NSMBA OR AAWIT OR "African American women in technology" OR NAACP OR "African American chamber")

There are many Black professional organizations and associations that you can use in your search. Following is just a small sample of them.

Technology and Design

All Star Code

Black Data Processing Associates

Black Girls Code

Code2040

/dev/color

Black Women Talk Tech

National Society of Black Engineers

Organization of Black Designers

Design

Organization of Black Designers

Business

National Association of Black Accountants

National Association of Black Administrative Professionals

National Economic Association

National Sales Network

National Association of African Americans in Human Resources

National Black MBA Association

Health Care

National Black Nurses Association

National Dental Hygienists' Association

National Medical Association

National Organization of Blacks in Dietetics and Nutrition

Association of Black Women Physicians

National Association for Black Veterinarians

Student National Medical Association

Education

National Alliance of Black School Educators

National Association of Black Male Educators

Cosmetology and Barbering

Black Beauty Association

Black Owned Beauty Supply Association

Professional Black Barbers Association

Government

Blacks in Government

Law and Criminal Justice

National Association of Blacks in Criminal Justice

National Organization of Black Law Enforcement Executives

Culinary

Black Culinarian Alliance

General Professional and Entrepreneurial Organizations

100 Black Men of America

Black Career Network

Black Career Women Network

Black Female Founders

Black Founders

The Hidden Genius Project

National Association of Negro Business and Professional Women's Clubs

National Coalition of 100 Black Women

National Black Business Council, Inc.

Asian Professional Associations & Organizations

Ascend

Asian American Advertising Federation (3AF)

Asian American Architects and Engineers Association (AAAESC)

Asian American Journalists Association (AAJA)

Asian American Professional Association (AAPA)

Asian American Hotel Owners Association (AAHOA)

Asian Pacific American Medical Student Association (APAMSA)

National Asian Pacific American Bar Association (NAPABA)

National Association of Asian American Professionals (NAAAP)

National Organization for Vietnamese American Leadership (NOVAL)

Society of Asian Scientists and Engineers (SASE)

LGBT Professional Associations & Organizations

Association of Lesbian, Gay, Bisexual, Transgender Addiction Professionals (NALGAP)

Association of LGBTQ Journalists (NLGJA)

Gay & Lesbian Medical Association (GLMA)

National Association of Gay and Lesbian Real Estate Professionals (NAGLREP)

Lesbians Who Tech

National Gay Pilots Association (NGPA)

National LGBT Bar Association (LGBT BAR)

National Organization of Gay and Lesbian Scientists and Technical Professionals (NOGLSTP)

Out in Science, Technology, Engineering, and Mathematics (oSTEM)

There are many other categories of organizations you can use to widen your search for diverse candidates. We will not go over all of the options, as the list is exhaustive. The goal is always for you to learn how to find this content for yourself; that way you can always ensure that you are accessing the most up-to-date information.

Affinity Groups

Affinity groups are often overlooked as a source for diverse candidates, but they can be very helpful. Many corporations have affinity groups, which means that there is already an established network of potential candidates for you.

For example, Amazon has thirteen groups,[207] including Amazon People with Disabilities, Amazon Women in Engineering, Asians@Amazon, Black Employee Network, Body Positive Peers, Families@Amazon, Glamazon, Indigenous@Amazon, Latinos@Amazon, Mental Health and Well-Being, Warriors@Amazon, Women@Amazon, and Women in Finance & Global Business Services (FGBS) Initiative (WiFi).

Furthermore, when you're sourcing for diverse candidates, you can get a better sense of their interests by looking at the organizations they're affiliated with. This information can be extremely valuable when trying to identify new organizations to target or when trying to learn more about a particular candidate's background and interests.

In short, affinity groups can be a great way to expand your pool of diverse candidates and to get more information about them. To get a first list of affinity groups, target big corporations like Amazon by adding their names into the search string:

(Amazon OR Facebook OR Meta OR Apple OR Google OR Twitter OR Uber) ("affinity group" OR "employee resource group" OR "resource group")

If you want to expand your search, use intitle: operators:

(intitle:"affinity group" OR intitle:"employee resource group" OR intitle:"resource group")

This will find you all the websites that are indexed by Google. Because the majority of the sites you will find will not be relevant, add more keywords:

---

[207] https://www.aboutamazon.com/affinity-groups

```
(intitle:"affinity group" OR intitle:"employee resource group" OR
intitle:"resource group") AND (Hispanic OR Latino OR Latina OR Latinx)
```

This string will help you find a group called "Latino Affinity Group." When you find a specific group that has candidates in the location where you need to find people, use that name in the LinkedIn search string:

```
site:linkedin.com/in "Latino Affinity Group"
```

No matter how hard you are trying to find your candidates you should always remember that some of the best talent is trying not to be found. Sometimes you won't find the best talent until the final page.

Sourcing will help you find diverse talent, but convincing them to sign on with your company could be hard if your social media presence is only full of stock photos of Caucasian men. Make your content more authentic, but don't rely on social media; work with diverse communities—whether online or offline. They are your best allies when you are trying to attract diverse talent to your company.

Image Searches

If you're looking for a more diverse pool of candidates to choose from, you might be tempted to use Google's image search function (or any other search engine's equivalent). Let's say you want to find more diverse candidates for your team, and you're specifically looking for a Java Developer in San Francisco who has Hispanic origins.

You try these search phrases:

- Hispanic "Java Developer" (SF OR "San Francisco")
- Latino "Java Developer" (SF OR "San Francisco")

Only people with images on the search engine who happen to have those images tagged with your keywords will show up.

You have several options on how to get more results with your search strings.

First, you can try to use the different keyword options, such as by replacing *developer* with *software engineer:*

```
"Software Engineer" Java "San Francisco" Hispanic
```

Or you could add more terms for ethnic categories:

```
"Software Engineer" Java "San Francisco" (Hispanic OR Latino OR Latina
OR Latinx)
```

Then you can make the search site specific:

site:linkedin.com/in "Software Engineer" Java "San Francisco" (Hispanic OR Latino OR Latina OR Latinx)

However this search will still not bring up too many options.

You can next try an advanced image search[208]:

1. Add your search phrase into "all these words:".
2. In "type of image," you will need to select Face.
3. You can select region.

If you need to limit your results to a domain, add the location-specific suffix into the "site or domain" field. You can use the site:linkedin.com/in in your search string to get results ONLY from LinkedIn or remove it and run it without the site: operator. If you do that, you will get more results and also find more sites where you can find more candidates.

To get even more results, return to the advanced image search dashboard to select "aspect ratio" for Tall or Square. Those are the two most common options for how profile photos are presented on the Internet. With square size you should have the most luck.

If you can't access the advanced image search dashboard, go to Google Images search, enter your search query, hit Enter, and then add &tbs=itp:face to the end of the search URL. This will further improve the results of your face-related search.

Try specifying image size with your search. You can add imagesize:WIDTHxHEIGHT to your search string:

"Software Engineer" Java "San Francisco" (Hispanic OR Latino OR Latina OR Latinx) imagesize:300x300

Then you need to switch to images and add &tbs=itp:face at the end of the URL or you can use the face option from the advanced image search dashboard.

Every website has a different size for its profile pictures so you'll have to take that into consideration as well. For example, LinkedIn shows profile pictures in various formats like 400 x 400 pixels and 165 x 165 pixels. You can also use operators like the intitle: operator or target phrases like "she is a developer" together with &tbs=itp:face or option for the Google Advanced Image Search Dashboard.

Consider phrases like

- "she is the author"

---

[208] https://www.google.com/advanced_image_search

- "she is responsible"
- "she was responsible"
- "her responsibility"

In the following example, you will target all pages that have the word *bio* in their title and *finance manager* and *she*. But you will also need to use &tbs=itp:face:

```
intitle:bio "Finance Manager" she
```

```
intitle:bio "Finance Manager" "she is the author"
```

The last option you have is to use other search engines like Bing[209] or Yandex[210] that have the ability to search based on a face filter.

On Bing, you can select from three different options: all, just faces, or head and shoulders. This gives you a lot of flexibility in terms of the results you see. Bing's reverse image recognition for faces is better than Google's. Bing Image Search provides its results under multiple tabs rather than all on one page.

Unless you live in Russia, the odds are pretty good that you've never heard of Yandex. This Russian search engine is one of the most popular on the Russian Internet. Yandex also offers a people filter, but you have to specifically select the "People" type in order to see results that include people. So if you're not specifically looking for images of people, you might not stumble upon this option. All in all, both search engines offer helpful filtering options, but Bing's is slightly more user-friendly in this regard.

Despite the potential to get some results from face searches, resist the urge. It's not an accurate or effective way to find diverse talent! You'll likely miss out on a lot of great candidates who don't show up in the top results. Although face search tools can turn up potential candidates, they tend to produce results that are biased toward individuals who are already well-represented in the workforce.

There are much better ways to find diverse candidates, so save yourself the hassle and use one of those instead!

Disability Sourcing

The way to access the widest pool of talent is by fostering an inclusive and flexible work culture that considers the needs and potential of all employees, including those who have disabilities. By recruiting people with disabilities, your company recognizes that everyone has unique

---

[209] https://www.bing.com/
[210] https://yandex.com/

abilities and strengths, which makes your workforce more diverse and innovative.

When you meet someone with a disability for the first time, you may not know what to say or do. This is normal, and there is no need to feel awkward or embarrassed. The best way to interact with someone with a disability is to treat them just like you would treat anyone else.

There are a few things to keep in mind, however, that can make the interaction smoother for both parties. First, remember that it is rude to ask personal questions about someone's disability unless they have offered to share this information.

Second, remember that everyone is an individual, and what works for one person may not work for another. The best way to learn more about interacting with people with disabilities is to learn more about Disability Etiquette.[211] Appropriate disability etiquette allows all employees to be more comfortable and productive. By following simple guidelines, you can ensure that everyone has a positive and respectful interaction.[212] Here are a few basic guidelines[213]:

- Ask before you help.
- Be sensitive about physical contact.
- Think before you speak.
- Don't make assumptions.
- Respond graciously to requests.

Put the person first. Say, "person with a disability" rather than "disabled person." Say "people with disabilities" rather than "the disabled." For specific disabilities, say, "person with Tourette's syndrome" or "person who has cerebral palsy." But remember that every individual will have their own preferences.[214]

Don't automatically refer to 'disabled people' in all communications – many people who need disability benefits and services don't identify with this term. Consider using 'people with health conditions or impairments' if it seems more appropriate.[215]

Job seekers with disabilities often face significant challenges in finding employment. One way to help them is to partner with local disability

---

[211] https://disabilityin.org/resource/disability-etiquette/
[212] https://askjan.org/topics/disetiq.cfm
[213] https://unitedspinal.org/disability-etiquette/
[214] https://unitedspinal.org/disability-etiquette/
[215] https://www.gov.uk/government/publications/inclusive-communication/inclusive-language-words-to-use-and-avoid-when-writing-about-disability

organizations and college and university career centers. By advertising job openings in these places, you can reach a large pool of potential applicants.

You can also post vacancies on websites and in publications that focus on disability-related issues. In addition, setting up internship and mentoring programs specifically for young people with disabilities can give them the skills and experience they need to compete for jobs in the future. By taking these steps, you can help increase opportunities for talented individuals with disabilities.

Sourcing Veterans

There are many benefits to hiring veterans. They tend to be reliable, hardworking, and disciplined. They also tend to be highly motivated and have a strong sense of loyalty and commitment. In addition, hiring veterans can help improve your company's image and boost morale among your employees.

Many business leaders endorse hiring veterans as a good business practice because these candidates bring many beneficial attributes and characteristics to the workplace. Veterans have skills and training that can be difficult to find in civilians, such as experience dealing with challenging situations, problem-solving skills, and leadership abilities.

Databases

To find veteran candidates, use job boards and databases dedicated to army personnel. One of the best is Recruitmilitary.com[216]. This database is the largest of its kind, and it offers many useful options. You can search profiles of qualified candidates, post jobs, reach out through targeted email campaigns, and even build a branded presence on their site.

Keywords

Finding veterans is all about using the right keyword. If you are looking for people who are associated with the United States Space Force (USSF), for example, which is the space service branch of the U.S. Armed Forces, you will have several options:

USSF OR "United States Space Force" OR "U.S. Space Force"

You can use all three options in your search string. This will give you better results.

---

[216] https://recruitmilitary.com/

The main U.S. military branches are Army, Marine Corps, Navy, Air Force, Space Force, Coast Guard, and National Guard. There are also several military service branches that you can use as keywords in your search:

- Army—Army Reserve, Army National Guard
- Marine Corps—Marine Corps Reserve
- Navy—Navy Reserve
- Air Force—Air Force Reserve, Air National Guard
- Space Force—currently without a service branch
- Coast Guard—Coast Guard Reserve

If you're looking for commands, use these search terms:

- **Army**
  — U.S. Army Forces Command (FORSCOM)
  — U.S. Army Training and Doctrine Command (TRADOC)
  — U.S. Army Materiel Command (AMC)
  — U.S. Army Futures Command (AFC)
- **Marine Corps (U.S. Marine Corps, USMC)**
  — U.S. Marine Corps Forces Command (COMMARFORCOM)
  — Fleet Marine Force, Atlantic (FMFLANT)
  — Marine Forces Pacific (MARFORPAC)
  — Fleet Marine Force, Pacific (FMFPAC)
- **U.S. Navy**
  — U.S. Fleet Forces Command (USFF)
  — U.S. Northern Command (USNORTHCOM)
  — U.S. Naval Forces Strategic Command (USPACFLT)
  — U.S. Naval Forces Central Command (NAVCENT)
  — U.S. Naval Forces Southern Command (USNAVSO)
  — U.S. Naval Forces Europe–Africa (CNE-CNA)
  — U.S. Fleet Cyber Command (USFCC)
  — U.S. Naval Special Warfare Command (NAVSPECWARCOM/USNSWC), also known as WARCOM
  — Military Sealift Command (MSC)
- **Air Force**
  — Air National Guard (ANG)
  — Air Force Reserve Command (AFRC)
  — Air Combat Command (ACC)
  — Air Education and Training Command (AETC)
  — Air Force Global Strike Command (AFGSC)
  — Air Force Materiel Command (AFMC)
  — Air Force Reserve Command (AFRC)
  — Air Force Special Operations Command (AFSOC)
  — Air Mobility Command (AMC)

— Pacific Air Forces (PACAF)

— U.S. Air Forces in Europe–Air Forces Africa (USAFE-AFAFRICA)

- **Space Force (U.S. Space Force, USSF)**

  — Space Operations Command (SpOC)

  — Space Systems Command (SSC)

  — Space Training and Readiness Command (STAR Command or STARCOM)

- **Coast Guard (U.S. Coast Guard, USCG)**

  — Coast Guard Atlantic Area (LANTAREA)

  — Coast Guard Pacific Area & Defense Forces West (PACAREA)

You can use any of the abbreviations in your search string:

"U.S.A.R." OR AETC OR USN OR USNR OR USAF OR USMC OR "U.S.M.C." OR USMCR OR "U.S.M.C.R." OR "MARFORRES" OR USCG OR "U.S.C.G." OR USCGR

If you want to simplify your search string, you can target more generic keywords:

Army OR Navy OR "Air Force" OR Marine OR "National Guard" OR Veteran OR "honorable discharge" OR "honorably discharged" OR "Army Reserve" OR "Army Reserves" OR "Force Reserve" OR "Force Reserves" OR "Naval Reserves" OR "Naval Reserve" OR "National Guard"

Veterans often face a number of challenges as they transition back into civilian life. They may have trouble finding steady employment, adjusting to new work environments, or dealing with physical or mental injuries sustained during their time in the military. Hiring veterans can make a huge difference in their lives and help them get back on their feet. It is not only a great way to show your gratitude for their service, but it can also make your business stand out from other companies.

Legal Concerns

During the hiring process, candidates can self-identify. That will happen via applicant tracking systems (ATS), which request standard demographic data—such as race, gender, and veteran status—as defined by the Equal Employment Opportunity Commission[217] (EEOC). But the U.S. federal government and other international governments prohibit employers from using selection processes that screen out individuals based on race or gender, and any race or gender is eligible for employment.

---

[217] https://en.wikipedia.org/wiki/Equal_Employment_Opportunity_Commission

Protecting race and gender from discrimination in hiring is important, as is not favoring one group over another through selection processes. This means that employers may not use any type of selection process that screens out individuals on the basis of their race or gender.

The purpose of this chapter is not to give you tools to help you to find candidates from a particular ethnic group but instead to give you tools for expanding your search to find more diverse candidates.

If you are presenting candidates that are all male Caucasians to employers, those employers will hire a male Caucasian as an employee. By expanding your recruitment pipeline with a diverse set of candidates, you are helping your company build a more inclusive environment that will be beneficial to all employees.

The best sources of diverse candidates are other minority employees. Asking your underrepresented employees for referrals will likely increase diversity at the top of your funnel and help you to get more diverse candidates. Of course, you still need to create an inclusive environment where all people feel welcomed.

As you cannot search for race, ethnicity, or gender within LinkedIn Recruiter, you will need to use relevant keywords for these searches, such as keywords for prospects who attended diverse schools or joined diverse sororities, fraternities, or alumni groups.

Before you start with your search, bear in mind that you should always select and hire the best candidate for the job. Just remember that the best candidate is not always the one with most skill and experience.

If you use technology (some sourcing tools) to extend your reach to diverse groups, document your efforts to show how you reached your qualified candidates. Document everything you do, what search strings you used, and what methods you employed. If a claim of discriminatory hiring is made, you will need to provide evidence that you followed legal practices. You and your employer must be prepared to defend your decisions—including using protected class information—and sourcing methods.

In addition to documenting everything, follow smart practices as well:

- When hiring, don't rely on just one source for candidates.
- Write inclusive job ads. Job descriptions can be biased, and even single words can be loaded with unintentional bias. It's always important to revise job descriptions to be clear, concise, and more inclusive.

Final Thoughts

When companies embrace diversity, they can outperform their competitors. A diverse workforce brings different perspectives and experiences to the table. In addition, businesses that embrace diversity are better able to withstand unexpected challenges, such as a pandemic. When it comes to the workplace, diversity is always a good thing.

It's important to remember that not everyone is comfortable self-identifying as part of an underrepresented group. As a result, companies need to be careful not to exclude these candidates accidentally when they're trying to increase diversity.

One way to avoid this problem is to focus on skills and qualifications instead of profile photos when sourcing candidates. It's important not to make assumptions about someone's background based on their appearance. Instead, give everyone a fair chance by judging them based on their merits.

By taking this approach, you'll be more likely to find the best candidates for the job, regardless of their background.

19. Epilogue

When you're at work or having a discussion with your friends or strangers it's important to be conscious of the language you use. The **words you choose can have a big impact on others, so it's important to be mindful of the message you're sending**.

Inclusive language doesn't contain biases, stereotypes, or derogatory or discriminating phrases against people of different races, genders, sexual orientations, health conditions, and backgrounds. The speaker typically aims to address the listeners in a more impartial way. Following are some examples of how you can start incorporating more inclusive language into your speech.

For example when referring to gender

- instead of saying "he/she," try using "they/them/theirs."
- instead of saying "guys/ladies," try using "team/folks/everyone/all."
- instead of saying "boss/chairman/businessman," try using "leader/executive/representative."

In a world where words matter more than ever, it's important to choose them carefully. The words we use can make a huge difference in the way we're perceived, and in the way we're able to connect with others.

I wrote this book with the hope of sparking important conversations about diversity and inclusion. These topics can be difficult to talk about, but I believe that it is essential that we do so. By increasing our understanding and awareness of these issues, we can make our world a more inclusive and welcoming place for everyone.

It's important to learn about other cultures and experiences so that we can be more understanding and inclusive of others. It's easy to get caught up in our own lives and perspectives, but if we take the time to learn about others, we can open ourselves up to new ways of thinking and become more compassionate and aware. There are so many different cultures and experiences out there, and each one has something valuable to offer.

I hope that you'll be able to use this information to help your company with its diversity hiring initiatives and help create a more inclusive environment at your workplace. The future of work is diverse, and the sooner you start embracing it, the better off you'll be.

If you have a minute to spare, I would really appreciate a short positive review on Amazon, Goodreads, or the site where you bought the book. You can write a short positive post on social media (LinkedIn, Twitter, Instagram, Facebook) about this book using this hashtag: #FullStackRecruiter.

Five-star reviews and positive feedback from readers like you make a huge difference in helping others find this book. Many thanks for considering my request.

Thank you again for reading!

Jan

P.S. If you do not have **_Full Stack Recruiter: The Ultimate Edition_**,[218] I recommend you get it as you will learn more from it about recruitment and sourcing.

---

[218] https://fullstackrecruiter.net/

Appendices

Diversity and Inclusion Glossary

Diversity and inclusion terms are everywhere, but do you know what they all mean?

- **Ableism:** Beliefs or actions based on the idea that being able-bodied is "normal" and that other states of being require "fixing" or alteration. This can lead to a loss of value or discrimination. People with physical, intellectual, or psychological disabilities are often discriminated against.
- **Accessibility:** The "ability to access" a system's or entity's functionality and benefit from it. The extent to which a product, service, or environment is available to the greatest number of people. *Accessible design* allows for both direct (unassisted) and indirect (aided) access via assistive technology, whereas *universal design* ensures that everyone can access, understand, and fully use an environment (as much as possible).
- **Accommodation:** An adjustment in an environment or to the way things are normally done that allows a person with a disability to have equal access, participation, and opportunity. Employers must accommodate qualified persons with disabilities unless doing so requires significant difficulty/expense.
- **ADHD:** Attention deficit hyperactivity disorder (ADHD), a neurodevelopmental disorder characterized by excessive amounts of inattention, carelessness, hyperactivity (which can evolve into inner restlessness in adulthood), and impulsivity that are pervasive, impairing, and otherwise age-inappropriate.
- **Agendered/Genderless:** Not identified with a specific gender. The identification falls under the nonbinary umbrella, which includes people who are neither male nor female; neither are they neutral, xenic, outherine, or any other gender. They may identify more strongly as an individual than as a specific gender.[219]
- **Alaska Native:** The indigenous people of Alaska. More than 200 federally recognized tribes speaking twenty different languages.
- **Ally:** Someone who advocates for people from underrepresented or underprivileged groups. An ally is not a member of a marginalized or disadvantaged group but expresses or supports their views.

---

[219] LGBTA Wiki. Retrieved January 28, 2022, from https://lgbta.fandom.com/wiki/Agender.

- **Allyship:** The process by which persons with privilege and power try to build support for oppressed or disadvantaged outgroups to advance their interests. Allyship is a component of the anti-oppression or anti-racist dialogue, which employs social justice theories and principles. The purpose of allyship is to foster a culture of support for underprivileged people.
- **Androgyne:** A person who identifies or expresses gender outside of the gender binary. Androgynes have a gender identification that is a mix of both binary genders or neither.
- **Anglo:** A person descended from Germanic people who ruled Britain until the Norman conquest in 1066. Describes White English-speaking people of European descent who live in England or North America and are not of Hispanic or French ethnicity.
- **Anti-Black:** The marginalization of Black people and the immoral disdain for Black institutions and supportive policies. Behavior that is discriminatory or hostile toward Black people.
- **Anti-Racism:** The stance of aggressively opposing racism through political, economic, and social change. It aims to combat racial prejudice, structural racism, and racial oppression of certain racial groups. Anti-racism is typically based on intentional efforts aimed at providing equal chances for all people on a personal and institutional level.
- **Anti-Racist Ideas:** The belief that, despite their differences, racial groupings are equals.
- **Arabs:** People with ethnic roots in Algeria, Bahrain, Egypt, Iraq, Jordan, Kuwait, Lebanon, Libya, Morocco, Oman, Palestine, Qatar, Saudi Arabia, Sudan, Syria, Tunisia, the United Arab Emirates, or Yemen.
- **Asperger's Syndrome:** An autism spectrum disorder that affects people's ability to communicate and engage with others. People with Asperger's syndrome can function well and may not have the learning impairments that people with other forms of autism do.
- **Assimilation:** The process through which an individual, family, or group abandons some characteristics of their culture to adapt to the beliefs, language, patterns, and behaviors of a new host country. An assimilated individual, family, or group will resemble a dominant group.
- **Autism Spectrum Disorder (ASD):** A range of neurological differences caused by abnormal brain connections that impair a person's development. These distinctions may result in exceptional growth, challenges, or special ability.
- **BAME:** An acronym that stands for "Black, Asian, and Minority Ethnic." It is used in the United Kingdom.

- **Belonging:** The sense of being welcomed and included by those around you. Having a sense of social connection and identification with others.
- **Benevolent Sexism:** A subtle form of sexism that stems from a good place and incorporates positive gender ideals yet can harm people (particularly women) and gender equality. The language or acts are usually subliminal, unconscious, and habitual.
- **Bias/Implicit Bias:** Prejudice in favor of or against one item, person, or group in comparison to another, usually in an unfavorable or negative sense. Unconscious bias involves attitudes and preconceptions that influence judgment, decision-making, and behavior in ways that are outside of conscious awareness and/or control.
- **Bicultural:** People who have the values, beliefs, languages, and habits of two different ethnic or racial groups.
- **Bigotry:** Stubborn or irrational commitment to an idea, opinion, or faction; specifically, prejudice against a person or persons because they belong to a specific group. Exaltation of one's own group while harboring prejudices toward members of other groups. A person who displays bigotry is a bigot.
- **Biphobia:** An unreasonable fear, hatred, or intolerance of people who identify as bisexual. It might take the form of denial that bisexuality is a real sexual orientation, or it can take the form of negative stereotypes about bisexuals (*Biphobia*, 2021[220]).
- **Biracial:** A person who identifies as being of two races or whose parents are from two separate race groups.
- **Biromantic Asexual:** A person who is romantically attracted but not sexually attracted to many genders.
- **Biromantic Demisexual:** A person who is sexually attracted to many genders. They may seek sexual relationships with people of more than one gender.
- **Birth Assigned Sex:** The biological, hormonal, and genetic makeup of a person at the time of birth. It is based on the child's external anatomy.
- **Bisexual/Bi:** A person who is attracted romantically and sexually to people of both male and female genders. People who identify as pansexual, queer, or fluid are sometimes included in the broad definition.
- **Black Lives Matter:** A human rights movement that began in the African-American community. It is dedicated to ending violence and institutional racism against Black people.

---

[220] Retrieved May 12, 2021, from Wikipedia: https://en.wikipedia.org/wiki/Biphobia.

- **Black:** Linked to persons of African ancestry or who are not of White European descent. In the United States, the terms Black and African American are frequently used interchangeably.
- **Bloomberg Gender-Equality Index (GEI):** An index that measures how equal men and women are in the workplace. Workplace diversity figures are shared in the annual report.
- **Butch:** A person who is overtly or stereotypically masculine but does not have the biological sex of a man.
- **Bystander Effect/Bystander Apathy:** When a person becomes discouraged or less likely to assist a distressed person due to the presence of other people. The bystander effect occurs when people expect that someone else will intervene and help; the result is that no one intervenes.
- **Chicanx:** A person who is related to Mexican Americans or their culture. Chicanx is a gender-neutral alternative of Chicano and Chicana.
- **Cisgender:** A person whose gender identity corresponds to the sex assigned to them at birth. Cisgender is derived from the Latin word "ci," which means "on this side."
- **Cissexual:** A person who identifies with the same biological sex as they were assigned at birth.
- **Classism:** Having biased attitudes or discriminating against a person or group based on disparities in socioeconomic status and income level.
- **Co-conspirators:** People who are willing to put their lives on the line to use their privilege to dismantle oppressive systems. Co-conspirators go beyond allies in their efforts. They not only educate themselves about systemic injustice and racism, but they also take personal risks to pursue real action.
- **Code-Switching:** When a person changes the way they express themselves culturally and linguistically according to the group they are with. An example may be a Muslim woman who wears her burka with other Muslims but takes it off with non-Muslim friends.
- **Colonization:** Invasion, dispossession, or control of a nation or group of people. Great Britain has colonized many countries.
- **Color Blindness:** The practice of treating individuals equally regardless of color, culture, or ethnicity. Can also refer to a resistance to recognize that underrepresented groups do indeed experience the world differently than the groups in power. A person can also have an eyesight impairment of the same name, which refers to not being able accurately to see colors.

- **Color Brave:** A dialogue about race that can help individuals better understand each other's viewpoints and experiences. This can build toward future inclusivity.
- **Color-Evasiveness:** A racial ideology in which people reject or reduce racial importance.
- **Coming Out/Coming Out of the Closet:** Describes the process of revealing one's sexual orientation to others. This is not a process for people who are heterosexual/straight as heterosexuality is commonly considered the "norm."
- **Communities of Color:** A term used to describe groupings of people who do not identify as White and who share common experiences of racism.
- **Corporate Social Responsibility (CSR):** Engaging at the organizational level in positive corporate citizenship to have a beneficial impact on communities rather than focusing solely on generating profits.
- **Covert Racism:** An indirect, more subtle form of racism. Examples include comments made quietly or out of earshot of the targeted group or offensive comments that are passed off as jokes.
- **Criminalization:** Making specific behaviors or actions illegal for the purpose of oppressing vulnerable communities. For example, legislation prohibiting serving food to homeless people in public parks.
- **Critical Race Theory (CRT):** A multidisciplinary intellectual and social movement of civil-rights researchers and activists who want to investigate the connection between race and law in the United States and question standard approaches to racial justice. For example, the CRT conceptual framework can be used to investigate how and why U.S. courts treat drug traffickers of certain races differently.[221]
- **Cross-Dresser:** Someone who dresses in attire that is traditionally associated with a gender other than the one with which they identify. An example may be a male who identifies as a man but sometimes wears stereotypically female clothing, such as high heels.
- **Cultural Appropriation:** Adopting features or practices or aesthetics of an underrepresented culture without a proper understanding of the context or respect for the original's meaning and value. An example is a White artist creating and selling art in the style of Native Pacific Northwest artists.
- **Cultural Identity:** The identity or sense of belonging to a group based on nationality, ethnicity, religion, socioeconomic class, generation,

---

[221] Retrieved January 27, 2022, from Wikipedia: https://en.wikipedia.org/wiki/Critical_race_theory#:~:text=The%202021%20Encyclopaedia%20Britannica%20describe.

identity, or locality. Food, sport, language, religious beliefs, festivals, and political beliefs are all ways to display our cultural identities.

- **Cultural Intelligence:** The ability to adapt to different cultures, relate to them, and work effectively with them. People with a high CI quotient are not necessarily cultural experts; instead, they can confidently enter new contexts and make informed decisions based on observations and data rather than stereotypes and biases.
- **Culture Adds:** People who cherish company culture and standards as well as provide a positive aspect of diversity to the workplace.
- **Culture:** A social system of customs, beliefs, and aesthetics formed by a group of people to secure their existence and adaptation.
- **Deadnaming:** The use of a transgender or nonbinary person's birth or other prior name without their consent. The birth or prior name is considered "dead."
- **Decolonization:** An indigenous culture group's active resistance to colonial powers. The concept is particularly relevant to the dismantling of colonial empires built prior to World War I.[222]
- **Deficit-Minded Language:** Language that blames children for their experiences rather than exploring the systemic reasons that lead to inequity.
- **Diaspora:** The voluntary or coercive migration of people from their home countries to other places. Historically, *diaspora* applied to the mass dispersion of Jewish people from their homelands.
- **Disability:** A physical or mental handicap that significantly limits one or more major life activities of an individual. Examples include Down's syndrome, visual or hearing impairments, mental health conditions, brain injury, and Dwarfism.
- **Disablism:** Promoting uneven or disparate treatment of people with actual or perceived disabilities, whether knowingly or unconsciously. Disablism is a kind of discrimination, oppression, and abuse motivated by the assumption that disabled people are inferior to others.
- **Discrimination:** The unfair treatment of individuals or groups based on factors such as race, gender, social class, sexual orientation, physical ability, religion, national origin, age, or physical or mental aptitudes. An employer cannot by law discriminate. Discrimination can occur because of either conscious or unconscious prejudice.
- **Diversity:** The state of being different or possessing differences in respect to race, sexual orientation, religion, age, class, ethnicity, gender, health, and physical and mental ability. Diversity includes any dimension that can be utilized to distinguish people from one another.

---

[222] Retrieved January 27, 2022, from Wikipedia: https://en.wikipedia.org/wiki/Decolonization

- **Dominating Culture:** A society's major cultural beliefs, values, and customs. In a dominant culture, the major practices are regarded as "natural" and "correct."
- **Drag Queen/King:** A drag queen portrays feminine stereotypes and a drag king portrays masculine stereotypes through dress, language, and behavior in a performance. The performance typically includes singing, dancing, and comedy.
- **Dyscalculia:** A condition in which a person has difficulties with numbers and computations.
- **Dysgraphia:** A condition in which a person has trouble spelling or putting thoughts on paper. It usually manifests itself when children are learning to write for the first time.[223]
- **Dyslexia:** Trouble reading. People with dyslexia may also struggle with reading comprehension, spelling, and writing.
- **Dyspraxia:** A movement and coordination disorder. Many people with dyspraxia also suffer with ADHD or other sensory processing disorders.
- **Echolalia:** The meaningless repetition of another person's spoken words as a symptom of a psychiatric disorder. Echolalia can also refer to the repetition of speech by a child learning to talk.
- **Emotional Tax:** The effects of being on high alert at work to avoid bias. Emotional tax has a negative impact on a person's health, well-being, and ability to succeed at work.
- **Employee Resource Group (ERG):** An identity- or experience-based group that is designed to foster a sense of community in the workplace. Affinity groups or diversity groups are other names for ERGS.
- **Enby:** An abbreviation for a nonbinary person. It is a phonetic pronunciation of the word "nonbinary," which refers to persons who do not identify as either male or female.
- **English as a Second Language (ESL):** First speaking or reading/writing another language other than English.
- **Equal Employment Opportunity (EEO):** A section of the 1964 Civil Rights Act of the United States, which forbids discrimination in the workplace based on race, color, religion, sex, or national origin. Other countries, such as the United Kingdom, have similar acts.
- **Equality:** Usually described as the condition of everyone having access to the same opportunities. It is sometimes used as a substitute for the word "inclusion." For example, equality might mean that by law a school cannot refuse to accept Black students.
- **Equity:** The situation of the playing field being leveled so that everyone can access the same opportunities. For example, equity might mean

---

[223] Retrieved January 28, 2022, from https://dsf.net.au/what-is-dysgraphia/

that a school offers scholarships to Black students to make it possible for them to attend.

- **Essentialism:** The technique of categorizing a whole group based on preconceptions about what makes up that group's essence. Individuals with essentialism are unable to remain open to individual distinctions within groupings.
- **Ethnic Diversity:** The presence of people of various ethnic backgrounds or identities. Employers are increasingly recognizing the benefits of an ethnically diverse workforce.
- **Ethnicity:** A method of classifying people into smaller social groupings based on factors such as values, cultural heritage, behavior, political opinions, and ancestry.
- **Ethnocentrism:** The propensity to assume that your own ethnic group is the most significant and to judge everyone else by your own standards and practices. An example may be a Christian person who believes all non-Christian celebrations to be insignificant.
- **Eurocentrism:** The use of Europe and European culture as a frame of reference or set of standard criteria. Eurocentrism privileges European cultural norms while ignoring the facts and experiences of other cultures.
- **Exclusion:** Leaving out a person because of their perceived differences. Race, age, gender, sexual orientation, disability, class, and other social groupings can all be the basis for these exclusions.
- **Feminism:** Advocating for the equality of women in society.
- **Femme:** A gender identification in which a person is aware of cultural femininity standards and intentionally adopts an ultrafeminine appearance or role. It is also the French word for woman.
- **Filipinx:** A person who is either a Filipino national or a descendant of a Filipino. Filipinx is a gender-neutral term.
- **First Nations:** Indigenous peoples in Canada who are not Inuit or Métis.
- **Gaslighting:** A purposeful attempt to weaken a victim's sense of reality or sanity by arguing that what actually happened did not. In the workplace, it usually refers to activities that jeopardize the target's success, self-confidence, self-esteem, or well-being. It is more likely to be used against underrepresented or less powerful groups.
- **Gay:** Those who are physically attracted to people of the same sex or gender. Gay is also an identification phrase for a male-identified person who is romantically, sexually, and/or emotionally attracted to other male-identified persons.
- **Gender Binary:** A classification system that divides people into two genders: male and female.

- **Gender Dysphoria:** Describes a sensation of discomfort and dissatisfaction experienced by people whose gender identification differs from their biological gender.
- **Gender Expansive:** Describes someone whose gender expression defies conventional norms or assumptions. A way to categorize people who do not identify with traditional gender norms but are not limited to a single gender narrative or experience.
- **Gender Expression:** A person's exterior presentations of gender (masculine or feminine) that are dependent on dress, demeanor, mannerisms, interests, or social interaction.
- **Gender Fluid:** Describes a person who may change their gender over time or may even switch daily from dressing as traditionally male or female. Those who are gender fluid often express the importance of flexibility.
- **Gender Identity:** A person's view of their own gender. Gender identity may or may not correspond to a person's sex assigned at birth.
- **Gender Neutral:** Describes legislation, language, clothing, and social institutions that avoid invoking gender. This helps avoid discrimination that may occur from traditional social roles.
- **Gender Non-Conforming (GNC):** Description of someone who does not adhere to society's gender expression requirements. GNC also refers to a person's gender expression being difficult to define as either male or female.
- **Gender Policing:** The application of gender norms to someone who is viewed as not behaving in a way that corresponds to their assigned gender at birth. An example would be telling girls to be more ladylike or telling boys they shouldn't cry.
- **Gender Queer:** Description of people who do not identify as either male or female.
- **Gender Role:** A socially imposed expectation or cultural gender standard that governs conduct, mannerisms, attire, and other aspects of one's life. An example is the expectation that a woman will raise children and not seek employment.
- **Gender Spectrum:** A model of gender based on the belief that there are many different genders besides male and female. According to Abrams,[224] there are sixty-four gender identities and expressions (2019).
- **Gender Transition:** A progression from external gender expression that is based on gender assigned at birth toward an expression based on personal gender identity.

---

[224] Abrams, M. (2019, December 20). *64 Terms That Describe Gender Identity and Expression.* https://www.healthline.com/health/different-genders.

- **Gender:** The socially constructed roles, attitudes, activities, and characteristics that society thinks "acceptable" for either men or women. Not to be confused with "sex," which is the biological classification of male and female based on physiological and biological characteristics.
- **Gentrification:** The process of people from a dominating group with a high socioeconomic status changing the economics or demographics of low-income, marginalized areas by building homes, businesses, and other structures that exclude and displace the people who live there.
- **Greygender/Graygender:** A person who is torn between gender identities and expressions. A gender identity and/or gender expression in which one identifies partially outside the gender binary and has strong ambivalence regarding one's gender identity and/or gender expression.
- **Greysexual/Graysexual:** A person who has a restricted sense of sexual attraction. Some greysexuals may experience sexual attraction only once or twice in their lives. Others may feel it on a more regular basis.
- **Groupthink:** The tendency of people to share beliefs and thoughts with the rest of their group instead of thinking for themselves. A perceived group consensus.
- **Gypsies/Travelers**[225]**:** An ethnic group recognized in the United Kingdom under the Race Relations Act. A race of people who traditionally have traveled in caravans, living in many different places.
- **Harassment:** Unwelcome, intimidating, exclusionary, threatening, or unfriendly behavior directed toward a person. It can occur alongside discrimination.
- **Health at Every Size (HAES):** A social and health promotion movement that tackles societal stigma based on weight, size, and shape. Rather than focusing on weight loss, the movement promotes body positivity, positive health outcomes, and healthy food and movement.
- **Hepeating:** Occurs when a man repeats a woman's ideas as if they were his own to receive credit or admiration. It is a type of microaggression.
- **Heteronormativity:** The belief that heterosexuality is the most natural, ideal, or superior sexual orientation.
- **Heterosexism:** A set of beliefs, biases, and prejudices that promote female-male sexuality and relationships. The view that heterosexuality is preferable or more "normal" than other types of sexuality or sexual orientation.

---

[225] https://commonslibrary.parliament.uk/research-briefings/cbp-8083/

- **Heterosexual:** A female-identified person who is attracted to a male-identified person or a male-identified person who is attracted to a female-identified person. Also referred to as "straight."
- **Hidden Bias/Implicit Bias:** An unintended, subtle, and unconscious expression of bias. Attitudes or stereotypes that unknowingly influence a person's knowledge, behaviors, or decisions toward or regarding persons from different groups.
- **Historically Black Colleges and Universities (HBCUs):** Colleges founded in the United States after the Civil War to serve the Black community. They accept students of all races.
- **Homophobia:** An irrational dread or hatred of people who are gay. A fear of LGBTQ+ people.
- **Homosexual:** A person who is sexually attracted to people of the same sex. The term has come to have a negative connotation due to its overuse by those opposed to LGBTQ+ populations.
- **Host Culture:** The prevailing culture in a place to which people have emigrated. Adapting to a host culture can often be difficult.
- **Hypersensitivity:** When a neurodivergent person has a particularly strong or powerful response to stimuli such as colors, scents, textures, and noises.
- **Identity First Language (IFL):** Language that prioritizes identity over personhood, often used in the context of disability. For example, calling someone a deaf person (instead of a person who has hearing impairment) is IFL.
- **Imposter Syndrome:** When high-achieving individuals are constantly afraid of being discovered as frauds and are unable to embrace their achievements. Members of underrepresented groups are more likely to experience imposter syndrome.
- **Inclusion:** The process of bringing people who have traditionally been excluded into decision-making processes, activities, or positions of authority. Individuals or groups can feel protected, respected, driven, and engaged when they are included.
- **Inclusive Vocabulary/Language:** Respectful language that promotes acceptance and value of people. The use of gender-neutral language to prevent assumptions about sexual orientation and gender identity.
- **Indigenous People:** The native people or first people to inhabit an area.
- **Individual Racism:** When a person acts in ways that perpetuate or encourage racism without realizing it. Racist comments, avoiding certain races, and tolerating racist acts are a few examples.
- **In-Group Bias:** When people respond more positively to people in what they consider to be "in-groups" than to people from "out-groups." Also known as "group favoritism."

- **Institutional Racism:** The inequality of certain racial groups having different experiences than other groups because of institutional practices and regulations. Although institutionally racist policies do not expressly target any ethnic group, they have the effect of benefitting White people and oppressing all other ethnicities.
- **Integration:** Maintaining one's own cultural identity while also becoming a member of the host culture.
- **Intersectionality:** The complicated, cumulative impacts of multiple forms of discrimination. The commonalities among different groups. An example is a Black lesbian who experiences homophobia like other lesbians but also experiences racism like other Black people and sexism like other women.
- **Inuit:** A member of an indigenous group from northern Canada, Greenland, or Alaska. Inuits are generally culturally similar.
- **Karen:** A stereotype of White women who abuse their status to demand things that are not essential. The word is used as a term of contempt for middle-aged White women.
- **Latinx:** Describes persons who are from Latin America or are descended from Latin Americans and living in the United States There is debate about whether Caribbean people identify as Latinx.
- **Lesbian:** A female-identified individual who is emotionally, physically, or sexually attracted to other female-identified individuals.
- **Lesbophobia:** An irrational fear or hate of lesbians or lesbian conduct as well as prejudice against them. Lesbophobia is common in South Africa.
- **LGBTQ+:** Lesbian, gay, bisexual, transgender, and/or queer, abbreviated as LGBTQ. The plus represents all other sexual identities.
- **Low Income:** According to federal criteria, households with incomes that do not exceed 150 percent of the poverty threshold.
- **Mansplain:** The act of a man telling a woman something she already knows in a condescending or patronizing manner. A blend of the words "man" and "explain."
- **Marginalization:** The process of excluding, ignoring, or relegating a group of individuals to a minor or powerless place in society. There are three types of marginalization: social, economic, and political.
- **Melting Pot:** A metaphor for a society in which different types of people blend as one. America is often regarded as a Melting Pot society.
- **Men-Loving-Men (MLM):** A phrase for gay, bisexual, and pansexual men who are attracted to other gay, bisexual, and pansexual men. This attraction does not have to be exclusive.
- **Merit:** A supposedly neutral assessment of academic achievement and surface qualifications. Nonetheless, merit is rooted in Whiteness ideology and perpetuates race-based structural inequity.

- **Métis:** A person of mixed descent. Used to describe a multi-ancestral indigenous people who live in regions of Canada and the United States between the Great Lakes and the Rocky Mountains.
- **Metrosexual:** A well-groomed heterosexual man, to differentiate him from a gay man. A metrosexual is a combination of "heterosexual" and "metropolitan."
- **Microaffirmation:** A small act of compassion, care, or inclusion. Listening, offering comfort and support, being an ally, and explicitly recognizing everyone's contributions and presence are examples.
- **Microaggression:** A comment or action that inadvertently or unintentionally conveys or reveals a biased attitude against a marginalized group. Microaggressions can isolate and alienate persons over time, affecting their health and well-being.
- **Middle Eastern:** Describing the geographical locations that encompass Arab countries, on the eastern and southern edges of the Mediterranean Sea, the Arabian peninsula, Iraq, Iran, Afghanistan, and northeast Africa.
- **Minority:** A racially, ethnically, or culturally unique group that is disempowered by more dominant groups. A minority in one situation does not always imply a minority in another. At historically Black colleges and universities, for example, Black students often make up the majority of students.
- **Misgender:** Inaccurately reflecting the gender with which a person identifies. An example is using she/her pronouns for a person who is trans male and prefers he/him pronouns.
- **Misogyny:** Hatred and prejudice directed toward women. Misogyny can also mean a belief that men are superior to women.
- **Mixed Race:** A person whose parents are of two or more racial or ethnic groupings.
- **Model Minority:** An underrepresented group of people who are thought to have a better level of socioeconomic success than the general population. A word coined by sociologist William Peterson to describe Japanese communities that could withstand oppression due to their cultural beliefs.
- **Movement Building:** Confronting systemic issues or injustices while presenting alternatives or different perspectives. It blends institutional reform with social force to bring about a systemic shift.
- **Multicultural Competency:** The process of learning about diverse cultures and becoming allies with individuals from various backgrounds. The capacity to comprehend and interact effectively with persons from various cultural origins.

- **Multicultural:** Belonging to more than one culture. It can also refer to a place with many different cultures present.
- **Multiethnic:** Having ancestors from two or more ethnic groups. A society with two or more ethnic groups.
- **Multiracial:** Having ancestors from two or more races. A society with people of different races.
- **Native American:** Indigenous people in the United States. Although many Native Americans find the term "Indian" objectionable and prefer to identify themselves by their tribe, the terms *Native American* and *American Indian* are sometimes used interchangeably.
- **Neopronoun/Neo-pronoun/Neo Language:** A category of English third-person personal pronouns that do not identify gender. Examples are "ze" and "zir."
- **Neuroatypical:** Not having a neurological divergence. Commonly used within the autistic community to refer to everyone else.
- **Neurodivergent (ND):** Having a brain that works in a way that differs significantly from the mainstream societal norms. Variations fall in the categories of sociability, learning, attention, and mood.
- **Neurodiversity:** When neurological distinctions, like any other type of human uniqueness or variation, are recognized and appreciated. Dyspraxia, dyslexia, and attention deficit disorder are examples of these variances.
- **Neurodiversity Movement:** A social justice movement dedicated to achieving equality, respect, inclusion, and civil rights for people with neurodiversity.
- **Neurominority:** A group of neurodiverse persons who are underrepresented in society and may experience obstacles or bias. Examples include people with schizophrenia, bipolar disorder, autism, and dyslexia.
- **Neurotypical:** A type of neurocognitive functioning that conforms to cultural norms of "normal."
- **Nonbinary:** Identifying with a gender that is neither exclusively male nor exclusively female but falls somewhere in the middle. Sexual identity not defined in terms of binary opposites.
- **Outgroup Prejudice:** When people in a group see persons outside their group as inferior, strange, or dissimilar and may have a negative bias toward them.
- **Pansexual:** A person who is attracted to someone regardless of their gender or sexuality. A pansexual may refer to themselves as "gender blind."

- **People of Color/Individuals of Color:** People who are not White. The phrase is intended to be inclusive of all non-White communities, based on commonality of experiences of racism.
- **Polyamory:** The practice of having several romantic relationships at once with mutual consent.
- **Polygender:** Having multiple gender identities. An umbrella term that includes people who identify outside gender binary (male/female).
- **Privilege:** An undeserved, long-term advantage based on race, gender, sexuality, aptitude, socioeconomic status, age, and other factors. White people are often believed to be more privileged.
- **Pronouns:** Words that are used in place of a person's name to refer to them. "She" and "he" are examples of gendered pronouns.
- **Queer:** People who do not identify as heterosexual or cisgender. An umbrella term for lesbian, gay, bisexual, and transgender.
- **Race:** A social construct that divides people into various groups based on criteria including physical appearance, ancestry, cultural affinity, history, and/or ethnic classification.
- **Racism:** The view that racial differences cause or contribute to intrinsic superiority or inferiority. Prejudice, discrimination, antagonism, or hatred motivated by race. Systemic racism, often known as *institutionalized racism,* refers to racism that is ingrained in society or organizations.
- **Religion:** A set of beliefs that is frequently formally articulated and structured.
- **Reparations:** An attempt to redress extensive previous government-caused human rights breaches. An example would be federal government payments to descendants of enslaved Americans.
- **Reverse Discrimination:** Unfair treatment of members of a dominant or majority group. Frequently used by opponents of affirmative action. The Supreme Court has ruled that considering race and other demographic factors in hiring and other employment-related decisions is unconstitutional.
- **Safe Space:** A place designed to help everyone feel comfortable, feel welcome, and express themselves. No one in a safe space should feel afraid or suffer ridicule.
- **Sex:** Primary and secondary sexual features as well as biological and physical differences used to classify people into sexes. Different from *gender,* which is founded on the societal creation of the categories "men" and "women."
- **Sexual Orientation:** Who we are romantically, emotionally, and/or physically attracted to. It is important to remember that a person's romantic orientation can differ from their sexual orientation.

- **Social Justice:** A vision of a society in which resources are distributed fairly and all individuals are physically and psychologically safe.
- **Sponsor:** A powerful internal advocate who looks after your interests, helps connect you to leaders and special projects, and amplifies your work to other senior people in your business. The difference between sponsors and mentors is that mentors give guidance and advice and lack some of the influence of a sponsor.
- **Stakeholder Capitalism:** A risk-and-opportunity paradigm that focuses on environmental and social risks and opportunities. It contrasts with the shareholder-primacy model, which focuses on financial and operational costs and benefits.
- **Stereotype:** Oversimplified opinions, prejudiced attitudes, and judgments regarding individuals of certain groups.
- **The Caren Act/CAREN Act:** A piece of legislation that was introduced in the United States and stands for Caution Against Racially Exploitative Non-Emergencies. The policy is identical to California Assemblyman Rob Bonta's statewide AB 1550 measure, which makes it illegal and punishable for a caller to "fabricate false racially-biased emergency reports." An example would be a person irritated that kids are playing music outside her apartment calling the police to report that Black people are threatening her with physical violence.
- **Tokenism:** Symbolic or performative practice of demographic diversity in venues where people from marginalized populations are not completely welcomed or allowed to participate. Their presence in very low numbers helps to deflect criticism about a lack of diversity.
- **Tolerance:** Acceptance of the behaviors, attitudes, and cultures of others. It does not necessarily imply agreement or support.
- **Transgender:** Having a gender identification that is different from sex assigned at birth (SAAB).
- **Transitioning:** The actions taken by a person to live as the gender with which they identify but that may differ from their sex assigned at birth. Medical intervention, such as hormone therapy and surgeries, that may be required for some trans persons. Not all trans people want or are able to have medical intervention.
- **Under-Represented Minorities (URM):** Sub-groups within larger racial/ethnic minority groups that are underrepresented in comparison to their size. For example, even though Hispanic persons are proportionately represented in a specific field, Mexican Americans may be underrepresented.
- **Veteran:** A person who served in the Armed Forces. The Army, Navy, Marine Corps, Air Force, Coast Guard, and National Guard are all considered parts of the Armed Forces.

- **White Fragility:** A term coined by Robin D'Angelo to characterize the privilege that White people have because of living in a culture that shields and insulates them from race-based stress. According to D'Angelo, this creates the expectation of constantly feeling comfortable and protected, which reduces the ability to withstand racial stress and activates a variety of defensive responses.
- **White Supremacy:** The belief that White people are superior to all others. Also, refers to White people exploiting or oppressing people who are not White to maintain and defend a system of wealth, privilege, and power.
- **Xenophobia:** The fear of or prejudice against persons from different countries. Xenophobia can also refer to a fear of strangers.
- **Zero-Sum:** A situation in which there can only be victors and losers. When it comes to gender equity, zero-sum bias encourages males to believe that they must give up their resources or achievements in order for women to prosper equally.

Historically Black Colleges and Universities (HBCUs)

Historically Black Colleges and Universities (HBCUs)[226] were founded in the mid-19th century as a way to provide higher education to Black Americans. There are more than sixty HBCUs across the United States. Many HBCUs are considered prestigious institutions, and many of their alumni have successful careers in business, government, and the arts.

ALABAMA

- Alabama A&M University
- Alabama State University
- Bishop State Community College
- C. A. Fredd Campus of Shelton State Community College
- Concordia College Selma
- Gadsden State Community College
- J. F. Drake Technical College
- Lawson State Community College
- Miles College
- Oakwood College
- Selma University
- Stillman College
- Talladega College
- Trenholm State Technical College
- Tuskegee University

ARKANSAS

- Arkansas Baptist College
- Philander Smith College
- Shorter College
- University of Arkansas at Pine Bluff

DELAWARE

- Delaware State University

DISTRICT OF COLUMBIA

- Howard University
- University of the District of Columbia

---

[226] https://nces.ed.gov/programs/digest/d15/tables/dt15_313.10.asp?current=yes

FLORIDA

- Bethune-Cookman University
- Edward Waters College
- Florida A&M University
- Florida Memorial University

GEORGIA

- Albany State University
- Clark Atlanta University
- Fort Valley State University
- Interdenominational Theological Center
- Morehouse College
- Morehouse School of Medicine
- Morris Brown College
- Paine College
- Savannah State University
- Spelman College

KENTUCKY

- Kentucky State University

LOUISIANA

- Dillard University
- Grambling State University
- Southern University and A&M College
- Southern University at New Orleans
- Southern University at Shreveport
- Xavier University of Louisiana

MARYLAND

- Bowie State University
- Coppin State University
- Morgan State University
- University of Maryland, Eastern Shore

MICHIGAN

- Lewis College of Business

MISSISSIPPI

- Alcorn State University
- Coahoma Community College
- Hinds Community College
- Jackson State University

- Mississippi Valley State University
- Rust College
- Tougaloo College

MISSOURI

- Harris-Stowe State University
- Lincoln University of Missouri

NORTH CAROLINA

- Barber-Scotia College
- Bennett College
- Elizabeth City State University
- Fayetteville State University
- Johnson C. Smith University
- Livingstone College
- North Carolina A&T State University
- North Carolina Central University
- St. Augustine's College
- Shaw University
- Winston Salem State University

OHIO

- Central State University
- Wilberforce University

OKLAHOMA

- Langston University

PENNSYLVANIA

- Cheyney University of Pennsylvania
- Lincoln University

SOUTH CAROLINA

- Allen University
- Benedict College
- Claflin University
- Clinton Junior College
- Denmark Technical College
- Morris College
- South Carolina State University
- Voorhees College

TENNESSEE

- American Baptist College
- Fisk University
- Knoxville College
- Lane College
- LeMoyne-Owen College
- Meharry Medical College
- Tennessee State University

TEXAS

- Huston-Tillotson University
- Jarvis Christian College
- Paul Quinn College
- Prairie View A&M University
- Saint Philip's College
- Southwestern Christian College
- Texas College
- Texas Southern University
- Wiley College

VIRGINIA

- Hampton University
- Norfolk State University
- Virginia State University
- Virginia Union University
- Virginia University of Lynchburg

WEST VIRGINIA

- Bluefield State College
- West Virginia State University

U.S. VIRGIN ISLANDS

- University of the Virgin Islands

Hispanic-Serving Institutions (HSIs)

Hispanic Serving Institutions (HSIs)[227] are nonprofit organizations that help Hispanic Americans access higher education and career opportunities. They provide scholarships, fellowships, and other financial assistance. Most HSIs also offer mentoring, networking, and job search assistance.

ARIZONA

- Arizona State University Downtown Phoenix campus
- Arizona State University West campus
- Arizona Western College
- Central Arizona College
- Chandler-Gilbert Community College
- Cochise County Community College District
- CollegeAmerica–Phoenix
- Estrella Mountain Community College
- GateWay Community College
- Glendale Community College
- Mesa Community College
- Phoenix College
- Pima Community College
- South Mountain Community College
- University of Arizona
- University of Arizona South

ARKANSAS

- Cossatot Community College

CALIFORNIA

- Allan Hancock College
- American River College
- Antelope Valley College
- Antioch University–Santa Barbara
- Azusa Pacific University
- Bakersfield College
- Barstow Community College
- Berkeley City College
- Brandman University
- Butte College

---

[227] https://www.edexcelencia.org/Hispanic-Serving-Institutions-HSIs-2019-2020

- Cabrillo College
- California Baptist University
- California Christian College
- California College San Diego, San Marcos
- California College San Diego, San Diego
- California Lutheran University
- California State Polytechnic University, Pomona
- California State University, Bakersfield
- California State University, Channel Islands
- California State University, Chico
- California State University, Dominguez Hills
- California State University, East Bay
- California State University, Fresno
- California State University, Fullerton
- California State University, Long Beach
- California State University, Los Angeles
- California State University, Monterey Bay
- California State University, Northridge
- California State University, Sacramento
- California State University, San Bernardino
- California State University, San Marcos
- California State University, Stanislaus
- Cañada College
- Casa Loma College
- CBD College
- Cerritos College
- Cerro Coso Community College
- Chabot College
- Chaffey College
- Charles R. Drew University of Medicine and Science
- Citrus College
- City College of San Francisco
- Clovis Community College
- Coastline Community College
- College of Alameda
- College of Marin
- College of San Mateo
- College of the Canyons
- College of the Desert
- College of the Sequoias
- Community Christian College
- Compton College

- Contra Costa College
- Copper Mountain College (Copper Mountain Community College)
- Cosumnes River College
- Crafton Hills College
- Cuesta College
- Cuyamaca College
- Cypress College
- DeAnza College
- Diablo Valley College
- East Los Angeles College
- East San Gabriel Valley Regional Occupational Program
- El Camino Community College District
- Evergreen Valley College
- Feather River Community College District
- Foothill College
- Fresno City College
- Fresno Pacific University
- Fullerton College
- Gavilan College
- Glendale Community College
- Golden West College
- Grossmont College
- Hacienda La Puente Adult Education
- Hartnell College
- Holy Names University
- Hope International University
- Humboldt State University
- Humphreys College—Stockton and Modesto Campuses
- Imperial Valley College
- John Paul the Great Catholic University
- La Sierra University
- Lake Tahoe Community College
- Las Positas College
- Lassen Community College
- Life Pacific College
- Loma Linda University
- Long Beach City College
- Los Angeles City College
- Los Angeles County College of Nursing and Allied Health
- Los Angeles Harbor College
- Los Angeles Mission College
- Los Angeles Pacific University

- Los Angeles Pierce College
- Los Angeles Southwest College
- Los Angeles Trade-Technical College
- Los Angeles Valley College
- Los Medanos College
- Marymount California University
- Mendocino College
- Menlo College
- Merced College
- Merritt College
- Middlebury Institute of International Studies at Monterey
- Mills College
- MiraCosta College
- Mission College
- Modesto Junior College
- Monterey Peninsula College
- Moorpark College
- Moreno Valley College
- Mount Saint Mary's College
- Mt. San Antonio College
- Mt. San Jacinto Community College District
- Napa Valley College
- National University
- Norco College
- Notre Dame de Namur University
- Orange Coast College
- Oxnard College
- Pacific Oaks College
- Pacific Union College
- Palo Verde College
- Palomar College
- Pasadena City College
- Porterville College
- Providence Christian College
- Reedley College
- Rio Hondo College
- Riverside City College
- Sacramento City College
- Saddleback College
- Saint Mary's College of California
- San Bernardino Valley College
- San Diego Christian College

- San Diego City College
- San Diego Mesa College
- San Diego Miramar College
- San Diego State University
- San Francisco State University
- San Joaquin Delta College
- San Jose City College
- San Jose State University
- Santa Ana College
- Santa Barbara City College
- Santa Monica College
- Santa Rosa Junior College
- Santiago Canyon College
- Sierra College
- Skyline College
- Solano Community College
- Sonoma State University
- Southern California University of Health Sciences
- Southwestern College
- Taft College
- University of California, Irvine
- University of California, Merced
- University of California, Riverside
- University of California, Santa Barbara
- University of California, Santa Cruz
- University of La Verne
- University of Redlands
- University of Saint Katherine
- University of the West
- Vanguard University of Southern California
- Ventura College
- Victor Valley College
- West Hills College Coalinga
- West Hills College Lemoore
- West Los Angeles College
- West Valley College
- Whittier College
- Woodbury University
- Woodland Community College
- Yuba College

COLORADO

- Adams State University
- Aims Community College
- Altierus Career College-Thorton
- CollegeAmerica-Denver
- CollegeAmerica-Fort Collins
- Colorado State University–Pueblo
- Community College of Aurora
- Community College of Denver
- Lamar Community College
- Metropolitan State University of Denver
- Morgan Community College
- Otero Junior College
- Pueblo Community College
- Trinidad State Junior College

CONNECTICUT

- Capital Community College
- Gateway Community College
- Housatonic Community College
- Naugatuck Valley Community College
- Norwalk Community College
- University of Connecticut–Stamford
- District of Columbia
- Trinity Washington University

FLORIDA

- Barry University
- Broward College
- Carlos Albizu University–Miami
- City College–Miami
- Florida Atlantic University
- Florida International University
- Florida Keys Community College
- Florida SouthWestern State College
- Hillsborough Community College
- Hodges University
- Indian River State College
- Johnson & Wales University–North Miami
- Keiser University–Ft. Lauderdale
- Miami Dade College
- Nova Southeastern University

- Palm Beach State College
- Polytechnic University of Puerto Rico–Miami
- Polytechnic University of Puerto Rico–Orlando
- SABER College
- Saint John Vianney College Seminary
- Seminole State College of Florida
- South Florida State College
- St. Thomas University
- Trinity International University–Florida
- University of Central Florida
- Valencia College

GEORGIA

- Dalton State College

IDAHO

- Stevens Henager College

ILLINOIS

- City Colleges of Chicago
- Dominican University
- Elgin Community College
- Morton College
- National Louis University
- Northeastern Illinois University
- Robert Morris University Illinois
- Saint Xavier University
- St. Augustine College
- Triton College
- University of Illinois at Chicago
- Waubonsee Community College
- Wilbur Wright College

INDIANA

- Calumet College of Saint Joseph

KANSAS

- Dodge City Community College
- Donnelly College
- Seward County Community College

MARYLAND

- Universidad del Este

- Universidad del Turabo

MASSACHUSETTS

- Northern Essex Community College
- Springfield Technical Community College
- Urban College of Boston

NEVADA

- College of Southern Nevada

NEW JERSEY

- Bergen Community College
- Cumberland County College
- Essex County College
- Fairleigh Dickinson University–Metropolitan Campus
- Felician University
- Hudson County Community College
- Kean University
- Middlesex County College
- New Jersey City University
- Passaic County Community College
- Pillar College
- Saint Peter's University
- Union County College
- William Paterson University

NEW MEXICO

- Central New Mexico Community College
- Clovis Community College
- Doña Ana Community College
- Eastern New Mexico University
- Eastern New Mexico University–Roswell
- New Mexico Highlands University
- New Mexico Institute of Mining and Technology
- New Mexico State University
- New Mexico State University Alamogordo
- New Mexico State University Carlsbad
- New Mexico State University Grants
- Northern New Mexico College
- Santa Fe Community College
- University of New Mexico
- University of New Mexico–Los Alamos
- University of the Southwest

- Western New Mexico University

NEW YORK

- Boricua College
- Borough of Manhattan Community College
- Bronx Community College
- City College of New York
- College of Mount Saint Vincent
- College of Staten Island
- Dominican College
- Guttman Community College
- Hunter College
- John Jay College of Criminal Justice
- Laguardia Community College
- Lehman College
- Mercy College
- New York City College of Technology
- Nyack College
- Orange County Community College
- Queens College
- Vaughn College of Aeronautics and Technology
- Westchester Community College

OREGON

- Blue Mountain Community College
- Chemeketa Community College
- Columbia Gorge Community College
- Mount Angel Seminary
- Treasure Valley CommunityCollege
- Warner Pacific University

OHIO

- Union Institute & University

PENNSYLVANIA

- Lehigh Carbon Community College
- Reading Area Community College
- The Workforce Institute's City College

PUERTO RICO

- American University of Puerto Rico
- Antillean Adventist University
- Atlantic University College

- Bayamon Central University
- Caribbean University
- Carlos Albizu University
- Escuela de Artes Plásticas y Diseño de Puerto Rico
- Inter-American University of Puerto Rico
- Polytechnic University of Puerto Rico
- Pontifical Catholic University of Puerto Rico
- San Juan Bautista School of Medicine
- Universidad del Este
- Universidad del Sagrado Corazon
- Universidad del Turabo
- University of Puerto Rico at Aguadilla
- University of Puerto Rico at Arecibo
- University of Puerto Rico at Bayamón
- University of Puerto Rico at Carolina
- University of Puerto Rico at Cayey
- University of Puerto Rico at Humacao
- University of Puerto Rico at Mayagüez
- University of Puerto Rico at Ponce
- University of Puerto Rico at Utuado
- University of Puerto Rico, Medical Sciences Campus
- University of Puerto Rico, Río Piedras Campus

TEXAS

- Alvin Community College
- Amarillo College
- Angelo State University
- Austin Community College District
- Baptist University of the Americas
- Brazosport College
- Brookhaven College
- Cisco College
- Coastal Bend College
- Del Mar College
- Eastfield College
- El Centro College
- El Paso Community College
- Galveston College
- Hallmark University
- Houston Baptist University
- Houston Community College
- Howard College

- Jacksonville College
- Laredo Community College
- Lee College
- Lone Star College System
- McLennan Community College
- Mountain View College
- North Lake College
- Northeast Texas Community College
- Northwest Vista College
- Northwood University
- Our Lady of the Lake University
- Palo Alto College
- Remington College
- San Antonio College
- San Jacinto Community College
- Schreiner University
- South Plains College
- South Texas College
- Southwest Texas Junior College
- Southwestern Adventist University
- St. Edward's University
- St. Mary's University
- Sul Ross State University
- Tarrant County College
- Texas A&M International University
- Texas A&M University–Corpus Christi
- Texas A&M University–Kingsville
- Texas Lutheran University
- Texas State University
- Texas Tech University
- Texas Woman's University
- University of Houston
- University of Houston–Clear Lake
- University of Houston–Downtown
- University of Houston–Victoria
- University of St. Thomas
- University of Texas at Arlington
- University of Texas at El Paso
- University of Texas at San Antonio
- University of Texas Health Science Center
- University of Texas of the Permian Basin
- University of Texas Rio Grande Valley

- University of the Incarnate Word
- Victoria College
- Western Texas College
- Wharton County Junior College

WASHINGTON

- Big Bend Community College
- Columbia Basin College
- Heritage University
- Wenatchee Valley College
- Yakima Valley Community College

Tribal Colleges and Universities (TCUs)

There are thirty-two fully accredited Tribal Colleges and Universities (TCUs) in the United States. These TCUs a total of 358 programs, including apprenticeships, diplomas, certificates, and degrees. They include 181 associate degree programs at twenty-three TCUs, forty bachelor's degree programs at eleven TCUs, and five master's degree programs at two TCUs.[228]

ALASKA

- Ilisagvik College

ARIZONA

- Diné College
- Tohono O'odham Community College

KANSAS

- Haskell Indian Nations University

MICHIGAN

- Bay Mills Community College
- Keweenaw Bay Ojibwa Community College
- Saginaw Chippewa Tribal College

MINNESOTA

- Fond du Lac Tribal and Community College
- Leech Lake Tribal College
- White Earth Tribal and Community College

MONTANA

- Blackfeet Community College
- Chief Dull Knife College
- Aaniiih Nakoda College
- Fort Peck Community College
- Little Big Horn College
- Salish Kootenai College
- Stone Child College

NEBRASKA

- Nebraska Indian Community College
- Little Priest Tribal College

---

[228] https://sites.ed.gov/whiaiane/tribes-tcus/tribal-colleges-and-universities/

NEW MEXICO

- Navajo Technical College
- Institute of American Indian Arts
- Southwestern Indian Polytechnic Institute

NORTH DAKOTA

- Cankdeska Cikana Community College
- Fort Berthold Community College
- Sitting Bull College
- Turtle Mountain Community College
- United Tribes Technical College

SOUTH DAKOTA

- Oglala Lakota College
- Sinte Gleska University
- Sisseton Wahpeton College

WASHINGTON

- Northwest Indian College

WISCONSIN

- College of Menominee Nation
- Lac Courte Oreilles Ojibwa Community College

Associate Status

OKLAHOMA

- College of the Muscogee Nation
- Comanche Nation College

WYOMING

- Wind River Tribal College

Sororities and Fraternities

Native American[229]

Fraternities

ΒΣΕ   Beta Sigma Epsilon

ΕΧΝ   Epsilon Chi Nu

ΦΣΝ   Phi Sigma Nu

ΣΝΑΓ   Sigma Nu Alpha Gamma

Sororities

ΑΠΩ   Alpha Pi Omega

ΓΔΠ   Gamma Delta Pi

ΣΟΕ   Sigma Omicron Epsilon

African-American[230]

Fraternities

Prince Hall Freemasonry

IBPOEW Improved Benevolent and Protective Order of Elks of the World

ΣΠΦ   Sigma Pi Phi

ΑΦΑ   Alpha Phi Alpha

ΚΑΨ   Kappa Alpha Psi

ΩΨΦ   Omega Psi Phi

ΦΒΣ   Phi Beta Sigma

Wine Psi Phi

Nu Gamma Alpha

ΙΦΘ   Iota Phi Theta

Phi Eta Psi

MALIK Fraternity

---

[229] https://en.wikipedia.org/wiki/Cultural_interest_fraternities_and_sororities#Native_American
[230] https://en.wikipedia.org/wiki/List_of_African-American_fraternities

ΦΔΨ   Phi Delta Psi

ΣΦΡ   Sigma Phi Rho

Delta Psi Chi

Beta Phi Pi

Megisté Areté (Christian)

ΦΡΗ   Phi Rho Eta

Sororities

ΑΚΑ   Alpha Kappa Alpha

ΔΣΘ   Delta Sigma Theta

ΖΦΒ   Zeta Phi Beta

ΣΓΡ   Sigma Gamma Rho

ΙΦΛ   Iota Phi Lambda

ΖΦΒ   Eta Phi Beta

ΤΓΔ   Tau Gamma Delta

ΓΦΔ   Gamma Phi Delta

ΖΔΦ   Zeta Delta Phi

ΚΘΕ   Kappa Theta Epsilon

Asian American[231]

Fraternities

ΑΚΩ   Alpha Kappa Omega

ΑΨΡ   Alpha Psi Rho

ΑΣΛ   Alpha Sigma Lambda (local)

ΒΩΦ   Beta Omega Phi

ΒΠΦ   Beta Pi Phi

ΒΤΩ   Beta Tau Omega

ΒΥΔ   Beta Upsilon Delta

ΧΡΟ   Chi Rho Omicron

ΧΣΤ   Chi Sigma Tau

---

[231] https://en.wikipedia.org/wiki/Cultural_interest_fraternities_and_sororities

ΔΧΨ	Delta Chi Psi
ΗΜΘ	Eta Mu Theta
ΓΒ	Gamma Beta
ΓΕΩ	Gamma Epsilon Omega
ΚΒΖ	Kappa Beta Zeta
ΚΠΒ	Kappa Pi Beta
ΛΑΦ	Lambda Alpha Phi
ΛΦΕ	Lambda Phi Epsilon 1 2
ΛΨΡ	Lambda Psi Rho
ΛΘΔ	Lambda Theta Delta
ΝΑΦ	Nu Alpha Phi
ΩΦΓ	Omega Phi Gamma
ΩΣΤ	Omega Sigma Tau
ΩΞΔ	Omega Xi Delta
ΦΔΣ	Phi Delta Sigma
ΠΑΦ	Pi Alpha Phi 1
ΠΔΨ	Pi Delta Psi 1
ΨΧΩ	Psi Chi Omega
ΡΨ	Rho Psi
ΤΚΩ	Tau Kappa Omega
ΘΔΒ	Theta Delta Beta
ΘΛΒ	Theta Lambda Beta
ΞΚ	Xi Kappa
ΖΕΤ	Zeta Epsilon Tau
ΖΦΡ	Zeta Phi Rho

Sororities

ΑΔΚ	Alpha Delta Kappa
αΚΔΦ	Alpha Kappa Delta Phi 1
ΑΦΓ	Alpha Phi Gamma 1

ΑΣΡ	Alpha Sigma Rho
ΧΑΔ	Chi Alpha Delta
ΧΔΣ	Chi Delta Sigma
ΧΔΘ	Chi Delta Theta
ΧΣΑ	Chi Sigma Alpha
ΔΧΛ	Delta Chi Lambda
ΔΛΧ	Delta Lambda Chi
ΔΦΓ	Delta Phi Gamma
ΔΦΚ	Delta Phi Kappa
ΔΦΛ	Delta Phi Lambda 1
ΚΓΔ	Kappa Gamma Delta
ΚΛΔ	Kappa Lambda Delta
ΚΦΛ	Kappa Phi Lambda 1
ΚΨΕ	Kappa Psi Epsilon
ΚΖΦ	Kappa Zeta Phi
ΛΔΨ	Lambda Delta Psi
ΦΑΟ	Phi Alpha Omicron
ΦΔΑ	Phi Delta Alpha
ΦΖΤ	Phi Zeta Tau
ΡΔΧ	Rho Delta Chi
ΣΟΠ	Sigma Omicron Pi 1
ΣΦΩ	Sigma Phi Omega
ΣΨΖ	Sigma Psi Zeta 1
ΣΣΡ	Sigma Sigma Rho
ΤΘΠ	Tau Theta Pi
ΘΚΦ	Theta Kappa Phi

Latinx

Coed

| ΑΨΛ | Alpha Psi Lambda 1 |

ΔΣΧ   Delta Sigma Chi 3

Fraternities

ΔΠΡ   Delta Pi Rho

ΓΙΟ   Gamma Iota Omicron

ΓΦΣ   Gamma Phi Sigma

ΓΖΑ   Gamma Zeta Alpha

ΛΑΥ   Lambda Alpha Upsilon

ΛΙΥ   Lambda Iota Upsilon

ΛΚΚ   Lambda Kappa Kappa

ΛΘΦ   Lambda Theta Phi

ΛΣΥ   Lambda Sigma Upsilon

ΛΥΛ   Lambda Upsilon Lambda

ΝΑΚ   Nu Alpha Kappa

OeMeT Oquichtli Macuilli Tonatiuh

ΦΔΨΗ Phi Delta Psi Eta

ΦΙΑ   Phi Iota Alpha

ΣΔΑ   Sigma Delta Alpha

ΣΛΒ   Sigma Lambda Beta

Sororities

ΑΠΣ   Alpha Pi Sigma

ΑΡΛ   Alpha Rho Lambda

ΑΣΩ   Alpha Sigma Omega

ΧΥΣ   Chi Upsilon Sigma

ΔΦΜ   Delta Phi Mu

ΔΤΛ   Delta Tau Lambda

ΓΑΩ   Gamma Alpha Omega

ΓCΥ   Gamma Ce Upsilon

ΓΦΩ   Gamma Phi Omega

ΚΔΧ   Kappa Delta Chi

ΛΦΔ	Lambda Phi Delta
ΛΠΧ	Lambda Pi Chi
ΛΠΥ	Lambda Pi Upsilon
ΛΘΑ	Lambda Theta Alpha
ΛΘΝ	Lambda Theta Nu
ΜΙΥ	Mu Iota Upsilon
ΩΦΒ	Omega Phi Beta
ΦΛΡ	Phi Lambda Rho
ΠΛΧ	Pi Lambda Chi
ΣΔ	Sigma Delta
ΣΔΛ	Sigma Delta Lambda
ΣΙΑ	Sigma Iota Alpha
ΣΛΑ	Sigma Lambda Alpha
ΣΛΓ	Sigma Lambda Gamma
ΣΛΥ	Sigma Lambda Upsilon
ΣΩΝ	Sigma Omega Nu
ΣΠΑ	Sigma Pi Alpha